# Autobiographical memory

# Autobiographical memory

*Edited by*

DAVID C. RUBIN
*Duke University*

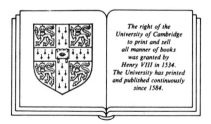

The right of the
University of Cambridge
to print and sell
all manner of books
was granted by
Henry VIII in 1534.
The University has printed
and published continuously
since 1584.

## CAMBRIDGE UNIVERSITY PRESS

*Cambridge*
*New York   Port Chester   Melbourne   Sydney*

Published by the Press Syndicate of the University of Cambridge
The Pitt Building, Trumpington Street, Cambridge CB2 1RP
40 West 20th Street, New York, NY 10011, USA
10 Stamford Road, Oakleigh, Melbourne 3166, Australia

First published 1986
First paperback edition 1988
Reprinted 1989

Printed in the United States of America

*Library of Congress Cataloging-in-Publication Data*

Main entry under title:
Autobiographical memory.
Includes index.
1. Autobiographical memory – Addresses, essays,
lectures.   I. Rubin, David C.
BF378.A87A88   1986   153.1'2   85-25479

*British Library Cataloging in Publication Data*

Autobiographical memory.
1. Memory
I. Rubin, David C.
153.1'2     BF371

ISBN 0 521 30322 2 hard covers
ISBN 0 521 36850 2 paperback

# Contents

## Part V   Temporal distributions of autobiographical memories

## Part VI   Failures of autobiographical memory

# Contributors

Alan Baddeley
Medical Research Council
Applied Psychology Unit
Cambridge

Craig R. Barclay
Graduate School of Education and
    Human Development
University of Rochester

John B. Black
Teachers College
Columbia University

William F. Brewer
Department of Psychology
University of Illinois at Urbana-
    Champaign

Norman R. Brown
I.B.M.
Thomas J. Watson Research Center

Nelson Butters
Psychology Service
San Diego VA Medical Center

Laird S. Cermak
Psychology Service
Boston VA Medical Center
Department of Neurology
Boston University School of Medi-
    cine

Herbert F. Crovitz
Durham, N.C., VA Medical Center
Department of Psychiatry
Duke University Medical Center
Department of Psychology
Duke University

Joseph M. Fitzgerald
Department of Psychology
Wayne State University

Peter Kalamarides
Department of Psychology
Yale University

Marigold Linton
Department of Psychology
University of Utah

Robert D. Nebes
Western Psychiatric Institute and
    Clinic

Ulric Neisser
Department of Psychology
Emory University

Brian J. Reiser
Department of Psychology
Princeton University

Lance J. Rips
Department of Behavioral Sciences
University of Chicago

John A. Robinson
Department of Psychology
University of Louisville

David C. Rubin
Department of Psychology
Duke University

Steven K. Shevell
Department of Behavioral Sciences
University of Chicago

John A. Sweeney
The New York Hospital
Cornell Medical Center

Scott E. Wetzler
Department of Psychology
Montefiore Hospital

Barbara Wilson
Rivermead Rehabilitation Centre
Oxford

# Preface

The purpose of this book is to bring together in one place and in an integrated fashion contemporary research on autobiographical memory. Included are chapters that use a general cognitive framework to understand the recollections people have for substantial portions of their lives. Taken as a whole, the book provides a tutorial on, and a context from which to view, our current understanding of autobiographical memory.

My role as editor was made easier, and much more enjoyable, by the cooperation and encouragement of my family, chapter authors, and publisher. Support during editing was provided by National Institute of Aging grant number AG04278. Portions of the book were presented during an invited symposium at the 92nd Annual Convention of the American Psychological Association and appeared in summary form in the September 1985 issue of *Psychology Today*.

*Part I*

# Overview

---

The first chapter of this book is an overview by the Editor. It begins with several trends and themes that are central to the study of autobiographical memory and that recur throughout the book. The introduction then acknowledges and provides references to additional topics that might have been included in a book with different goals but the same title and concludes with a chapter-by-chapter preview of the book. The preview makes explicit the intended organization of the book and the more obvious relationships among the chapters that follow.

# 1    Introduction

*David C. Rubin*

All attempts at a scientific explanation of human behavior are ambitious. This book is no exception. Consider the challenge. A complete understanding of autobiographical memory would require: a knowledge of basic memory processes in the individual as well as of the influences of the society in which the individual lives; a knowledge of memory processes in the individual at one age and time as well as of the effects of changes in development and environment over a lifetime; a knowledge of the intact as well as of the impaired individual; a knowledge of cognition as well as of affect. This book is an attempt to begin meeting this challenge. Together the chapters represent a set of interwoven interests. Each chapter views autobiographical memory from a different perspective, but shares with the others a common approach that encourages the free exchange of ideas.

## Recurring themes

### Phenomenological reports as data

Several themes run through the book. One is a heavy reliance on phenomenological reports. Brewer (Chap. 3), for instance, makes explicit his claim that phenomenological reports are data that must be accounted for in the same sense as more objective measures, such as amount recalled or reaction time. In order to begin formulating theories of autobiographical memory, Linton (Chap. 4) considers her own process of recall; Neisser (Chap. 5) makes a basic distinction between descriptions of occurrences and the awareness of those occurrences; and Reiser, Black, and Kalamarides (Chap. 7) analyze what their subjects have to say about their process of recall. Similarly, Brown, Shevell, and Rips (Chap. 9) use subjects' protocols while dating events to test hypotheses about the structure of autobiographical memories. In these cases, it is not the recall but what is reported about the process of recalling that is considered as primary data, on a par with more traditional measures. Other

3

types of phenomenological reports, such as Robinson's reports of mood (Chap. 10), also find their way into the book. In the clinical studies, however, phenomenological reports take on a whole new role. The problem with the patient described by Crovitz (Chap. 15) is not that he cannot recall the details of an event but rather that he does not feel he can recall them from his own memory. If this phenomenological distinction is not allowed, the phenomenon of interest disappears.

## Verifiability

Intertwined with the increased reliance on phenomenological report is an expanded view of the role of verifiability. A few years ago researchers in this area were receiving reviews asking how they could call their work memory research when they were not at all sure of the relation between the verbal reports they were collecting and the initial events that led to them. Memory research, to these critics, required the presentation of a known stimulus, a delay, and a report of that known stimulus. The reports could be partial or they could contain distortions, but their relation to a known stimulus was essential. The study of memory included here is broader. Some of us (Linton, Chap. 4; Barclay, Chap. 6; Brown, Shevell, & Rips, Chap. 9; Butters & Cermak, Chap. 14) are probing the issue of how memories distort, change, and are lost over time, using known, verifiable, initial stimuli. The rest of us are often content to try to understand the internal structure of the memory system without asking the methodologically difficult question of how that internal structure relates to past realities. Once Bartlett (1932), with a little help from others such as Neisser (1967), had convinced us that memory is much more often a reconstruction than a reproduction, questions began to arise about the constructive abilities of our memories that are independent of those memories' relations to past events (e.g., Robinson, Chap. 2, and Barclay, Chap. 6). If memory creates as well as distorts, the principles of that creation need to be understood, and this does not always require knowledge of a particular stimulus presentation.

The issue of verifiability and phenomenological report mix in part because it is often more important that our memories seem real than that they be real. Brewer (Chap. 3) makes use of this distinction in his taxonomy of memory, Barclay (Chap. 6) makes this distinction clear in his discussion of literary autobiography, and Baddeley and Wilson (Chap. 13) as well as Crovitz (Chap. 15) use clinical case studies to provide some painfully vivid examples. There are at least two independent criteria for judging the autobiographical memories: how well they reflect past occurrences, and how real they seem to the rememberer. Verifiability addresses only one of these criteria.

*An increase in the description of behavior*

Another theme or attitude that runs through the book is a clear willingness to stand back and begin describing memory almost as if it had never really been studied before. In doing so, the contributors tend to use the metaphor of a botanist, or an ethologist, to describe their activities. Cognitive psychologists are beginning to study autobiographical memory, and, reasonably enough, the first step they often take is to try to describe the phenomena under study. Several chapters provide broad initial taxonomies of aspects of autobiographical memory, including descriptions of the kinds of memories recalled (Linton, Chap. 4), the place of autobiographical memories in memory as a whole (Brewer, Chap. 3), search strategies (Reiser, Black, & Kalamarides, Chap. 7), and clinical deficits (Baddeley & Wilson, Chap. 13). In addition, the chapters by Rubin, Wetzler, and Nebes (Chap. 12) and by Wetzler and Sweeney (Chap. 11) consist mostly of descriptions of the shape of curves with only tentative attempts at theoretical explanations of those curves.

Much of current psychology involves the statistical testing of hypotheses, often in relatively artificial situations. If our recent history is any indication in the area of memory research, many of these hypotheses, and the theories from which they come, are not worthy of the empirical research they generate (Meehl, 1978). One of the most encouraging indications that real progress may be made in autobiographical memory is the willingness of psychologists to delay committing themselves to particular theories and detailed hypotheses until phenomena worth their theorizing have been more fully described. This is not to say that existing theories are ignored. They are included in an extremely eclectic and searching manner. What is avoided, however, is the tendency to test one theory, or one version of a theory, against a null hypothesis before evidence is considered that could falsify the whole class of theories of which the theory being tested is a member. The techniques used to try to understand nature must be appropriate to the problem and to the degree of theoretical sophistication and empirical knowledge available. This book's preponderance of taxonomies is appropriate for our current level of understanding and should help lead to more solid and lasting advances.

**Varied theoretical perspectives**

In order to begin understanding the broad range of phenomena uncovered when autobiographical memory is viewed without strong theoretical blinders, it is necessary to integrate a broad range of research and theory. The research presented in the chapters that follow is a varied and efficient mix of sophisticated laboratory techniques and complex "real-world" problems. The theoretical perspectives employed, however, are what most clearly show the eclectic nature of this volume. Rather than contrasting, the various perspectives complement each other, the insights gained from each perspective adding to our total understanding.

## *The influence of experimental psychology*

The most widely used theoretical perspective is that of the experimental psychology–verbal learning view of human memory. This traditional perspective serves to couch many of the questions asked and provides laboratory-tested accounts for much of the data. Thus, autobiographical memory can be said to include encoding, retention, and retrieval as measured in the laboratory. Moreover, to the extent measured, these terms operate in autobiographical memory much the way they do in the laboratory. Studies of retention functions and encoding specificity apply directly to describing the distribution of adults' autobiographical memories (e.g., Rubin, Wetzler, & Nebes, Chap. 12; Wetzler & Sweeney, Chap. 11) and to consideration of developmental changes (e.g., Fitzgerald, Chap. 8). Even the classic debate about differences between recall and recognition turns out to be important. A person recalls an autobiographical memory, but if that recalled memory is not recognized as the person's own it will not add to the person's theory of self or sense of continuity (e.g., Barclay, Chap. 6; Baddeley & Wilson, Chap. 13; and Crovitz, Chap. 15). Theories of recognition that stress judgments of familiarity (Mandler, 1980) are certainly appropriate here.

At the more cognitive end of the experimental psychology–verbal learning perspective, the concept of schema, in its many forms, pervades this book. Autobiographical memory is organized in more ways than just a time line; specifying that organization is a major goal of most of the research presented here. A sign of progress is the introduction of affect into that organization.

## *The influence of developmental psychology*

The theoretical perspective of developmental psychology enters on a somewhat argumentative note. Those of us of the experimental psychology–verbal learning persuasion tend to study healthy college sophomores who develop at most a semester, and usually less than an hour, during our experiments. As these subjects are supposed to be near their intellectual prime, we feel that we can safely ignore their development during this brief interval. Autobiographical memory forces a different view (e.g., Fitzgerald, Chap. 8). Even studies using only one age group and lasting only an hour often ask for memories from the entire lifespan. In all memory studies, the relationship of the person at the time of retrieval to the person at the time of encoding is important. For autobiographical memory, the person is often markedly different in development at these two times. The study of autobiographical memory is the study of memory for a lifetime and therefore must be informed by what is known about memory development. Another argument for the developmental perspective comes from the observation of autobiographical memory itself. Questions about childhood amnesia (Wetzler & Sweeney, Chap. 11) and reminiscence (Rubin, Wetzler, & Nebes, Chap. 12) predate experimental psychology, and careful observers have noted other, more subtle changes in autobiographical memory with development (e.g., Barclay, Chap. 6; Linton, Chap. 4).

## The influence of personality and social psychology research

The theoretical perspective of personality and social psychology speaks to one of the central aspects of autobiographical memory. Autobiographical memory is about the self; it is about such technical terms as self-theories, self-reference, and identity (Barclay, Chap. 6). Autobiographical memory is the source of information about our lives, from which we are likely to make judgments about our own personalities and predictions of our own and, to some extent, others' behavior. Autobiographical memory, however, also provides a sense of identity and of continuity, a sense that can, but need not, be lost along with the neuropsychological loss of other aspects of autobiographical memory functioning (Baddeley & Wilson, Chap. 13; Butters & Cermak, Chap. 14; Crovitz, Chap. 15).

Although cognitive psychology has provided concepts for personality and social psychology, it has been slow to incorporate ideas from personality and social psychology. Part of this lack of reciprocity is due to reductionist tendencies. Part is also due to the choice of research questions. Our understanding of many of the laboratory tasks used in cognitive psychology might not benefit from such borrowing. In any case, in studying autobiographical memory, cognitive psychologists are faced with issues similar to those that personality and social psychologists have pondered. Although novel solutions would certainly be appreciated, it appears that psychology's tendency to ignore its past will be avoided.

## The influence of the humanities

A refreshing aspect of this volume is the inclusion of a humanistic perspective from outside the normal scope of psychology. Some of the questions psychologists are now asking have been pondered by scholars whose interests are in literature (Barclay, Chap. 6), history (Brown, Shevell, & Rips, Chap. 9), and philosophy (Brewer, Chap. 3) rather than in memory per se. Although the humanists' methods often differ from those of psychologists, their descriptions of the behavior of individuals who are constructing autobiographies and histories provide a good source of both data and hypotheses to pursue. Considering the literary autobiographies and the histories themselves as complex human behaviors enriches our data base.

### Paths not taken

As is pointed out by Brewer, different implicit and explicit definitions of autobiographical memory are used in the 15 chapters of this book. At present, autobiographical memory is a topic of study, a book title, a set of phenomena, and not a clearly defined part of a system of memory. For the purposes of this book, the examples of research and theory define the term *autobiographical memory,* not a formal definition. In selecting the chapters, I tried to choose research from a cognitive background that adds to what we know about the recollections people have for a substantial portion of their lives. Without a formal definition of autobiographical memory, other selections were possible. A different book with different goals, but the same title, could have just as well included chapters on the aspects of psychoanalysis that provide an indepth probing of an individual's autobiography; on how one decides that a memory is one's own memory of an actual event (Johnson, in press; Johnson & Raye, 1981); on the reports of individuals who have constructed their own autobiographies either in a literary attempt or during individual or group psychotherapy (Allport, 1942; Myerhoff, 1978); on the technique of survey literature used to access particular aspects of autobiographical memory (Dijkstra & van de Zouwen, 1982; Moss & Goldstein, 1979); on the sociological and psychological description of the life course (Back, 1980; Reese & Smyer, 1983); on how people recall a small number of particular episodes from their lives, such as earliest childhood memories (Adler, 1937; Langs, 1965), eyewitness testimonies (Loftus, 1979), and flashbulb memories (Brown & Kulik, 1977; Neisser, 1982; Pillemer, 1984; Rubin & Kozin, 1984; Winograd & Killinger, 1983).

### A preview of the book

Each of the 14 chapters that follow attempts to understand the recollections people have of a substantial portion of their lives. Together they are a tutorial on the cognitive psychology of autobiographical memory. The outline of the book is quite simple. Part II contains introductions to the topic of autobiographical memory from three perspectives: historical, theoretical, and methodological. Within the framework set up by these introductory chapters, Parts III, IV, and V explore the schematic and temporal organization of autobiographical memory. Several clinical case studies are examined in Part VI.

The remainder of this introduction previews the book chapter by chapter. The purpose is not to provide a summary; there is much more covered in each chapter than will be mentioned here. Rather, the overall organization of the book will be laid out, the role of each chapter in that organization specified, and some indication given of the type of information presented in each chapter. The reader with a knowledge of contemporary research in this area, after examining the Table of Contents, could skim the rest of this chapter and miss little.

*Historical, theoretical, and methodological contexts*

Robinson's introductory chapter (Chap. 2) traces the study of autobiographical memory back to Ebbinghaus, Freud, and Galton. It is a long history but one marked with long periods of stagnation. The divergent traditions that followed from the work of these three scholars have affected, in varying degrees, the chapters of this book. In contrast, Brewer (Chap. 3) provides a contemporary context for the study of autobiographical memory. He probes the possible meanings of autobiographical memory, its likely components, and its relation to other forms of memory. Whether autobiographical memory is ultimately viewed as a separate form of memory with its own functional properties, and possibly its own physiology, is not at all clear. Nonetheless, at any point in the progress of science, and especially as a new area of research is being undertaken, a scholarly and efficient approach requires defining terms and searching related literatures for concepts and data. Brewer accomplishes this by providing a taxonomy of all of human memory, indicating where the functions discussed in this book would fall. Both Robinson and Brewer end with a consideration of the reconstructive and reproductive aspects of autobiographical memory. Robinson stresses the former, Brewer the latter.

Linton (Chap. 4) provides the methodological context for the book. She begins her chapter innocently enough by asking, "What do we know about the contents of human memory?" Like Brewer, she attempts an inventory but concentrates on autobiographical memory. She finds that the contents of autobiographical memory appear to change systematically with the method of observation used. Her extensive research on her own autobiographical memory leads not only to comparisons among methods but also to taxonomies of the kinds of memories retrieved and the types of search strategies that are effective under various conditions.

One of the most interesting aspects of Linton's chapter is her taxonomy of autobiographical memories. Unlike Brewer, who places autobiographical memory in a taxonomy of human memory in general, Linton classifies the different kinds of autobiographical memories she recalls. Most research limits the temporal and thematic scope of the memories studied, either by asking subjects to try to recognize descriptions of events of a certain format (Barclay, Chap. 6) or by asking questions that require knowledge of a certain kind (Brown, Shevell, & Rips, Chap. 9; Butters & Cermak, Chap. 14) or by using cues and instructions to evoke only certain kinds of memories (Reiser, Black, & Kalamarides, Chap. 7; Fitzgerald, Chap. 8; Wetzler & Sweeney, Chap. 11; Rubin, Wetzler, & Nebes, Chap. 12; Baddeley & Wilson, Chap. 13; Crovitz, Chap. 15). In her more open-ended searches of autobiographical memory, Linton does not limit what she will consider as a memory and so arrives at a classification of her recalls that ranges from the most general level of *mood tone* through *themes, extendures, episodes,* and *elements* down to *details.* Some of these levels match up with the earlier literature; others, like *extendures,* which are sets of memories loosely bound by the coexistence of some significant persistent orientation, do not.

Together, the chapters by Robinson, Brewer, and Linton provide a broad introduction to autobiographical memory and the existing background literature. Once this is accomplished, direct probes are made into how autobiographical memory is organized. In Part III Neisser; Barclay; Reiser, Black, and Kalamarides; and Fitzgerald examine the role of organization in autobiographical memory; and in Part IV Brown, Shevell, and Rips and Robinson examine the role of one kind of organization that has been held to be central to autobiographical memory: temporal organization.

## *The general organization of autobiographical memory*

Neisser (Chap. 5) provides a theoretical framework for the taxonomy of autobiographical memory observed by Linton, as well as an alternative framework for much of the rest of the book. Neisser extends Gibson's approach to perception to the study of autobiographical memory. Just as objects in the world have nested structure, the events that make up our lives have nested structure. Just as grains of sand, for example, are nested in sand castles which are nested in dunes which are nested in a beach, small movements are nested in actions which are nested in events which are nested in whole periods of our lives. Neisser initially tries to describe the structure of such nesting in the world instead of in mental representations. The emphasis on describing observables in the environment with greater precision is not a return to the behaviorism Neisser (1967) once argued against. The behaviorists did not attempt to describe carefully the environment in which animals and people evolved and normally live. Rather, Neisser's description of the environment is the start of a new endeavor, the beginning of an ecological theory of memory.

Whether the organization is described in terms of the external world or internal cognitive schemata, all the authors in Part III take as part of their challenge the description of how that organization affects behavior. Barclay (Chap. 6) musters the strongest arguments for the role of organization in autobiographical memory, arguments that complement Brewer's attempt to resurrect the copy theory of memory for recent memories. Barclay's thesis is that most autobiographical memories are reconstructions of past events, reconstructions that are driven by highly developed self-schemata. He begins by reviewing cases in which people believed their inaccurate memories to be accurate. The errors in memory reviewed are not random but rather fit into reasonable stories the rememberers might construct. Barclay then proceeds to review the ways in which literary autobiographies are constructed and criticized. Literary autobiographies, he says, "must convey precisely and honestly the autobiographer's intentions"; they need not, in fact cannot, convey an accurate record of the past. The events reported must be plausible and consistent, not veridical. The psychological literature on the self is then summoned to demonstrate that the forces acting to schematize autobiographical memories are much the same as those forces acting on an autobiographer. If Barclay's thesis and the evidence used to support it are correct, people should be willing to recognize, as their own, memories that are not theirs and should do so with increasing frequency as the events become more remote from and more similar to actual occurrences in their lives. Barclay reports such data from a group of students who kept diaries for him. His chapter provides theory and data that help us understand the paradox of why we believe our own memories to be true, yet know from extensive research that they cannot be accurate.

Reiser, Black, and Kalamarides (Chap. 7) take a very different approach to studying memory organization. Rather than arguing that autobiographical memories are constructed to be consistent with an overall self-schema, they begin describing what the structure is like. Their methodological approach is to analyze the search process people take in finding specific memories. Reiser, Black, and Kalamarides' subjects were asked to recall specific events, such as an instance of when they went to a public library or felt impatient or had bad weather during a vacation. The subjects talked aloud as they searched for a particular instance, and their protocols were analyzed to uncover their search strategies. If the way in which memory is searched is known, so is its functional organization. Aided by artificial intelligence theories of the structure of knowledge, Reiser, Black, and Kalamarides develop a taxonomy of autobiographical memory search strategies. Like the taxonomy offered by Linton for the different kinds of autobiographical memories she retrieved and the taxonomy offered by Brewer for different types of human memory including autobiographical, Reiser, Black, and Kalamarides' taxonomy of search strategies provides a starting point for future work.

Fitzgerald (Chap. 8) reminds us of the changes schemata must undergo with experience, with the development of the individual, and with changes in the society in which the individual lives. Under any theoretical framework peoples' schemata change as their experiences and the world they live in change. In addition, if Piaget, Bruner, and others are correct, the whole qualitative nature of schemata must change with development.

In general, the Fitzgerald chapter provides a somewhat more holistic approach to the study of autobiographical memory than most of the other chapters. For instance, in most research, I try to simplify the analysis by restricting myself to one time, one age group, and one cultural cohort. Fitzgerald cautions that such simplification can lead to misleading results even for the one time, age group, cultural cohort under study. I study prose memory (as well as list learning) as an implicit model for all memory. Fitzgerald notes that in doing so I strip real-world stimuli of their physical, sensual cues, and so my findings may not generalize beyond stimuli written on pieces of paper or on computer screens. I view a subject as encoding and retrieving memories. Fitzgerald notes that autobiographical memories are a transaction between an individual and that individual's memories: The individual can change his or her memories, and the memories can change the individual by providing a context for interpreting new experiences. I would typically try to find the simplest theory to account for the data at hand. Fitzgerald suggests that "the success of the autobiographical memory paradigm is dependent upon the richness of the theoretical framework that grows up around the data" (Chap. 8). The plurality of research strategies is characteristic of psychology. In time we will know which strategy or combination of strategies was the most fruitful. Fitzgerald has wagered a substantial amount of effort that his strategy is correct; so have I.

## The temporal organization of autobiographical memory

One kind of schematic organization has attracted special attention in studies of autobiographical memory: temporal organization. A reasonable initial hypothesis about autobiographical memory is that it is primarily organized along a time line. Time-line organization is certainly a factor, as is seen in the search strategies described by Linton and by Reiser, Black, and Kalamarides; the distribution of cued memories in the chapters by Rubin, Wetzler, and Nebes and by Wetzler and Sweeney; and the description of and the recovery from amnesias in the chapters by Baddeley and Wilson, Butters and Cermak, and Crovitz. In Part IV, Brown, Shevell, and Rips and Robinson, however, indicate that, at a deeper level, considering autobiographical memory as organized along a time line may be a fundamental error. Rather than autobiographical memory being organized along a time line, the time line may be organized in terms of the events and schemata recorded in autobiographical memory. When the confounding of the time line as measured by the calendar and the temporal succession of events is teased apart, the temporal succession of events is shown to have the greater role.

The two chapters in Part IV take two different approaches to this problem. Brown, Shevell, and Rips (Chap. 9) provided their subjects with a description of a public event, such as Prince Charles's marriage to Diana Spencer, and asked them to think aloud as they dated the event. The protocols produced were then analyzed to find the types of strategies employed. Among the many findings, Brown, Shevell, and Rips note that about 40% of the protocols they collected used autobiographical events to date the public event. That is, their subjects often told time in terms of the events of their own lives. For political events, which Brown, Shevell, and Rips note tend to belong to extended narratives, similar to the extendures in Linton's recalls, subjects referred to other events in the narrative to which the event belonged about one third of the time. That is, in these cases, subjects often told time in terms of political events. Further support for the claim that events and not time provide the time line for dating memories comes from one of the cleverest experimental manipulations in all of the reaction time literature. I will not steal Brown, Shevell, and Rips's thunder, but I will tell you that the prince's marriage took place in July of 1981.

Robinson's approach to investigating the effects of events on the temporal organization of autobiographical memory was to study the effect of a well-practiced and widespread temporal reference system: the school year (Chap. 10). For Robinson's subjects this consisted of three major blocks of time: fall semester, winter–spring semester, and summer vacation. The boundaries between these blocks are times of transition in activity and social status. Robinson shows that this reference system affects his subjects' judgments of their moods, their ability to recall events from the past year, the order of the events recalled, and their ability to date events reliably. The school year even provided a mnemonic organization that improved performance in paired-associate learning. For Robinson's subjects the school year consisted of a series of events that had effects on autobiographical memory beyond those of the simple passage of time. The beginning of classes, Thanksgiving, Christmas vacation, graduation, and similar occurrences combined to provide an ordered structure that allowed autobiographical memory to be organized in a temporal fashion. Both for Brown, Shevell, and Rips's subjects and for Robinson's, events rather than the passage of time or dates on a calendar provided a means of temporal organization.

## Temporal distributions of autobiographical memories

Having examined ways in which autobiographical memory is organized, the book considers the periods in a person's life from which these autobiographical memories come. The simplest hypothesis, and one that provides an excellent approximation for many situations, is that most autobiographical memories come from the recent past, with a smooth monotonically decreasing function into the distant past. If it is assumed that people record approximately the same number of autobiographical memories every day of their life, then a retention function showing how many of these memories are lost as a function of time would be enough to predict the shape of the distribution. The chapters in Part V note deviations from such a retention function. Wetzler and Sweeney (Chap. 11) demonstrate a sharp decrease in autobiographical memory from the first several years of life, and Rubin, Wetzler, and Nebes (Chap. 12) demonstrate an increase in memories coming from the childhood and young adult period of their older subjects. The decrease is often termed *childhood amnesia;* the increase, *reminiscence.* In providing quantitative definitions of what are usually considered as qualitative phenomena, these two chapters uncover descriptions that are inconsistent with some existing theories and general wisdom.

## Failures of autobiographical memory

By this point in the book, theoretical contexts for studying autobiographical memory have been provided, the schematic nature of autobiographical memory explored, especially with respect to temporal organization, and the distribution of autobiographical memories as a function of their age described. The three chapters in Part VI examine ways in which autobiographical memory fails to function. Trying to understand neurological memory deficits in terms of the theories and methods of cognitive psychology and trying to improve the theories and methods of cognitive psychology by studying neurological deficits have proven to be very tricky undertakings but ones with marked success. Autobiographical memory is especially suited to these undertakings. The various clinical syndromes of amnesia are, after all, primarily failures in autobiographical memory, and they help to raise fundamental questions that might otherwise be overlooked.

As in several of the preceding chapters, Baddeley and Wilson (Chap. 13) explicitly provide the beginnings of a taxonomy, in this case a tentative taxonomy of autobiographical memory deficits. Results from 10 amnesic and 2 nonamnesic patients are presented to demonstrate and begin classifying the variety of autobiographical memory deficits that can occur. The overview provided by comparing 10 amnesic patients is helpful in providing the background for the remainder of Part VI. The rest of Chapter 13, Chapter 14, and Chapter 15 each study one etiology present in Baddeley and Wilson's sample of subjects.

From their tentative taxonomy, Baddeley and Wilson select one dimension, that of confabulation, and one etiology, that of frontal lobe amnesics, for more detailed study. Baddeley and Wilson suggest that amnesia can be due to either a lack in the necessary active memory search processes, such as those studied by Reiser, Black, and Kalamarides (Chap. 7), or to a lack in the mnemonic information to be searched. Baddeley and Wilson argue that the frontal lobe patients, when compared to other amnesics, have more of a deficit in memory search processes.

Butters and Cermak (Chap. 14) discuss retrograde amnesia, that is, amnesia that occurs for events prior to an injury or the onset of an illness. Partly because studying retrograde amnesia involves knowing about a patient before the time that patient presents symptoms, such work has been exceedingly difficult. Butters and Cermak report on a unique case study that allowed an opportunity to study and verify the loss of previously noted memories. A few years after writing an autobiography, a famous scientist developed a dense amnesia as a result of Korsakoff's syndrome. Moreover, because the scientist's extensive publications and correspondence were available to Butters and Cermak, additional information that the famous scientist once knew could be obtained. From these multiple sources, Butters and Cermak developed tests to measure the degree of loss of various types of information learned during various periods of this scientist's life.

Crovitz (Chap. 15) also provides data from a single subject, a patient with a severe closed-head injury. An important event occurred, which was lost in the patient's period of retrograde amnesia. The patient had been told about the event by his brother and so knew about it but could not remember it for himself. This curious state of affairs serves to isolate two functions of autobiographical memory: its function as a source of information and its function as a basis for a feeling of self and of continuity. The patient has the former function available for a particular event but not the latter. Crovitz succeeds in restoring the patient's memory only to ponder what has been restored.

Together the three chapters on failures in autobiographical memory serve to provide a primer on amnesia and, more importantly for the book as a whole, force us to wonder about issues we might otherwise tend to ignore.

Memory hardly ever fails in ways we might expect from the theories that emanate from the laboratory or the armchair. In amnesia, as well as in aphasia and other neurological disorders, patients simultaneously display the ability to perform one task and the inability to perform a related, often simpler task. Through extreme practice, for instance, amnesics can learn complex motor tasks or the solutions to complex problems, not even recognizing the task as one they performed earlier. Failures of memory therefore have the potential to teach us a great deal we would not learn easily in other ways.

## References

Adler, A. (1937). The significance of early recollections. *International Journal of Individual Psychology, 3*, 283–287.

Allport, G. W. (1942). *The use of personal documents in psychological science.* New York: Social Science Research Council.

Back, K. W. (Ed.) (1980). *Life course: Integrative theories and exemplary populations.* AAAS Selected Symposium No. 41. Boulder, CO: Westview Press.

Bartlett, F. C. (1932). *Remembering: A study in experimental and social psychology.* Cambridge: Cambridge University Press.

Brown, R., & Kulik, J. (1977). Flashbulb memories. *Cognition, 5*, 73–99.

Dijkstra, W., & van der Zouwen, J. (1982). *Response behavior in the survey-interview.* London: Academic Press.

Johnson, M. K. (in press). The origin of memories. In P. C. Kendall (Ed.), *Advances in cognitive-behavioral research and therapy* (Vol. 4). New York: Academic Press.

Johnson, M. K., & Raye, C. L. (1981). Reality monitoring. *Psychological Review, 88*, 67–85.

Langs, R. J. (1965). Earliest memories and personality: A predictive study. *Archives of General Psychiatry, 12*, 379–390.

Loftus, E. F. (1979). *Eyewitness testimony.* Cambridge, MA: Harvard University Press.

Mandler, G. (1980). Recognizing: The judgement of previous occurrence. *Psychological Review, 87*, 251–271.

Meehl, P. E. (1978). Theoretical risks and tabular asterisks: Sir Karl, Sir Ronald, and the slow progress of soft psychology. *Journal of Consulting and Clinical Psychology, 46*, 806–834.

Moss, L., & Goldstein, H. (1979). *The recall method in social surveys.* London: University of London Institute of Education.

Myerhoff, B. (1978). *Number our days.* New York: Dutton.

Neisser, U. (1967). *Cognitive psychology.* New York: Appleton-Century-Crofts.

(1982). Snapshots or benchmarks? In U. Neisser (Ed.), *Memory observed: Remembering in natural contexts* (pp. 43–48). San Francisco: Freeman.

Pillemer, D. B. (1984). Flashbulb memories of the assassination attempt on President Reagan. *Cognition, 16*, 63–80.

Reese, H. W., & Smyer, M. A. (1983). The dimensionalization of life events. In E. J. Callahan & K. A. McCluskey (Eds.), *Life-span developmental psychology: Normative life events* (pp. 1–33). New York: Academic Press.

Rubin, D. C., & Kozin, M. (1984). Vivid memories. *Cognition, 16*, 81–95.

Winograd, E., & Killinger, W. A., Jr. (1983). Relating age at encoding in early childhood to adult recall: Development of flashbulb memories. *Journal of Experimental Psychology: General, 112*, 413–422.

*Part II*

# Historical, theoretical, and methodological contexts for the study of autobiographical memory

The three chapters of Part II provide a framework for the study of autobiographical memory. Robinson (Chap. 2) traces the study of autobiographical memory back to its prestigious roots, Brewer (Chap. 3) places autobiographical memory in the context of the study of memory in general, and Linton (Chap. 4) provides a general methodological overview of the kinds of memories and memory organizations that are seen when different memory search techniques are employed.

# 2 Autobiographical memory: a historical prologue

*John A. Robinson*

When we speak of autobiographical memory we are referring to the memories a person has of his or her own life experiences. Like many other aspects of human behavior, the study of personal recollections predates the emergence of psychology as a discipline. From the beginning biographers and historians have used personal recollections to construe the individual and collective past. The archival function of memory has often been given primary emphasis in biographical and historical work. According to this view, life memories are time capsules, records of an unrepeatable past. As such they can be used both to recount the past and to teach lessons for the future. The intimate association between memory and narrative arises from this urge to use the past to instruct present and future generations. An awareness of the fallibility of memory, however, is as old as man's fascination with memory itself, and efforts to authenticate and verify recollections by various means (e.g., documents, corroborative reports from contemporaries) are among the factors that distinguish history and biography from legend and folklore. Historians and biographers were and remain concerned with the construction of judicious accounts of the past. They are not concerned with remembering per se; that has become the province of psychology.

We can trace the beginnings of systematic empirical research on autobiographical memory to Galton and Freud. Both were contemporaries of Ebbinghaus, but both established traditions of memory research quite different from his, and quite different from each other's. Life memories tell us something about remembering and about the rememberer. An interest in this double aspect of memory has, from the beginning, distinguished work on autobiographical memory from the research on learning and memory that has flowed from the Ebbinghausian tradition.

Galton and Freud both favored the direct study of personal recollections, but they differed in method and purpose. Galton's approach to memory was that of the botanist whereas Freud's approach was that of the biographer. Galton was fascinated with variety and sought to describe, quantify, and codify

19

it in each domain of his psychological inquiries. His investigation (Galton, 1883) into his own recollections illustrates the botanical orientation quite clearly. Galton describes the various forms of his recollections (sensory images, words and names, general impressions) and then proposes that the words used as memory prompts could be classified in terms of the relative frequency with which each elicited the several types of association. Galton also recorded the reaction time for each prompt and grouped his recollections according to the period of his life when the experience originally occurred. In retrospect, it is obvious that Galton's method was a type of ecological survey, a procedure for sampling the domain of recollections to discover what is there. Implicit in Galton's informal study is the prospect of a taxonomy of recollections with attendant questions about the causes and significance of the various types, and of individual differences in their predominance. It is a short step from such questions to the study of life history and personality.

Freud's interest in memory arose from his efforts to explain and treat neurosis. He concluded that the neurotic person was driven by experiences he or she could not forget and struggled to avoid remembering. In true biographical tradition Freud identified formative experiences and projected these as themes in the psychological development of the person. The treatment of neurosis through psychoanalysis entails reconstructing a person's life history, a process heavily dependent upon the recollections and associations of the analysand. Although individual recollections are of intrinsic interest, the relationships between them (as discerned by the analyst) are of primary concern, for these may disclose patterns from which causal inferences can be made about the person's psychic life. For Galton, recollections were tokens of prospective types. For Freud, however, any formal similarity between recollections was only one of many possible types of relationship of interest. Causal relationships may exist even where appearances do not disclose them. Hence, the analysis of memories had to go beyond the literal level of content and circumstance. Freud's distinctive blending of the case history method of medicine and the interpretive methods of humanistic studies was ideally suited to the biographical thrust of his work.

Neither Galton nor Freud pursued the study of personal recollections as a systematic problem. Galton's curiosity led him to continually study new topics, whereas Freud was convinced that his clinical methods were superior to the controlled experiments favored by academic psychologists. Galton's legacy can be traced through the questionnaire studies of recollections published intermittently since the publication of his own work (e.g., Colgrove, 1899). The continued importance of the botanical enterprise is explained by Marigold Linton (Chap. 4). Freud's impact was more direct and durable. There is a large literature in which personal memories were used as data for evaluating various of Freud's theoretical proposals about personality, development, and psychopathology. The biographical method of personality research (e.g., White, 1962) was, in part, inspired by the blend of case history and interpretive techniques that Freud pioneered. There have been many studies of memory per se prompted by Freud's theories, most notably those on the relationship of affect to retention or forgetting.

Judging from the published literature in psychology, one would have had to conclude that by the 1950s this topic and these two traditions were moribund. The empirical study of memory for life events never really ceased, however, though there were shifts of direction and emphasis. Developmental psychologists continued their investigations of the life history data parents provide about their children. Typically, those studies were concerned to determine the accuracy and authenticity of such reports. Recently, however, Field (1980, 1981) has taken advantage of the rich informational base provided by one of those longitudinal studies to explore parents' recall of their own histories. During this same period naturalistic studies of stressful life events appeared in substantial numbers (e.g., Uhlenhuth, Haberman, Balter, & Lipman, 1977). Most of that research relied on questionnaires, that is, structured retrospective reports about a person's health, family relations, and job experiences. In other disciplines, such as public health and marketing, sophisticated studies of memory for life experiences were undertaken to address the practical concerns of industry and government (cf. Cannell, Fisher, & Bakker, 1965; Cartwright, 1963; Parry & Crosley, 1950; Sudman & Bradburn, 1973). Also, the emergence of the subdiscipline of oral history both renewed interest in the study of memory among historians and provided another arena for the empirical study of autobiographical memory (cf. Lummis, 1981; Neuenschwander, 1978; Thompson, 1978).

While the research cited above was being carried out – without much notice by memory researchers – the climate of opinion within psychology was gradually changing. Theoretical models of memory and memory processes have become more complex and versatile. Concern about representativeness and the ecological validity of psychological constructs has intensified. Increased longevity has focused attention on adulthood and old age. The virtual identification of memory with the acquisition of knowledge has been challenged. Thus, when Crovitz and Schiffman (1974) revived Galton's prompting technique many psychologists were receptive to their message. Their article initiated a series of studies in which the Galtonian method and its botanical orientation are clearly evident. For example, the study of memories elicited by contrasting types of words (Robinson, 1976), the study of individual differences in visual imagery in relation to memory recency and retrieval speed (Karis, 1979), and interest in the distributional properties of recollections across the lifespan (e.g., Franklin & Holding, 1977) all reflect the taxonomic orientation initiated by Galton.

There are also signs that the biographical tradition is reemerging. It has been interesting to observe the gradual shift in Linton's work from her initial concern with questions of retention and accuracy to an interest in the transformation, organization, and significance of her recollections (Chap. 4). Khilstrom (1981) has advocated renewed study ⌐f the relationships between personality and memory and, with Harackiewicz (1982), has begun to reexamine childhood recollections from this perspective. Studies of reminiscing in middle-aged and older adults are raising questions about the structure and functions of our personal histories (e.g., Butler, 1963; Lieberman & Tobin, 1983; Myerhoff, 1978). Finally, efforts to develop a normative taxonomy of life events (Brim & Ryff, 1980) may help define the experiential structure of personal histories and provide a new bridge between the study of memory and the study of human development.

From either the Galtonian or the Freudian perspective, the rigorous study of meaningless memories advocated by Ebbinghaus will seem paradoxical. However, these three approaches to the study of memory are not necessarily incompatible. Ebbinghaus's invention of the nonsense syllable is an early example of simulation methodology. Those who rejected the direct study of personal recollections questioned the claim that such investigations provided reliable empirical descriptions of the domain their own experiments sought to simulate and thereby explain. On the other hand, the assumption that a nonsense syllable is a representative token of all types of remembrances has been repeatedly criticized. As subsequent generations of researchers have shown, however, it is possible to introduce more and more properties of ordinary recollections into simulation material without compromising the controls required in true experiments. Conversely, as current research on autobiographical memory readily demonstrates, the Galtonian method can be coupled with hypothesis testing and thus go beyond mere description. And what could be more Ebbinghausian than Linton's (1975, 1979) longitudinal self-study of everyday memory? In her work the biographical orientation, though not Freudian in character, has been coupled with the quantitative and controlled testing procedures of traditional memory research. Linton's experiment will probably not be duplicated, simply because of the extraordinary demands on time and commitment required by her procedures. Nevertheless, her findings can be compared with those of related investigations that have used diaries and other corroborative documents to assess a person's memory for his or her own history (e.g., Smith, 1952). This convergence of traditions and methods is a healthy development that bodes well for future progress in understanding autobiographical memory.

I would like to end this historical sketch by placing an issue on the agenda for future investigators. Memory research has traditionally focused on the accuracy of recall and the sources or causes of error and forgetting. No one should question the importance of this question, but it is not the only interesting question about memory, particularly about autobiographical memory. As Neisser (1978) pointed out, it is just as important to understand the uses of memories, the work they do in everyday life. One's factual and practical knowledge is used routinely in daily life. And plain observation will confirm that people regularly use memories of personal experiences to plan, solve problems, instruct and guide others, and justify and explain their actions to themselves and others. This matter of the uses of memory is, of course, connected to the question of accuracy. Bartlett expressed it well: "The critical questions [remain] as they have been ever since remembering began to be investigated: how to understand and reconcile the conflicting demands for the accurate and literal reinstatement of events and experiences at the time when they 'go into storage,' and the equally urgent requirement that when they come 'out of storage,' it should be in forms sufficiently flexible to meet the challenges of a constantly changing world" (1963, p. 235). Bartlett is suggesting that our notions of accuracy will need to become more sophisticated, and he implies that the study of memory in use holds the key to this advance. There is a generative dimension to remembering that mediates the matching of past and present. This observation applies with equal force to factual and autobiographical memory. There is another aspect of the generativity of memory, which I shall call *discovery*. By this I mean spontaneous conscious insights into one's history brought about when chance or circumstance evoke latent memories that reveal connections or themes in one's experience. Of course, certain forms of psychotherapy deliberately aim to achieve these moments of insight, but they occur in everyday life as well. Autobiographical memory is not only a record, it is a resource.

# References

Bartlett, F. C. (1963). *Encyclopaedia Britannica* (Vol. 15), s.v. "Memory." Encyclopaedia Britannica.

Brim, O. G., Jr., & Ryff, C. D. (1980). On the properties of life events. In P. B. Baltes & O. G. Brim, Jr. (Eds.), *Life-span development and behavior* (3:367–388). New York: Academic Press.

Butler, R. N. (1963). The life review: An interpretation of reminiscence in the aged. *Psychiatry, 26*, 63–76.

Cannell, C. F., Fisher, G., & Bakker, T. (1965). Reporting of hospitalization in the health interview survey. *Vital and Health Statistics* (series 2, no. 6, pp. 1–61). Washington, DC: National Center for Health Statistics.

Cartwright, A. (1963). Memory errors in a morbidity survey. *Millbank Memorial Fund Quarterly, 41*, 5–24.

Colgrove, F. W. (1899). Individual memories. *American Journal of Psychology, 10*, 228–255.

Crovitz, H. F., & Schiffman, H. (1974). Frequency of episodic memories as a function of their age. *Bulletin of the Psychonomic Society, 4,* 517–518.

Field, D. (1980, November). *Recollections of childhood: Changing perspectives.* Paper presented at the meeting of the Gerontological Society, San Diego, CA.

——— (1981). Retrospective reports by healthy intelligent elderly people of personal events of their adult lives. *International Journal of Behavioural Development, 4,* 77–97.

Franklin, H., & Holding, D. (1977). Personal memories at different ages. *Quarterly Journal of Experimental Psychology, 29,* 527–532.

Galton, F. (1883). *Inquiries into human faculty and its development.* London: Macmillan.

Karis, D. (1979). *Individual differences in autobiographical memory.* Paper presented at the 87th Annual Meeting of the American Psychological Association, New York.

Khilstrom, J. F. (1981). On personality and memory. In N. Cantor & J. F. Khilstrom (Eds.), *Personality, cognition, and social interaction* (pp. 123–149). Hillsdale, N.J.: Erlbaum.

Khilstrom, J. F., & Harackiewicz, J. M. (1982). The earliest recollection: A new survey. *Journal of Personality, 50,* 134–148.

Lieberman, M. A., & Tobin, S. S. (1983). *The experience of old age.* New York: Basic Books.

Linton, M. (1975). Memory for real-world events. In D. A. Norman & D. E. Rumelhart (Eds.), *Explorations in cognition* (pp. 376–404). San Francisco: Freeman.

——— (1979). Real-world memory after six years: An in vivo study of very long term memory. In M. M. Gruneberg, P. E. Morris, & R. N. Sykes (Eds.), *Practical aspects of memory* (pp. 69–76). London: Academic Press.

Lummis, T. (1981). Structure and validity in oral evidence. *International Journal of Oral History, 2,* 109–119.

Myerhoff, B. (1978). *Number our days.* New York: Dutton.

Neisser, U. (1978). Memory: What are the important questions? In M. M. Gruneberg, P. E. Morris, & R. N. Sykes (Eds.), *practical aspects of memory* (pp. 3–24). New York: Academic Press.

Neuenschwander, J. A. (1978). Remembrance of things past: Oral historians and long-term memory. *Oral History Review,* pp. 45–53.

Parry, H. J., & Crosley, H. M. (1950). Validity of responses to survey questions. *Public Opinion Quarterly, 14,* 61–90.

Robinson, J. A. (1976). Sampling autobiographical memory. *Cognitive Psychology, 8,* 578–595.

Smith, M. E. (1952). Childhood memories compared with those of adult life. *Journal of Genetic Psychology, 80,* 151–182.

Sudman, S., & Bradburn, N. M. (1973). Effects of time and memory factors on response in surveys. *Journal of the American Statistical Association, 68,* 805–815.

Thompson, P. (1978). *The voice of the past: Oral history.* Oxford: Oxford University Press.

Uhlenhuth, E. H., Haberman, S. J., Balter, N. D., & Lipman, R. S. (1977). Remembering life events. In J. S. Strauss, H. M. Babigian, and M. Roff (Eds.), *The origins and course of psychopathology.* New York: Plenum Press.

White, R. W. (1962). *Lives in progress: A study of the natural growth of personality.* New York: Holt.

# 3 What is autobiographical memory?

*William F. Brewer*

The purpose of this chapter is (*a*) to describe the forms of autobiographical memory and contrast them with other forms of memory; (*b*) to give a theoretical account of autobiographical memory in terms of the self; (*c*) to argue for the importance of phenomenal reports in the study of autobiographical memory; (*d*) to examine some of the experimental findings on autobiographical memory in the context of this analysis; (*e*) to give a detailed account of personal memory, one of the important forms of autobiographical memory; and (*f*) to outline a partially reconstructive view of personal memory.

## The problem

The study of autobiographical memory is one of the least well-developed areas in the study of human memory; there is considerable divergence both in what is being investigated and in the terminology used to describe what is being investigated. There is still much work to be done in describing and classifying the basic phenomena in the area. In order to gain an immediate impression of the complexities involved in studying this topic, I want to examine a concrete example.

Currently the most popular technique for studying autobiographical memory is a method developed by Sir Francis Galton (1879*a*, 1879*b*) in which the subject is presented with a word and asked to find a memory related to that word. This simple task nicely reveals one of the major problems that will be addressed in this chapter – the multiple forms of autobiographical and non-autobiographical memory. It seems to me that if I were a subject in an experiment of this type and if I were presented with a word such as *California,* I might give any one of the following very different kinds of response (depend-

I would like to thank Don Dulany, Demetrios Karis, John Pani, Brian Ross, David Rubin, Thom Srull, Tricia Tenpenny, and Ellen Brewer for reading an earlier version of this chapter. These loyal folk helped improve this work considerably and are obviously responsible only for the good parts of the final chapter.

25

ing upon the experimenter's instructions and/or upon my own self-imposed
retrieval strategy):

1. *Personal memory.* I might experience a mental image that corresponds to a particular episode in my life, such as the time in California, while visiting Mt. Palomar, when I made a snowball and threw
   it down the trail at my sons, starting a snowball fight.

2. *Autobiographical fact.* I might simply recall the fact (with no accompanying imagery) that I drove to Mt. Palomar on another occasion
   when I was a senior in high school.

3. *Generic personal memory.* I might have a mental image of what, in
   general, it was like to drive north on Highway 1 in California's Big
   Sur region: an image that does not appear to be of any specific moment during the drive but is a generic view from the driver's seat of
   the car with the sharp jagged cliffs to my right and the Pacific stretch-
   ing out to the horizon on my left.

4. *Semantic memory.* I might recall (with no accompanying imagery)
   that in California in 1978 the voters passed a limitation on property
   tax called Proposition 13.

5. *Generic perceptual memory.* I might have a visual image of the outline of the shape of the state of California.

In the next several sections of this chapter I will attempt to provide a structure that brings some order to this diverse set of memory phenomena. I will
argue that the first three responses are forms of autobiographical memory and
the last two are not, and I will organize these forms of memory in terms of
their acquisition conditions (single instance vs. repeated); their form of representation (imaginal vs. nonimaginal); and their content (self vs. depersonalized).

*The self*

Although the study of autobiographical memory has included a variety of
topics, it seems to me that the set of issues usually treated under this label
*does* have an internal coherence that leads investigators to want to distinguish
these topics from the more traditional laboratory memory phenomena. In particular, I think we can define autobiographical memory as memory for information related to the self.

In order to "cash in" this definition of autobiographical memory, however,
one has to be able to give a coherent account of the self. The construct of the
self has not been a topic of interest in modern cognitive psychology, yet it has
a long history in psychology (cf. the chapter on the self in James, 1890), and

it has recently been revived as a topic of interest in the area of social cognition (Greenwald, 1981; Markus, 1980). I would like to outline a position on the self that could provide a working position for cognitive psychologists interested in the topic of human memory. In brief, I intend to argue that the self is composed of an experiencing ego, a self-schema, and an associated set of personal memories and autobiographical facts.

*Ego.* By *ego* I mean the conscious experiencing entity that is the focus of our phenomenal experience. The ego is the aspect of a person that experiences things from the "inside." The ego is the conscious aspect of the mind that moves through space and time. It is the memory for the ego's moment-to-moment experience that we call personal memories.

*Self-schema.* The self-schema is the cognitive structure that contains generic knowledge about the self. In the same way that individuals have knowledge about the solar system or knowledge about Walter Cronkite, individuals have knowledge about themselves. This knowledge is presumably organized into unconscious mental structures that interact with incoming information about the self (Brewer & Nakamura, 1984; Rumelhart, 1980). Some of the information that goes into making up the self-schema is private and available only to the self; other information is public and available to an observer. The self-schema must be one of the richer knowledge structures in an individual's long-term memory; hence, once it has developed, it probably changes only slowly, thus providing consistency to the self over time.

*Self.* The self is the complex mental structure that includes the ego, the self-schema, and portions of long-term memory related to the ego-self (e.g., personal memories, generic personal memories, and autobiographical facts).

*Individual.* The individual is the larger entity that includes the self, the depersonalized (nonself) aspects of the mind, and the body. Thus, it is the individual who has depersonalized knowledge about biology (e.g., a robin has wings) and who possesses cognitive skills (e.g., can carry out long division), motor skills (e.g., can ride a bicycle), and rote skills (e.g., can recite Lincoln's Gettysburg Address).

My point in sketching out a position on the nature and organization of the self is simple. I believe that an experimental psychologist who wishes to give an account of human memory that includes autobiographical memory must include a set of constructs something like those outlined above. (I must confess, however, that I certainly did not believe this point until I began working on this chapter.)

## Autobiographical memory: description and classification

The next sections of this chapter give a definition of autobiographical memory in terms of memory for the self, provide a basic description of the forms of autobiographical memory, and contrast autobiographical memory with other types of memory.

### Brewer and Pani's analysis of human memory

In a recent paper Brewer and Pani (1983) argued that much of the experimental work on human memory jumped too rapidly into the detailed examination of a few particular forms of memory and suggested that this style of research be tempered with more attempts to step back and do basic descriptive work (for a similar view, see Neisser, 1978). We used the metaphor of descriptive biology to make this point and suggested that it might be productive if more effort were devoted to research in which investigators attempted to describe the naturally occurring forms of memory. Note that Linton (Chap. 4) and Robinson's discussion of Galton (Chap. 2) use the biology analogy to make a similar point. One wonders if this is the beginning of a trend away from experimental psychology's bad case of physics envy.

In the Brewer and Pani (1983) paper we provided a description of what we thought were the major forms of naturally occurring memory (personal memory, semantic memory, generic perceptual memory, motor skill, cognitive skill, and rote linguistic skill). We then gave a somewhat more analytic account in which we attempted to use our understanding of the forms of representation and processes that influence these forms of representation to sketch out a logical structure for the forms of human memory (a case of periodic-table envy?). In retrospect, however, it is clear that our analytic scheme, as presented, is not able to handle autobiographical memory, for we were not ready to include a concept of self in our analysis of human memory. The following section is an attempt to modify the analysis of Brewer and Pani to capture autobiographical memory. If this new analysis is successful, it should provide an account of the different forms of memory outlined in the example given at the beginning of this chapter.

### A structural account of autobiographical memory

The new classification of forms of human memory that incorporates autobiographical memory is given in Table 3.1. The table is structured with types of input to the memory system in the column heads and with types of acquisition conditions in the left-hand column. The cells contain the forms of memory

Table 3.1. *A structural account of autobiographical memory*

| Acquisition conditions & forms of representation | Types of input | | | |
|---|---|---|---|---|
| | Ego-self | Visual-spatial (objects, places) | Visual-temporal (events, actions) | Semantic |
| *Single instance* | | | | |
| Imaginal | Personal memory | Particular image (depersonalized) | Particular image? (depersonalized) | (Image of input modality) |
| Nonimaginal | Autobiographical fact | Instantiated schema or mental model | Instantiated script or plan | Facts |
| *Repeated (with variation)* | | | | |
| Imaginal | Generic personal memory | Generic perceptual memory | Generic perceptual memory | No image |
| Nonimaginal | Self-schema | Schema | Scripts | Knowledge |

*Note:* As used in this chapter, autobiographical memory includes those forms of memory listed in the ego-self column.

representation that are hypothesized to result from the interaction of the acquisition conditions and the memory inputs. Two acquisition conditions are considered: exposure to a single instance of some input and exposure to input that is repeated with variation. This particular aspect of the acquisition process is included because it appears to lead to different forms of memory representation.

Within each input condition there is a systematic analysis of the resulting memory representations into imaginal and nonimaginal forms of mental events. This reflects an explicit methodological commitment to the belief that a complete account of the human mind must include an account of the subject's phenomenal experience. Clearly, there has been a recent trend toward the acceptance of phenomenal data in experimental psychology (e.g., Ericsson & Simon, 1980; Hilgard, 1980; Natsoulas, 1970); however, in Brewer and Pani (1983) we take a very hard line on this issue. We argue that data from phenomenal experience are not to be used just to suggest further analyses or to support reaction time data. Instead, they are to be considered data for theory construction, just like any other class of data. Thus, if subjects' phenomenal reports are at variance with reaction time data or number-correct data, one does not throw out the subjects' reports but must develop a larger theoretical structure that covers the entire pattern of data. This methodological commitment seems particularly valuable in the study of autobiographical memory because of the important role of (phenomenally experienced) personal memory in this domain.

The columns of Table 3.1 are organized according to the form of input to the memory system; this table includes only the forms of input that appear to be needed to give an account of autobiographical memory and omits many forms of input that are more important in accounting for the broader range of depersonalized memory phenomena.

We now turn to an examination of the forms of memory representation that are hypothesized to occur in each combination of acquisition condition and memory input (i.e., each cell of the table). We will work through each column of the table starting with the first cell of the ego-self column.

*Ego-self: single.* When an individual experiences a single event of some type, the phenomenal aspect of the recall of the particular experience is a personal memory. Personal memories are experienced as a partial reliving of the original experience and typically have a strong visual imagery component. This form of memory has played a major role in research on autobiographical memory and so will be discussed in more detail later in the chapter.

In addition to the image form of representation, it is assumed that each experience also leads to nonimage representations of information about the self (e.g., I can recall that I had cereal for breakfast this morning without having a personal memory of myself sitting at the breakfast table). These autobiographical facts are presumably stored in some form of abstract nonimage representation (e.g., propositions).

*Ego-self: repeated.* Repeated exposure to a set of related experiences can give rise to a generic image of the experiences. For example, I have a generic personal memory of hiking up a mountain in Vermont. I simply am not able to produce a specific personal memory of any particular moment of the trip up the trail; yet the generic image I have is detailed enough to distinguish it from other hikes (e.g., the trail is in a tall forest, the trail is not along a ridgeline, I am using a branch I picked up as a hiking stick). This generic personal memory is thus different from the specific personal memory I have of the moment during the end of the hike when the hiker in the van next to us opened up his hood and found that porcupines had eaten all the rubber off his water hose. Generic personal memories are constrained by the abstracting properties of the relevant perceptual systems. Thus, I can have a generic personal memory of "going out on the beach" during some vacation but not of "going on vacation," where that includes going hiking in the mountains, going swimming at a beach, and visiting a major city.

As an individual has repeated experiences related to the self, a self-schema is formed. The assumption here is that the information about the self forms a complex knowledge domain and, like information in other domains, it comes to be organized into generic knowledge structures (cf. Brewer & Nakamura, 1984; Rumelhart, 1980). This self-schema then comes to modify perception and recall of new information related to the self and underlies many forms of action relating to the self (Epstein, 1973; Greenwald, 1981; Markus, 1980). Thus, if an individual is told that hard work is good and is frequently rewarded for hard work, over time "being a hard worker" becomes part of the self-schema, so that the individual tends to work hard, to pay attention to how hard others work, to misremember how much they have worked, and so on. This discussion of the self-schema completes the ego-self column of Table 3.1, and now I will turn to a brief treatment of three input conditions that give rise to nonautobiographical forms of memory.

*Visual-spatial: single.* Single exposure to a visual-spatial input (an object or place) leads to a particularized visual image. To the degree that a memory of an object includes information about the experiencing ego (e.g., ego location, ego feelings, etc.) it is a personal memory, but to the degree that information about the ego is not present one would have depersonalized memory of particular objects. It seems to me that most particularized visual images of objects are part of full personal memories; however, we need additional data on the existence and frequency of depersonalized particular images in memory.

My position on the form of nonimage representation for single visual-spatial inputs has changed somewhat from that presented in Brewer and Pani (1983). I now would like to distinguish inputs that are instances of a developed schema and inputs that are not. If the input is a new exemplar of a well-developed schema, then the information is hypothesized to be represented in the form of an instantiated schema (cf. Brewer & Nakamura, 1984); but if it is a new configuration, the information is hypothesized to be in the form of a mental model (Johnson-Laird, 1983).

*Visual-spatial: repeated.* Multiple exposures to a number of instances of a class of objects leads (within the constraints of the perceptual system) to a generic visual image. Under these conditions, the nonimage form of representation is assumed to be an object schema (e.g., knowledge about cars) or place schema (e.g., knowledge about church buildings).

*Visual-temporal: single.* It is not clear what type of image representation is produced through single exposures to visual-temporal input (events, actions).

Brewer and Pani (1983) speculated that most individuals cannot form a mental "video recording" of a complex action, but this remains open for investigation. In addition, there is a problem here similar to that with visual-spatial input because it is not obvious to what degree particular event memories occur as parts of full personal memories or as independent, depersonalized images.

I now think that the nonimage form of representation for instances of a repeated action will be in the form of an instantiated script (Schank & Abelson, 1977), whereas the representation for a unique intentional action will be in the form of an instantiated plan (Brewer & Dupree, 1983; Lichtenstein & Brewer, 1980).

*Visual-temporal: repeated.* Repeated exposures to visual-temporal input may lead to generic event images, but, because events appear to show more perceptual variability than objects, the possibility for generic event images is reduced. However, the nonimage form of representation for repeated actions should be in the form of scripts (Schank & Abelson, 1977).

*Semantic: single.* The analysis of the form of representation for nonautobiographical semantic memory is complex. Clearly, most semantic information arrives through some perceptual modality (reading, listening, television), but by convention (cf. Brewer & Pani, 1983, pp. 24–25) the image properties of the surface form of the input are treated in other parts of the structure, so there are no image properties for this cell. Single instances of semantic information are assumed to be represented in some nonimage form (e.g., propositions).

*Semantic: repeated.* Semantic information that is repeated with variation is assumed to have no image properties, and the nonimage representations are hypothesized to be more elaborated abstract knowledge structures.

*Terminology*

There has been enormous confusion in the terminology used in discussions of autobiographical memory. It seems to me that one of the benefits of the attempt to outline an overall framework for the analysis of human memory is that it allows us to clear up some of the confusion.

Many researchers in the area of autobiographical memory have stated that they were studying episodic memory as discussed by Tulving (1972). Examination of current texts on memory will show that the section on episodic memory is devoted to data from list-learning experiments coming from the Ebbinghaus Empire. This is a serious problem, because few people want to consider the development of rote skill at repeating a list as an example of autobiographical memory.

It seems to me that the root of the problem is that Tulving attempted to accomplish too much with a single binary distinction. Tulving's great insight in his 1972 paper was that memory investigators needed to distinguish the new experimental studies of the structure of long-term semantic knowledge from the traditional Ebbinghaus memory experiments. He proposed the terms *semantic memory* to cover the first and *episodic memory* to cover the second. Now, in retrospect, it seems that there were problems with Tulving's analysis of episodic memory. In the 1972 paper Tulving stated that episodic memory "stores information about temporally dated episodes or events and temporal-spatial relations among these events" (p. 385) and proposed that instances of episodic memory refer to "a personal experience that is remembered in its temporal-spatial relation to other such experiences" (p. 387). It seems clear that this abstract definition of episodic memory describes the type of memory that is called personal memory in our classification scheme. However, when one looks carefully at the examples given to make the definition more concrete, not one seems to be a clear example of personal memory, and at one point in the paper (p. 402) Tulving explicitly states that traditional verbal learning experiments are studies of episodic memory. Thus, the *definition* of episodic memory seems to refer to the phenomenon of personal memory (a topic not under investigation by experimental psychologists at that time), but in *actual usage* the term *episodic memory* was taken to cover a wide range of phenomena, particularly the study of rote verbal skill. Given these problems with the episodic-semantic memory distinction, it seems best not to define autobiographical memory as episodic memory, as that term has come to be used in current cognitive psychology.

In this chapter I have defined autobiographical memory to be memory for information relating to the self, where memory for the self is given more complete definition by the structural account of memory. Thus, in terms of Table 3.1, autobiographical memory is taken to cover the entire ego-self column (e.g., personal memory, autobiographical facts, generic personal memory, and the self-schema). It seems to me that this account of autobiographical memory succeeds in distinguishing autobiographical memory as a natural class from the various forms of depersonalized memory and that, if one takes the present volume as a concrete example of what is studied by scientists working on autobiographical memory, this definition does a fairly good job of mapping that set of phenomena.

Finally, it should be noted that defining autobiographical memory in terms of the self avoids problems that occur when several competing approaches are tried. Thus, if one tried to define autobiographical memory in terms of the occurrence of mental imagery, one would be forced to exclude autobiographical facts and the self-schema and to include generic perceptual memory (e.g., one's image of a capital $E$). This approach does not seem to carve out an appropriate subclass of memory phenomena. One could try to define autobiographical memory as memory that can be organized along a time line or that can be assigned absolute dates. However, this approach also leads to problems, because memory for public events and memory for historical events would also have to be included. Thus, an analysis of autobiographical memory in terms of the self seems to provide an internally consistent account of the topic, and its only defect is that it requires the introduction of the construct of the self, something that experimental psychologists have been reluctant to allow.

### Characteristics of personal memory

It seems to me that a unique contribution of the study of autobiographical memory to the overall study of human memory is the analysis of personal memory, so this section will include a full description of the characteristics of personal memory. One of the few theoretical discussions of personal memory in recent cognitive psychology is the treatment in Brewer and Pani (1983); however, this topic has been of considerable interest to philosophers, and extensive discussions can be found in Russell (1921) under the label "true memory"; in Furlong (1951) under "retrospective memory"; in Ayer (1956) under "event memory"; in Smith (1966) under "occurrent memory"; and in Locke (1971) under "personal memory."

A personal memory is a recollection of a particular episode from an individual's past. It frequently appears to be a "reliving" of the individual's phenomenal experience during that earlier moment. The contents almost always include reports of visual imagery, with less frequent occurrences of other forms of imagery. Other aspects of the earlier mental experience, such as occurrent thoughts and felt affect, are also found in the reports of personal memories. The strong component of visual imagery in personal memory suggests that it might be of interest to study personal memory in blind individuals. Personal memories are experienced as occurring at specific times and locations. This does not mean that the individual can assign an absolute date, just that the memory is experienced as having occurred at a unique time.

A personal memory is accompanied by a belief that the remembered episode was personally experienced by the self. It would be interesting to see if individuals suffering from "depersonalization" (cf. Kihlstrom, 1984; Reed, 1979) have personal memories in which this characteristic of the personal memory is reduced or eliminated. A personal memory is accompanied by a belief that it occurred in the self's past. The issue of why one rarely confuses personal memories with current perceptions has been one of the major topics in philosophical discussions of memory (cf. Ayer, 1956; Furlong, 1951; Locke, 1971; Russell, 1921; Smith, 1966). These philosophers have suggested a wide range of solutions. For example, it has been proposed that the distinction is made on the basis of attributes of the personal memory (e.g., vividness of the image); contents of the personal memory (e.g., "this personal memory includes a house I used to live in, so it must be from the past"); and direct, phenomenally experienced past markers (e.g., feelings of familiarity; see James, 1890). It seems to me that this issue is currently ripe for empirical study, and in fact Johnson and Raye's (1981) recent work on "reality monitoring" is directed at aspects of this problem.

Finally, personal memories are typically accompanied by a belief that they are a veridical record of the originally experienced episode. This does not mean that they are, in fact, veridical, just that they carry with them a very strong belief value. In order to see this, it is instructive to compare the denial of an autobiographical fact with the denial of a personal memory. Thus, if someone were to tell me that my memory that I attended my sister's wedding on July 6, 1980, was wrong and that it was really on July 13, 1980, I could easily be convinced that my factual autobiographical memory was wrong. However, if someone were to tell me that my personal memory of seeing my sons decorate her car with shaving cream is wrong and that it did not occur, I would be hard to convince. In fact, even if someone provided photographs showing that the car was perfectly clean as it was driven away, I would almost certainly claim that the pictures were faked and would not give up my belief in that particular personal memory. This strong belief in the truth of personal memories is important to keep in mind when investigating the degree to which the recall of personal memories is veridical.

This account of the characteristics of personal memory is based on (*a*) my own introspections, (*b*) the discussion of the issue within philosophy, and (*c*) data from several of my own (unpublished) empirical studies of autobiographical memory. This is obviously not a very satisfactory data base, and it is clear that we need much more empirical work on the basic descriptive aspects of this important form of human memory.

## Flashbulb memories versus personal memories

In an important paper in 1977 Brown and Kulik focused on a form of memory they refer to as *flashbulb memories*. The description of personal memory just outlined suggests the need for a partial reevaluation of their analysis of this form of memory. Brown and Kulik state that flashbulb memories are "memories for the circumstances in which one first learned of a very surprising and consequential (or emotionally arousing) event" (p. 73). They state that these memories have "a primary, 'live' quality that is almost perceptual. Indeed, it is very like a photograph that indiscriminately preserves the scene . . . when the flashbulb was fired" (p. 74). Brown and Kulik present data to show that events such as the assassination of John Kennedy produce memories that fit their description of flashbulb memories, a finding supported by a number of later studies (Winograd & Killinger, 1983; Yarmey & Bull, 1978).

If, however, one compares Brown and Kulik's description of flashbulb memories with the description of personal memory in the previous section, it is not obvious that these are two different forms of memory (see Rubin & Kozin, 1984, for a similar argument). Personal memories for trivial events (e.g., what your breakfast table looked like this morning) seem to have most of the characteristics of memories for the dramatic events that produce flashbulb memories. Thus, in terms of the overall analysis of autobiographical memory the question is not why flashbulb memories have the characteristics described by Brown and Kulik but why these particular personal memories are not forgotten as rapidly as are most personal memories for trivial events. The issue of forgetting personal memories will be discussed later in this chapter.

### Analysis of empirical studies

In this section I would like to use some of the distinctions developed in the structural account of autobiographical memory to clarify several issues in the study of autobiographical memory.

*Galton's breakfast questionnaire.* Sir Francis Galton initiated the empirical study of autobiographical memory. In his work Galton developed two different techniques, the breakfast questionnaire and the word technique. The breakfast technique (Galton, 1880) consisted of asking subjects to recall the appearance of their breakfast table from that morning's breakfast. In terms of our analysis this technique was a pure test of personal memory. The approach of directing subjects to a particular episode in their lives was for a very long time rarely used in experimental studies of memory but has shown a burst of new activity in the last few years (see Brewer & Pani, 1982; Nigro & Neisser, 1983; Rubin & Kozin, 1984; and Reiser, Black & Kalamarides, Chap. 7).

*Galton's word technique.* Galton's (1879a, 1879b) word technique is a more complex case. As Galton originally described and used the technique, it was not intended to be strictly a test of autobiographical memory. The procedure

Galton used was to display a word, to "allow about a couple of ideas to successively present themselves" (1879*b*, p. 426), and then to record the resulting ideas. In looking over these early papers, it seems clear that Galton devised the word technique as an open-ended sampling of the contents of his mind, not as a method restricted to the examination of personal memories. If Galton's technique was successful in sampling the contents of his mind, one might expect his responses to include many different types of memory, and that is just what he reports. It appears that his most frequent responses were examples of rote verbal memory (e.g., verses from Tennyson) and generic perceptual memory (e.g., generic mental landscapes). Ironically, there are no clear examples of personal memory in Galton's report of his data with the use of the word technique!

*The Crovitz technique.* After a rather impressive pause (95 years), Crovitz and Schiffman (1974) modified Galton's word technique to study autobiographical memory. Their paper contains no theoretical discussion of the types of memory, but it is clear from the shift in methodology that Crovitz and Schiffman were interested in the study of personal memories. Thus, they told their subjects that the experiment "was a study of their personal memories" (1974, p. 517) and instructed them to "think of a specific memory associated with each word" (Crovitz & Quina-Holland, 1976, p. 61). In fact, given the conceptual importance of this shift in methodology, it seems to me that the use of the word technique modified to study personal memories ought to be referred to as the Crovitz technique, to be distinguished from Galton's technique of using a word as a probe for an open-ended sampling of information from memory.

The development of the Crovitz technique has given rise to one of the main themes of work on autobiographical memory (cf. Robinson, Chap. 10; Wetzler & Sweeney, Chap. 11; Rubin, Wetzler, & Nebes, Chap. 12). Most of the researchers in this area have clearly been interested in obtaining data on personal memory and have frequently modified their instructions to be even more specific about the issue (e.g., Robinson, 1976; Rubin, 1982). Thus, Robinson instructed his subjects to "think of an experience from your own life which the word reminds you of" (1976, p. 581); if the subject gave some other form of response, the subject was told "to continue thinking until a specific incident associated with the word came to mind" (p. 581).

A few studies in this area, however, have deviated from the strict Crovitz technique. Franklin and Holding (1977) instructed subjects to give "an immediate association involving personal reference" and found that 31% of their responses were "recurrent events." In the terms of the memory classification scheme in Table 3.1, it appears that under these somewhat general instructions subjects were giving generic personal memories in addition to specific personal memories. Karis (1979, 1981) deliberately modified the Crovitz technique to elicit both personal memories and generic personal memories. In his instructions he states, "The main thing is to write down whatever memory comes first to mind – it can be very specific, like breaking a window on a certain day, or quite general, like the memory that you used to wash windows every Saturday morning (without having a particular Saturday in mind)" (1980, pp. 140–141).

*Mental imagery research.* The original Galton technique was also adapted to the study of visual imagery. Perky (1910) read words to subjects who had been instructed "to give themselves up to the visual imagery evoked by the word" (p. 435). She found that the responses fell into two basic types, one type characterized by "particularity (in the sense of a particular sample, placed and dated) and the other by absence of personal reference" (p. 436). These two forms of response clearly correspond to personal memories and generic perceptual memories. Clark (1916) used a similar technique; she found in her responses a class she called memory *F*-images and another group called *G*-images that correspond respectively to personal memory and generic perceptual memory as described in this chapter. Thus, it appears that when the original Galton technique is modified to restrict the subjects to image responses they tend to produce a mixture of personal memories and generic perceptual memories.

*Word association studies.* In terms of empirical research generated, the most popular modification of the original Galton procedure was the word association technique, a technique that appears to shift the task to the study of phenomena outside the area of autobiographical memory. In this experimental paradigm subjects are presented with words and asked to respond with the first word that comes to mind (Deese, 1965; Postman & Keppel, 1970; Woodworth, 1938). This modification of Galton's instructions probably taps some complex mixture of conceptual and linguistic skills. In terms of the structure of memory scheme presented earlier, it is impressive to see that "slight" changes in instructions from the original Galton word technique lead to dramatic differences in what type of memory is sampled. There is an interesting contrast between the results of the Crovitz technique and the classic word association technique. One of the major findings with the Crovitz technique (e.g., Crovitz & Shiffman, 1974; Rubin, 1982) is that the reported personal memories tend to give a negatively accelerated decreasing retention function. One of the basic findings with the word association technique, however, is that subjects tend to respond with high-frequency words, which also tend to be the earliest words in acquisition. Thus, in terms of the age of acquisition, the distribution of responses on the word association task will be the reverse of the personal memory response distribution, with the largest number of responses coming from the earliest acquisition period. Clearly, as the original Galton technique is modified to sample different aspects of the overall memory system, one appears to find very different processes at work.

*Temporal organization.* A final set of studies that can be looked at in terms of the framework for the structure of memory are studies of temporal organization and temporal dating. The study of memory for public events (Squire & Slater, 1975; Underwood, 1977; Warrington & Silberstein, 1970) is a semantic memory domain that can be organized temporally; it thus forms an interesting comparison with studies of personal memory and autobiographical facts, which also can be organized temporally. Brown, Shevel, and Rips (Chap. 9) provide data showing that memory for public events and memory for autobiographical information are organized somewhat separately and that subjects can use information from one system to help date events in the other system.

### History of the study of personal memory

Finally, I would like to consider why it has taken so long for experimental work on autobiographical memory to take hold in psychology. It seems to me that the long delay in continuing Galton's initial research in this area is due to two basic problems – methodological difficulties in studying autobiographical memory and a research tradition that focused on individual differences to an unusual degree.

*Methodological problems.* Consider Galton's two methods for the study of personal memory, the breakfast questionnaire (Galton, 1880) and the word technique (1879*a*, 1879*b*). Both of these procedures rely strongly on the subject's phenomenal experience, the memories are hard to verify, and it is difficult to see how to gain experimental control over the phenomena. Contrast this with Ebbinghaus's approach to the experimental study of memory. Ebbinghaus explicitly rejected the study of personal memory on the grounds that the study of consciousness was bad methodology (Ebbinghaus, 1885/1964, p. 1). His experimental procedures allowed easy verifiability of the form of memory being investigated, and he showed how to gain experimental control over a number of aspects of rote memory. Experimental psychologists looked at these two options and overwhelmingly chose the Ebbinghaus route. It is only recently, with the reduction in the methodological constraints of behav-

iorism and the elaboration of Galton's techniques, that the study of autobiographical memory has been able to make a comeback.

*Individual differences in imagery.* The other factor that retarded the development of this area was an early focus on individual differences. Although very
little basic research on autobiographical memory was carried out after Galton's pioneering efforts, there was a vigorous research tradition devoted to the
study of individual differences in mental imagery. The researchers in this area
expanded Galton's breakfast questionnaire into a number of more general imagery questionnaires and carried out studies attempting to relate differences
in the vividness of imagery to a variety of subject characteristics and cognitive
tasks (cf. reviews in Ernest, 1977; Richardson, 1969; and White, Sheehan,
& Ashton, 1977). The study of individual differences is an interesting problem, but in this area the topic was investigated to the exclusion of experiments
directed at the basic processes in autobiographical memory.

   Thus, when we began to carry out work on personal memory (Brewer &
Pani, 1982, 1983, in preparation), we expected to find very fragile experimental phenomena with enormous variability across subjects. However, we
discovered that we could manipulate variables in this area just as one can in
more traditional areas of human memory. For example, we found that, within
the same group of subjects, a question designed to tap personal memory (e.g.,
"Where were you the last time you spent cash for something?") gave essentially 100% imagery responses, whereas a question designed to tap semantic
memory (e.g., "In English, what word is the opposite of the word *answer?*")
gave only 10–15% imagery responses. Clearly, here it is not the characteristics of the subjects that are crucial but the type of memory processes that the
subjects are asked to carry out. Overall, it seems to me that the extreme focus
on individual differences in the study of personal memory has given the impression that this area is somehow different from other aspects of human
memory and has slowed the search for an understanding of the basic memory
processes in this area.

## Memory processes in autobiographical memory

The next sections of this chapter focus on mechanisms and processes in autobiographical memory. In terms of the biology metaphor mentioned earlier
there is a shift from descriptive anatomy to physiology.

*Personal memory: copy theories versus reconstructive theories*

The reader should beware: In this section I intend to have my cake and eat it
too. One important theoretical issue relating to personal memory is the degree

to which the personal memory is a copy of the earlier experience versus the degree to which it is a possibly nonveridical reconstruction of the earlier experience.

*Copy theories*. Copy theories of memory have a long history in philosophy. Thus, for example, Hobbes (1651/1952) gave an account of memory images in terms of decaying sensations. For him, personal memories were copies of the original sensations, but they were not as vivid because they faded over time. A number of more recent philosophers have continued to hold copy theories of one variety or another. Furlong (1951) took a position that personal memories were effectively a representation of an individual's "whole state of mind on the past occasion" (p. 83). Earle (1956) proposed a direct realist view of memory in which he argued that personal memories were "a direct vision of the genuine past, and veridical to the extent it is clear" (p. 10).

Most of the early theories of memory coming out of the Ebbinghaus verbal learning tradition were copy theories (see Bartlett, 1932, for an attack on them on those grounds); however, these experiments were directed not at personal memory but at various forms of rote verbal skills (cf. Brewer & Pani, 1983). The paper by Brown and Kulik (1977) on flashbulb memories does seem to be about personal memories and adopts an explicit version of a copy theory. Brown and Kulik discuss these memories in terms of a "now print!" mechanism that "indiscriminately preserves the scene" (p. 74).

There is very little evidence to support the copy theory. It seems to me that there have been three intellectual forces leading researchers to adopt the copy view: (*a*) a theory of memory that has this position as a natural consequence (e.g., Hobbes's decaying sensation); (*b*) the theorists' strong belief in the veridicality of their personal memories (cf. the earlier discussion of the strong belief value for personal memories); and (*c*) the fact that personal memories include irrelevant detail, a finding that would not be expected from most schema-based reconstructive theories of memory (cf. Brewer & Nakamura, 1984).

*Reconstructive theories*. In the last few years copy theories of personal memory have come under strong criticism (cf. Barclay, Chap. 6; Neisser, 1981, 1982). The usual line of attack is to provide an anecdotal example of a personal memory that was thought to be veridical and then later was discovered not to be correct (cf. Linton, 1975, p. 387; Neisser, 1982, p. 45). In addition to this form of evidence Neisser has provided two empirical studies relevant to the issue. In a 1981 paper Neisser compared John Dean's Watergate testimony about his conversations with President Nixon with the actual tapes of those conversations. He found that Dean was essentially correct about what the basic views of each individual were but that most of the details of Dean's memory about the conversations were incorrect. In a more recent paper Nigro and Neisser (1983) investigated the phenomenal properties of personal memories. They found that a number of personal memories were reported as being experienced from the individual's point of view during the original episode, as would be expected from a copy theory. A larger number, however, were reported to be experienced from the perspective from which some other person would have viewed the scene, and therefore they could not have been copies of the individual's original perceptions. Thus, although there is not a large amount of evidence in favor of the reconstructive view, it appears to be somewhat stronger than the evidence for the copy view of personal memories.

*Evaluation of reconstructive evidence.* Even though I have occasionally been known to take a fairly hard line in favor of the reconstructive view of memory, I think it will be instructive to take a critical look at this new reconstructive position for the area of personal memory. First, of course, it seems best not to put too much weight on anecdotal examples. In fact, the protocol provided by Linton (1975) does not seem like a clear case of personal memory. It contains very little recall of irrelevant context and includes phrases such as "I probably looked up and said, What?" (p. 387), which give it the ring of a reconstructed factual memory.

A closer examination of the evidence from John Dean's testimony (Neisser, 1981) also suggests problems with using it to show that personal memory is reconstructed. First, the bulk of the memory in this case is the report of the content of a number of long conversations. Descriptions of personal memory tend to emphasize that personal memory is memory for a spatial-temporal episode. I know of no examples of a theorist claiming that one can have personal memories of the contents of long conversations. Second, even if we ignore this problem, it would seem that the circumstances involved in the John Dean case were particularly ill suited for the development of unique personal memories. The original events consisted of a large number of repeated discussions of the same issues. After the original events were over John Dean spent a long time trying to reconstruct the events while preparing to testify (cf. Dean's discussion of using newspaper clippings as a guide to reconstructing the events; Neisser, 1981). In the analysis of personal memory outlined earlier in this chapter, I argued that unique episodes tend to lead to strong personal memories, and so the circumstances of the John Dean case seem antithetical to the development of clear personal memories. Note that James makes an argument similar to this one in his *Principles*. He states that the most frequent source of false memory is distortion introduced through the process of giving successive accounts of a particular personal memory episode (1890, pp. 373–374). Third, it is not clear to what degree John Dean felt his reports were based on personal memories versus reconstructed autobiographical facts. Finally, the evidence provided by the tape recordings is mute with respect to several of the aspects of Dean's testimony that do seem like personal memories. Dean notes, for example, that in his first major meeting with the president on the containment of the Watergate affair he sat in the right-hand chair. A test of the veridicality of information of this type would seem to be a more direct test of the copy theory of personal memory. Thus, overall the evidence for the reconstructive position does not seem as strong as it might have looked at first.

*A partial reconstructive view.* Now I would like to outline a partially reconstructive position of personal memory, starting with a modified version of the copy view. It seems to me that the basic materials for a copy theory have to be the individual's perceptions, and, because perceptions are not always veridical with respect to the physical world, no copy theory can be veridical in terms of the events in the world. In other words, a copy theory that postulates that memory is based on uninterpreted copies of the sensory input cannot succeed. I am thus arguing against any form of copy theory that assumes that personal memories are uninterpreted copies of the sensory input (cf. Pylyshyn, 1973, 1981, for a justification of this assertion). However, with this provision out of the way, I propose that recent (days to weeks) personal memories are, in fact, reasonably accurate copies of the individual's original phenomenal experience. One could look at this as a claim that those aspects of personal memories that correspond to the surface structure of a linguistic utterance have a much slower rate of forgetting than do their linguistic counterparts. Under this hypothesis, the strong belief value given to personal memories has a partial basis in fact. There is not much evidence, at present, to support this version of the copy view of personal memory. However, the reports of irrelevant detail in personal memories remain suggestive evidence for this position. Most current schema-based reconstructive approaches would have difficulty in accounting for the recall of this type of information (cf. Brewer & Nakamura, 1984). Note also that proponents of the reconstructive view never give anecdotal examples of completely nonveridical personal memories for events that occurred a few minutes earlier.

Now, having argued for a copy component to personal memory, I want to turn to the reconstructive issue. First, it is known that schema-based reconstructive processes occur in many forms of memory, and there is no reason to believe that personal memory is isolated from these memory processes. One might expect that childhood memories that have been recalled and discussed a number of times would be strong candidates for reconstructive processes. And, in fact, a large number of anecdotal accounts of personal memories of childhood that have turned out not to be veridical have been given by psychologists (Galton, 1879*b*, p. 429; Neisser, 1982, p. 45), by philosophers (Leyden, 1961, p. 78; Smith, 1966, pp. 22–23), and by literary scholars (Salaman, 1970/1982, p. 61).

The evidence presented by Nigro and Neisser (1983) that many personal memories are not experienced from the ego's original viewpoint seems like strong evidence for reconstructive processes at work in personal memory. And their finding that very recent personal memories do tend to be experienced from the ego's point of view seems to support the copylike aspects of recent personal memories.

Overall, the partially reconstructive position suggests that recent personal memories retain a relatively large amount of specific information from the original phenomenal experience (e.g., location, point of view) but that with time, or under strong schema-based processes, the original experience can be reconstructed to produce a new nonveridical personal memory that retains most of the phenomenal characteristics of other personal memories (e.g., strong visual imagery, strong belief value).

*Variables that influence recall of personal memories*

Only a few studies have investigated the forgetting of personal memories over time. These studies are in moderate agreement about the characteristics of the events that lead to well-recalled personal memories: (*a*) uniqueness (Linton, 1979, p. 85; Smith, 1952, p. 166; White, 1982, p. 176); (*b*) consequentiality (Rubin & Kozin, 1984, p. 92); (*c*) unexpectedness (Linton, 1979, p. 85; Rubin & Kozin, 1984, p. 92; Smith, 1952, p. 167); and (*d*) emotion-provoking (Rubin & Kozin, 1984, p. 92; Smith, 1952, p. 168; White, 1982, p. 176). The characteristics of events that lead to poor recall are frequently the mirror image of those that make for good recall. Thus, these studies have reported poor recall for personal memories resulting from events that are (*a*) repeated (Linton, 1975, p. 396; Smith, 1952, p. 164) and (*b*) trivial (Linton, 1975, p. 396; Smith, 1952, p. 164).

The first thing to note about the events that lead to good personal memories is that in the real world they tend to co-occur. Thus, the Kennedy assassination, the source of very long-lived personal memories, would be very high on each of the above dimensions that lead to strong recall. However, even though the correlation is high, it is not perfect (e.g., buying a hammock might be unique but not emotion-provoking), so with proper care it may be possible to disentangle these dimensions. Alternately, it may be possible to set up laboratory situations that attempt to unconfound these variables.

There have been few accounts of how these variables work in personal memory. It is possible, however, to develop a partial explanation of the impact of uniqueness and repetition. The structure of memory framework outlined earlier in this chapter suggests that single exposures to an event lead to personal memories, whereas multiple exposures can lead to generic personal memories. An interesting question is what happens to the individual personal memories when a generic personal memory is formed. Brewer and Dupree (1981, in preparation) have studied this issue in a somewhat different domain. They carried out a series of experiments on the development of generic mental maps using recognition memory for videotaped places. They found that there was some loss in recognition memory for the original individual instances during the course of the development of the generic place representations. As applied to the area of personal memory one could hypothesize that repetition of events leads to the development of generic personal memories at the expense of the individual personal memories that were repeated. This process would successfully predict good personal memories for unique events and poor personal memories for repeated events. The hypothesis also predicts that an originally unique event will show reduced personal memory strength if it is followed by other similar events.

*Organization of autobiographical memory*

Much of the work on the organization of autobiographical memory has made use of the fact that it is possible to array these memories along a time line, perhaps with the implicit assumption that autobiographical memories are organized temporally. Although it is true that time is one aspect that may organize autobiographical memories (and nonautobiographical memories such as knowledge about ancient history), it is also true that many other forms of organization may be involved. Thus, autobiographical memories might be structured in terms of individuals that one knows professionally and individuals that one knows through family relationships. It seems clear that we need much more work on this topic.

A related issue is the nature of the self-schema, compared with other depersonalized schemata. Rogers, Kuiper, and Kirker (1977) carried out memory experiments in which they seemed to claim special memory properties for the self-schema. In later work Bower and Gilligan (1979) and Keenan and Baillet (1980) provided data that suggested that the self-schema behaved like other schemata. We need more theoretical and empirical work on the structure of the self-schema, person schemata, and other, more "cold" cognitive schemata. It seems to me that the self-schema may differ in a number of important ways from other forms of schemata. Thus, Greenwald (1980) has suggested that the self-schema may show a strong bias toward positive self-evaluation.

Neisser's (1981) analysis of John Dean's testimony suggests that this mechanism was one of the powerful distorting forces in the errors in Dean's reconstructive recall.


## Conclusion

This chapter has been an attempt to carry out some of the preliminary descriptive and organizational work necessary to move the study of autobiographical
memory into the mainstream of research on human memory. I have tried to
make explicit a number of the implicit methodological and theoretical assumptions in this area. I have argued that autobiographical memory should
be defined as the study of memory for information relating to the self. The
core of the chapter is an attempt to organize autobiographical memory and
several forms of nonautobiographical memory in terms of their acquisition
conditions (single instance vs. repeated), their form of representation (imaginal vs. nonimaginal), and the type of information (self vs. nonself). This
analysis points out the unique place of personal memory in the overall structure of human memory and suggests the need for more research on this form
of memory. Throughout the chapter I have tried to consider both the phenomenal and the nonphenomenal aspects of memory, an exercise that seems to me
to be particularly valuable in the area of autobiographical memory. Finally, I
have proposed a partially reconstructive position in the debates on the veridicality of personal memories.


## References

Ayer, A. J. (1956). *The problem of knowledge*. Baltimore: Penguin Books.
Bartlett, F. C. (1932). *Remembering: A study in experimental and social psychology*. Cam-
    bridge: Cambridge University Press.
Bower, G. H., & Gilligan, S. G. (1979). Remembering information related to one's self. *Jour-
    nal of Research in Personality, 13*, 420–432.
Brewer, W. F., & Dupree, D. A. (1981, November). *Episodic and generic memory for places*.
    Paper presented at the 22nd annual meeting of the Psychonomic Society, Philadelphia, PA.
    (1983). Use of plan schemata in the recall and recognition of goal-directed actions. *Journal
        of Experimental Psychology: Learning, Memory, and Cognition, 9*, 117–129.
    (in preparation). *Schema acquisition: Episodic and generic memory for places and events*.
Brewer, W. F., & Nakamura, G. V. (1984). The nature and functions of schemas. In R. S.
    Wyer, Jr., & T. K. Srull (Eds.), *Handbook of social cognition* (Vol. 1, pp. 119–160).
    Hillsdale, NJ: Erlbaum.
Brewer, W. F., & Pani, J. R. (1982, November). *Personal memory, generic memory, and skill:
    An empirical study*. Paper presented at the 23rd annual meeting of the Psychonomic Society,
    Minneapolis, MN.
    (1983). The structure of human memory. In G. H. Bower (Ed.), *The psychology of learning*

*and motivation: Advances in research and theory* (Vol. 17, pp. 1–38). New York: Academic Press.

(in preparation). *Phenomenal reports during memory recall.*

Brown, R., & Kulik, J. (1977). Flashbulb memories. *Cognition, 5,* 73–99.

Clark, H. (1916). Visual imagery and attention: An analytical study. *American Journal of Psychology, 27,* 461–492.

Crovitz, H. F., & Quina-Holland, K. (1976). Proportion of episodic memories from early childhood by years of age. *Bulletin of the Psychonomic Society, 7,* 61–62.

Crovitz, H. F., & Schiffman, H. (1974). Frequency of episodic memories as a function of their age. *Bulletin of the Psychonomic Society, 4,* 517–518.

Deese, J. (1965). *The structure of associations in language and thought.* Baltimore: Johns Hopkins University Press.

Earle, W. (1956). Memory. *Review of Metaphysics, 10,* 3–27.

Ebbinghaus, H. (1964). *Memory.* New York: Dover. (Original work published 1885)

Epstein, S. (1973). The self-concept revisited, or a theory of a theory. *American Psychologist, 28,* 404–416.

Ericsson, K. A., & Simon, H. A. (1980). Verbal reports as data. *Psychological Review, 87,* 215–251.

Ernest, C. H. (1977). Imagery ability and cognition: A critical review. *Journal of Mental Imagery, 1,* 181–215.

Franklin, H. C., & Holding, D. H. (1977). Personal memories at different ages. *Quarterly Journal of Experimental Psychology, 29,* 527–532.

Furlong, E. J. (1951). *A study in memory.* London: Thomas Nelson.

Galton, F. (1879a). Psychometric experiments. *Brain, 2,* 149–162.

(1879b). Psychometric facts. *Nineteenth Century, 5,* 425–433.

(1880). Statistics of mental imagery. *Mind, 5,* 301–318.

Greenwald, A. G. (1980). The totalitarian ego: Fabrication and revision of personal history. *American Psychologist, 35,* 603–618.

(1981). Self and memory. In G. H. Bower (Ed.), *The psychology of learning and motivation: Advances in research and theory* (Vol. 15, pp. 201–236). New York: Academic Press.

Hilgard, E. R. (1980). Consciousness in contemporary psychology. *Annual Review of Psychology, 31,* 1–26.

Hobbes, T. (1952). *Leviathan.* Great Books of the Western World, Vol. 23. Chicago: Encyclopaedia Britannica. (Original work published 1651)

James, W. (1890). *The principles of psychology* (Vol. 1). New York: Macmillan.

Johnson, M. K., & Raye, C. L. (1981). Reality monitoring. *Psychological Review, 88,* 67–85.

Johnson-Laird, P. N. (1983). *Mental models.* Cambridge, MA: Harvard University Press.

Karis, G. D. (1979, September). *Individual differences in autobiographical memory.* Paper presented at the meeting of the American Psychological Association, New York.

(1981). Individual differences in autobiographical memory (Doctoral dissertation, Cornell University, 1980). *Dissertation Abstracts International, 41,* 3215B–3216B.

Keenan, J. M., & Baillet, S. D. (1980). Memory for personally and socially significant events. In R. S. Nickerson (Ed.), *Attention and performance, VIII* (pp. 651–669). Hillsdale, NJ: Erlbaum.

Kihlstrom, J. F. (1984). Conscious, subconscious, unconscious: A cognitive perspective. In K. S. Bowers & D. Meichenbaum (Eds.), *The unconscious reconsidered* (pp. 149–211). New York: Wiley.

Leyden, W. von. (1961). *Remembering.* New York: Philosophical Library.

Lichtenstein, E. H., & Brewer, W. F. (1980). Memory for goal-directed events. *Cognitive Psychology, 12,* 412–445.

Linton, M. (1975). Memory for real-world events. In D. A. Norman & D. E. Rumelhart (Eds.), *Explorations in cognition* (pp. 376–404). San Francisco: Freeman.

(1979, July). I remember it well. *Psychology Today*, pp. 80–86.

Locke, D. (1971). *Memory*. Garden City, NY: Doubleday (Anchor Books).

Markus, H. (1980). The self in thought and memory. In D. M. Wegner & R. R. Vallacher (Eds.), *The self in social psychology* (pp. 102–130). New York: Oxford University Press.

Natsoulas, T. (1970). Concerning introspective "knowledge." *Psychological Bulletin, 73*, 89–111.

Neisser, U. (1978). Memory: What are the important questions? In M. M. Gruneberg, P. E. Morris, & R. N. Sykes (Eds.), *Practical aspects of memory* (pp. 3–24). New York: Academic Press.

(1981). John Dean's memory: A case study. *Cognition, 9*, 1–22.

(1982). Snapshots or benchmarks? In U. Neisser (Ed.), *Memory observed: Remembering in natural contexts* (pp. 43–48). San Francisco: Freeman.

Nigro, G., & Neisser, U. (1983). Point of view in personal memories. *Cognitive Psychology, 15*, 467–482.

Perky, C. W. (1910). An experimental study of imagination. *American Journal of Psychology, 22*, 422–452.

Postman, L., & Keppel, G. (Eds.). (1970). *Norms of word association*. New York: Academic Press.

Pylyshyn, Z. W. (1973). What the mind's eye tells the mind's brain: A critique of mental imagery. *Psychological Bulletin, 80*, 1–24.

(1981). The imagery debate: Analogue media versus tacit knowledge. *Psychological Review, 88*, 16–45.

Reed, G. (1979). Everyday anomalies of recall and recognition. In J. F. Kihlstrom & F. J. Evans (Eds.), *Functional disorders of memory* (pp. 1–28). Hillsdale, NJ: Erlbaum.

Richardson, A. (1969). *Mental imagery*. New York: Springer.

Robinson, J. A. (1976). Sampling autobiographical memory. *Cognitive Psychology, 8*, 578–595.

Rogers, T. B., Kuiper, N. A., & Kirker, W. S. (1977). Self-reference and the encoding of personal information. *Journal of Personality and Social Psychology, 35*, 677–688.

Rubin, D. C. (1982). On the retention function for autobiographical memory. *Journal of Verbal Learning and Verbal Behavior, 21*, 21–38.

Rubin, D. C., & Kozin, M. (1984). Vivid memories. *Cognition, 16*, 81–95.

Rumelhart, D. E. (1980). Schemata: The building blocks of cognition. In R. J. Spiro, B. C. Bruce, & W. F. Brewer (Eds.), *Theoretical issues in reading comprehension* (pp. 33–58). Hillsdale, NJ: Erlbaum.

Russell, B. (1921). *The analysis of mind*. London: Allen & Unwin.

Salaman, E. (1982). A collection of moments. In U. Neisser (Ed.), *Memory observed: Remembering in natural contexts* (pp. 49–63). San Francisco: Freeman. (Reprinted from E. Salaman, *A collection of moments*. London: Longman Group, 1970)

Schank, R. C., & Abelson, R. P. (1977). *Scripts, plans, goals and understanding*. Hillsdale, NJ: Erlbaum.

Smith, B. (1966). *Memory*. London: Allen & Unwin.

Smith, M. E. (1952). Childhood memories compared with those of adult life. *Journal of Genetic Psychology, 80*, 151–182.

Squire, L. R., & Slater, P. C. (1975). Forgetting in very long-term memory as assessed by an improved questionnaire technique. *Journal of Experimental Psychology: Human Learning and Memory, 104*, 50–54.

Tulving, E. (1972). Episodic and semantic memory. In E. Tulving & W. Donaldson (Eds.), *Organization of memory* (pp. 381–403). New York: Academic Press.

Underwood, B. J. (1977). *Temporal codes for memories.* Hillsdale, NJ: Erlbaum.

Warrington, E. K., & Silberstein, M. (1970). A questionnaire technique for investigating very long term memory. *Quarterly Journal of Experimental Psychology, 22,* 508–512.

White, K., Sheehan, P. W., & Ashton, R. (1977). Imagery assessment: A survey of self-report measures. *Journal of Mental Imagery, 1,* 145–169.

White, R. T. (1982). Memory for personal events. *Human learning, 1,* 171–183.

Winograd, E., & Killinger, W. A., Jr. (1983). Relating age at encoding in early childhood to adult recall: Development of flashbulb memories. *Journal of Experimental Psychology: General, 112,* 413–422.

Woodworth, R. S. (1938). *Experimental psychology.* New York: Holt.

Yarmey, A. D., & Bull, M. P., III. (1978). Where were you when President Kennedy was assassinated? *Bulletin of the Psychonomic Society, 11,* 133–135.

# 4 Ways of searching and the contents of memory

*Marigold Linton*

What do we know about the contents of human memory? A preliminary listing might be obtained by surveying the literature. Such a review shows, however, that we know precious little about the denizens of that natural habitat, the mind. It quickly becomes clear that in such a quest we cannot inquire about contents generally – the question must be narrowed. An image that helps to focus my ideas is the following.

I see myself as an ethologist or a population biologist. I might be Darwin arriving at the Galapagos Islands. It is not idle for a biologist/botanist freshly come to a new shore to ask what organisms live in the new environment. What organisms make permanent homes here? Which are migratory, coming and going throughout the seasons? Which use the land during the day, which during the night? How large are the populations now? Which beasts thrive? Which will be here tomorrow, and which in a hundred tomorrows? The census of the Galapagos, like the census of New York, yields data obtainable from no other source, giving us hints about how life in a complex system works and providing a basis for understanding other relationships in the world. A census of the contents of the mind might give us, as the census does for biology, some sense of the fitness of ideas for survival and the shapes that items assume before reaching stable configurations.[1]

Why has cognitive psychology not begun with a basic understanding of what inhabits the mind? Why have we so few population mnemonists? Have we come to fear that, like the introspectionists, what we see will depend too heavily on what we expect? A census of the contents of memory should tell us about the functioning of the mind as censuses in other areas have informed

[1] As with all analogies, there are difficulties with this one. Some aspects of cognitive functioning, including unconscious control processes assumed by cognitive psychologists, are not modeled by the behavior of the population biologist. They seem much closer to the molecular biologists' concerns with jumping genes and DNA fragments and will almost certainly require different approaches.

50

these domains. Despite the formidable difficulties, there is much to be learned from the serious survey of contents of memory.

The perspective of a population biologist helps to clarify a number of issues. As a cognitive researcher committed to single-subject designs, I am frequently asked: "Do you imagine that other people remember the same things or in the same way as you do?" (or, "Do your results generalize to other individuals?"). Empirical evidence for answering this question is largely lacking. Moreover, a precise answer probably depends on the level at which the question is directed. My guess is that at a molar level people remember things in very different ways. What they remember and how these memories are organized vary widely. Such an assertion is usually taken by my questioners as an admission that a single-subject approach cannot yield meaningful data. Viewing myself as an analogue population biologist helps me deal more comfortably with the issue of individual differences. The specific contents of memory and the way in which they fit together may well be unique for every individual, just as the Australian deserts will yield a different population census than the Florida swamps. Biologists are not disturbed by these variations – they are inevitable. That common principles govern the systems is demonstrated by the general similarities among the deserts of Australia, the American West, and Africa; the similarities of the fauna in and near the great waterways of the continents; and the like. Under similar pressures originally disparate populations converge; under dissimilar pressures related populations diverge.

From my vantage point as a population mnemonist the questions to be asked about memories become clear. The questions relevant to a serious study of the mind include: What memories survive, thrive, and populate the domain? Whither do they come and where go, and what forms do they take during their tenure? Answers to these questions, I believe, have the greatest possibility for providing links to the total individual and the widely disparate areas of psychology that together map the totality of the individual: developmental, personality, social, biological, and cross-cultural. There are other questions we *might* ask: How well might a beast from another environment survive if transplanted here? How do we select beasts that would thrive in this ecological niche? Or even, How might we change this terrain to permit our target species to survive? These questions are legitimate ones – and each of them (and others) has a cognitive counterpart in laboratory studies that introduce "alien" materials or tasks into the system and then examine survival of the breed. The biologist may indeed count the thousands of fish produced in a spawn. But one cannot be satisfied with estimates of population viability that have meaning for only a day or a week. If our studies of the basic functioning of the mind are to illumine the organism's more complex functioning, we must examine the mature denizens of memory. The longer an organism survives, the more actively it interacts with its neighbors, the greater its potential impact. Much of traditional cognitive psychology deals with "organisms" that scarcely last the night. When we consider contents of memory we should be concerned not only with the cognitive analogue of a Petri dish, a zoo, or an arboretum; we must consider not only what *might possibly* survive but what *does* survive in a particular ecological niche.

There are a multitude of kinds of memories, each of which has an imaginable biological analogue, ranging from motor programs (e.g., riding a bicycle), conditioned responses (e.g., an acquired fear of height), semantic knowledge (the broad range of general knowledge that we each have), and episodic information (the distinctive events of our lives). Although all these areas deserve consideration, only the latter two classes will be considered in this paper. It should be clear that the methods are likely to be quite specific to the kinds of memories we wish to consider. There is no implication that the way to access a fond old memory is similar to the method for accessing a poorly learned mathematical rule, just as different methods must be used to visualize a virus and a squid.

## Some methods for accessing contents of the mind

How might we begin our census of the contents of the mind? Remember that we wish to see the mind as it commonly functions. We must distinguish sharply between what we *can* remember and what we *do* remember – between those creatures that can inhabit the pond and those that do. Let me consider some methods by which we may access these contents. In this survey I move from the open-ended to the narrowly restricted (or generally from unconstrained recall to recognition) methods. Some of these methods I have used extensively; some I have thought to use and have given up beforehand or they have failed in execution. Later I shall consider variations in the census that result from these methods.

*Memory watching*. Memory watching is a technique particularly appropriate for obtaining a census of our migratory autobiographical memory. As in any census the count may be restricted to particular subsets; for example, the age of qualifying memories may be specified. Restricting topics of memory to be recorded makes the task easier. Memory watching requires the subject to carry a note pad or recorder continuously for a period of time. Then, whenever a qualifying memory occurs, its specific content and other characteristics are noted. The age of memories qualifying for inclusion depends on the purpose of the study. Restricting topics of memory to be recorded makes the task easier.

Although this "ideal" means of watching the ebb and flow of memories may be successful for some individuals, it has not been so for me. The procedure involves a particularly insidious vigilance task. One must remain alert or miss the target – but the vigilance itself may *produce* the target, as if the recording device with which we enumerated the ducks landing on a lake were itself a duck call signaling them to land. The method fails for me because I cannot maintain the appropriate set. The typical form of the failure is particularly galling to a well-disciplined observer. After a period of time I simply forget to keep the records. (It is perhaps worth noting that I have enjoyed somewhat greater success when I have employed this method to observe other classes of memory phenomena. With some success I have tracked memory failures, including slips of the mind [Norman, 1981], tips of the tongue [Brown & McNeill, 1966], and failures to remember the names associated with familiar faces.)

*Thoughts that come unbidden.* Are there perhaps more efficient ways of accessing portions of our old memories? The following comments refer only to the class of memories I shall call "thoughts that come unbidden." Throughout my life I have noted delicate memory fragments that recur year after year – coming unbidden, sometimes when my "mind is silent" but also as by-products of searches for other information. These may be the involuntary memories (the precious fragments) that Salaman (1970, p. 45) writes about. Many stand almost as homey epigrams or proverbs. They seem to encapsulate some thing of particular significance. They might represent *X,* or my *understanding,* of *X.* For example, they might represent the fact that John loves Mary – *or* they might capture my crucial empathy for the bond between John and Mary. Sometimes my whole relationship with people spanning years or decades seems encapsulated in a series of such fragments. Perhaps Salaman is correct; these elements may be associated with a kind of crystalline emotion. Whatever their source, their meaning, and their relationship with other memories, can they be deliberately called to memory? I have succeeded in generating these fragments in the following way: I select a general topic – an individual or a theme – and then "float about" in those memories rather than deliberately "search." Rather soon an ore bearing these unbidden memories begins to surface.

The resulting list is relatively brief, often the memories are poorly specified, and items on this list are strikingly different from those produced by deliberate searches. They are more fragmentary and less episodic. When I muse about Judy, these memories come. If someone asks me to describe Judy or to tell about her, a remarkably different list is generated. The relationship of these memories to those elicited in more standard ways is not clear; however, their apparent minimal overlap with standard listings underlines how sensitive our accessed contents are to the method we employ.

*Temporally cued free recall.* Engaging in free recall for the population mnemonist is like taking a casual census of the flora or fauna: If you examine your garden closely on a dewy morning you see aphids, snails, a worm or two; at a hundred feet you may see a bird, and at greater distances you see only the large animals or the moving ones. We miss the small beast – or the still one. Is our goal a census of snails or of stags? To be meaningful, no experimental recall can be truly "free," but the methods I label "free" have fewer constraints than do the methods that follow. Although this sense of freedom from constraints may be deceptive, the most minimal prompt to memory would seem to be a temporal one (and, to be sure, the broader the temporal range, the more genuine this freedom is). In a reminiscent mode, among friends, we might dredge up "when I was a child . . ." memories. Experimentally, it is possible to ask, as I have, "Tell me everything you remember from 1976 or 1980," and so on. Similarly, I can ask for the contents of memory from January 1972. (Robinson, Chap. 10, shows the differential effectiveness as cues of various months.) Although I have never formally requested recall of memory contents from a specific week of my life, week-by-week recall occasionally occurs as a subset or strategy for obtaining contents from longer temporal units. I have never attempted recall for smaller units, such as that suggested by Lindsay and Norman (1977): "Query: What were you doing on Monday afternoon in the third week of September two years ago?" (They provide a plausible but fabricated recall.)

A date provides a searchable domain but itself does not directly color or cue the contents to be accessed (although as Robinson, Chap. 10, has shown, the schema associated with each month differs and hence the internally elicited cues are quite different). A more exact specification – for example, cuing by topic – may dramatically change the contents that are available.

*Categorical recall.* Categorical recall is simpler: It permits us to focus our gaze, to limit our search to the mammals or the reptiles, to the spiders or the worms. Somewhat greater constraints are placed by the requirement to search within categories – broad or narrow. Although my method does not impose categorical limitations, self-imposed categorical searches within temporal limitations are a valuable aid. (The transition from temporal to categorical searches will be described in the section on my observations.)

A number of investigators have combined temporal with categorical cues – for example, Brown and Kulik (1977), Linton (1975), and Yarmey and Bull

(1978) in their questions about the death of President Kennedy. Crovitz and Quina-Holland (1976) have used the method most extensively with their temporal/category cues such as "Remember a clock from childhood."

*Cued recall.* It is likely that the completeness and exactness of recall is dependent on the aptness of the cues. In much research a single cue is provided; for example, Crovitz (Chap. 15), and Rubin, Wetzler, and Nebes (Chap. 12) describe research that examines responses to discrete cues. Using a succession of cues may be more informative and would more closely mimic natural usage. (See Linton, 1979*b*, for a description of an as yet unimplemented scheme for using multiple cues.) This procedure is an analogue of a real-world procedure that we all recognize. Skilled conversationalists in attempting to renew old memories in the minds of friends try a variety of cues, "Do you remember when we . . ." "No." "Remember, there were trumpets . . ." Most natural searches yield some consensus between conversationalists, multiple cues seem more effective than discrete ones, and surely the effectiveness of particular classes of cues depends on the memory sought and the particular searcher.

Salaman (1970) comments interestingly on this sharing of memories:

> It has happened many times that as soon as I have told a memory to persons who have memories of the same period I am immediately asked if I remember other moments – things which they remember about me. I am often interested, amused, and sometimes even flattered, but when pressed to recognise the events I feel almost hostile. Other people's memories of us no more belong to us than their dreams of us. [P. 112]

Cued recall merges almost imperceptibly into recognition, a closely related and familiar procedure.

*Recognition.* Recognizing a picture or a word seen before is very different from "recognizing" an event, because the representation of the event or episode is more abstract and symbolic. My long-term memory study (Linton, 1975, 1979*a*, 1982) employed brief verbal descriptions of events. (Others who have used this method include Barclay, Chap. 6, and Thompson, 1982.) It has been suggested that video or audio tapes might provide more adequate cues. But even taped materials provide an abstract representation of a complex unit and may not adequately cue the stored material.

## A brief description of the study

In the preceding section I discussed a variety of methods for accessing the contents of memory. I would now like to describe the configuration of these methods that I have employed in my autobiographical memory study. These formal findings are occasionally complemented by observations of my memory in nonlaboratory settings.

Some 14 years ago in an effort to track old memories I began an examination of my own memory. To recapitulate very briefly, for many years I recorded events from my own everyday life, and then, once a month, I tested descriptions of events drawn randomly from this pool for recognition and attempted to date them. The procedures embodied in this brief description comprise two of the methods I have described: (*a*) a recognition method (Did I uniquely recognize the event described?); and (*b*) a cued recall procedure (Was I able to date the event on the basis of the brief (three-line) cue provided?). Fuller descriptions of these procedures appear in Linton (1975, 1979*a*, 1982).

Although the cued recall and recognition techniques provide the bulk of the data in this study, I wish to focus in this paper on another procedure – a simple "free recall" task (preceding the tasks described above) in which, at some level of generality, I listed all the unique events I could remember from the occurrences of the preceding year. The recall task was a minimally structured activity whose purpose was simply to "warm up" the memory system before the experiment proper. These free recall data are "special," or at least have an unusual status, because they were primarily collected as a means of maintaining experimental constancy – to avoid order effects between the first recognition items and the 50th or 100th. My directions were to freely recall all the events I could from the preceding year. Although "freely recalling" past events has always seemed perfectly reasonable to me, the task sounds impossible to some individuals. What was I doing last year at this time? Given this temporal cue I simply step back a year, comb through events, find landmarks, check hypotheses, and produce a listing of events. (Robinson's study, Chap. 10, concerns the impact of schemata on such searches.) To be sure, memories sometimes come easily, sometimes with difficulty, and, like anyone else, I make errors. My point is that the task seems quite natural to me, and I employ a general algorithm for finding the target material.

The free recall data just described were collected from 1972 to 1978. (These are described as Phase 1 data in Table 4.1.) In 1978, for another purpose, I performed a second, somewhat different, set of free recalls: I attempted to recall the events that had occurred during randomly selected *months* from this 6-year period. In this procedure I focused on the events from a much more restricted period – a single month rather than a year. (These are Phase 2 data.) Finally, in 1983, I performed a series of additional free recalls for events from the years 1971 to 1982 in random order (Phase 3 data).

Thus, I have three assessments of the contents of memory that use a temporal specification as the primary cue. The age of memories recalled were 1–

Table 4.1. *Summary of recall characteristics*

| Phase | Data collected | Maximum age of memories | Target | Temporal recall unit |
|---|---|---|---|---|
| 1 | 1972–78 | 12 months | Preceding | 1 year |
| 2 | 1978 | 6 years | Random | 1 month |
| 3 | 1983 | 12 years | Random order | 1 year |

12 *months* in the first phase, 1–6 *years* in the second phase, and 1–12 *years* in the third phase, and the recall units were 1 year, 1 month, and 1 year for the three phases respectively. The parameters of the study are summarized in Table 4.1.

## The structure of memories

My observations on the contents of memory may be better understood if I formalize my hypothesis about the general structure of events in long-term memory. Figure 4.1 provides a roughly "hierarchical" outline of the categories of memory most relevant to my observations. In each case, the simple labels are intended to represent a complex overlapping fabric in which the events of our memory are embedded. At the most general level there is *mood tone*. All events are classifiable by mood (labels such as negative or positive are simple representatives of much more extensive sets), and the impact on event memory of mood tone has been extensively studied. Mood tone cuts across all other categories in the hierarchy but is usually too general to provide an efficient cue by itself. At the next levels are *themes* and *subthemes*. These are the coherent directions or unifying aspects of life. Consistent themes may run throughout one's life, for example, interactions with loved ones. Some themes are complex and not easily expressible, but two, work/ professional contrasting with social (or ego-serving), are quite persistent. Not surprisingly, the boundaries of these categories are often blurred.

At the next level are what I have labeled *extendures*. These units are smaller and more temporally bound than are themes. They are sets of memories loosely bound by the coexistence of some significant persistent orientation. Extendures are ordinarily labelable: for example, "my marriage to Susan," "when I was doing graduate work," and "after I became a cognitive psychologist." Extendures thus reflect large defining units of our lives. An extendure may end, marking the end of some specific aspect of one's life. Some extendures end and are not replaced – unless one views "replacement" very ab-

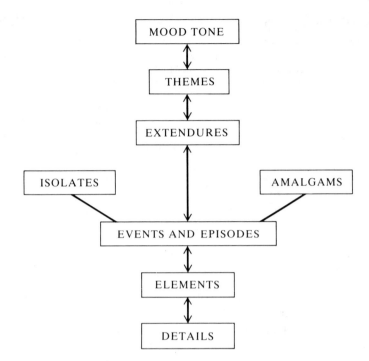

Figure 4.1. Hierarchical outline of memory categories

stractly. (Our formal education may end, but we may consider learning to be lifelong, or teaching and learning to be not very different.) In other cases, one extendure may rapidly follow another so that the representation for the larger theme contains a sequence of related subextendures. Our personal employment histories generally provide a sequence of closely packed extendures; for example, "when I worked for L.A. County General Hospital," ". . . San Diego State," ". . . the University of Utah," and so on. These extendures are discrete units that subsume associated memories.

At the next level we find *events* or *episodes*, which are representations of self-contained sets of actions, occurrences, and so on, that have independent coherence. Like extendures, events are usually labelable: for example, "our trip to Cancun." Although these units may (and frequently do) have extended antecedents and consequences, the units may be understood as discrete wholes even in the absence of explicit orienting information. For example, an episode in which one has an automobile accident may be understood, recalled, and described as a unit. This discrete unit *may* stand alone, unaffected by such surrounding features as one's destination or whose insurance company paid the damages. Events and episodes create the highlights and texture of extendures, against the background of more general semantic or generic knowledge and what Neisser (1981) has called repisodes, or similar repetitious events.

All events in memory need not be embedded in extendures. Some (*isolates*) may stand alone, maintaining solitary coherence independent of the unifying elements of one's life. Other events or episodes enter into *amalgams*. In amalgams an episode is attached to a logically unrelated episode or extendure. Amalgamated events are consistently found together in recall (probably as the result of simple temporal contiguity). Because there is no logical or necessary association in amalgams (except perhaps temporal proximity), it is not surprising that amalgams are unstable over time and that after long time periods events are remembered independently, or not at all.

Events and episodes comprise *elements* – that is, features or components of the event or episode. These include: who, what, where, and the like. Finally, there are *details* that clothe the elements and events – nuances of color, sound, texture, exact location, and so on. These are often implicit in memories but rarely appear, except fragmentarily, in explicit recall either natural or contrived.

This rough outline omits explicit mention of semantic memories, which provide the fundamental structure on which episodic memories and other details rest (see Linton, 1979*a*, for a brief discussion of the relationship of episodic and semantic memories), but does provide a basis for discussing the results of my recall sessions. What can we learn about the contents of memory from a survey of a dozen years? What does this lengthy exploration tell us about the contents of memory and how they are accessed? What patterns or regularities emerge?

## Contents of memory: some observations

*Negative memories.* In the first months of the study in 1972, evidence began to emerge for systematic nonavailability of one class of items, namely, negative ones (Linton, 1975). The "contents of memory" as represented by the *recall* protocols are curiously silent about specific negative events. Fewer than 13% of events ever recalled were negatively toned (some estimates are as low as 7%). The probability of negative events being repeatedly recalled was 24% as compared with 30% for positive items. Even surprisingly large, "world-shaking" negative events often failed to appear in these recall protocols. Furthermore, search type (to be described) had no effect on the number of negative items recalled. The two most common methods yielded equal numbers of negative items; however, the specific items recalled did differ with method. To be sure, the ending of relationships is noted, papers or books take forever to write, one teaches classes, but the niggling daily items, such as quarrels with loved ones, disagreements with colleagues, the first pained response to a negative review, a broken treasure – these are lost or modified by memory. They do not, for the variety of reasons summarized by Matlin and Stang (1978) in the *Pollyanna Principle,* remain active features of memory contents. Recalled contents are robust, coherent, forward-looking – a generally integrated, cheerful view of a life.

I am certain, nevertheless, that were I to perform a deliberate search of my memory for negative events I could access a substantial number of them without difficulty (Bower's 1980 study suggests that a particular mood tone might be as effective in eliciting general negative memories as an appropriate verbal cue). Undoubtedly, provided proper cues, I could recall specific negative memories. They comprise a class of *my* memories, however, that do not appear in temporally cued recall. On the other hand, in the recognition–cued recall task, I found no evidence that negative items were lost more rapidly than positive ones. These observations are consistent with recent findings that recall is more sensitive to systemic vagaries than is recognition (Bower, 1980).

*Strategies for conducting a free recall memory search.* When asked to "freely recall" old memories and given no restrictions except comfort and habitual usage, I used four different strategies for accessing memories. (I summarize here data only from the 6 years of recall in Phase 1, during which a total of 69 searches of 1-year domains were conducted.) Each strategy yielded somewhat different contents for the same time period. The strategies are listed in order of my preference in recalling material *during the first year* after the memories were laid down.

1. *Simple chronological order (62.3%).* I began with the most remote time period, listed the oldest items, and simply worked forward to the present. Fewer than 5% of the items were recalled out of their temporal sequence.
2. *Categorical summaries (23.2%).* Here I selected dominant themes from my life, often embedding extendures within themes, and recorded information (often chronologically) on a particular theme for the entire target time frame.
3. *Reverse chronological order (5.8%).* This method, closely related to the first, began with recent memories and moved backward in time.
4. *Graphical and time-line expressions (5.8%).* In this form of recall a graphical representation conveyed the shape or configuration of my

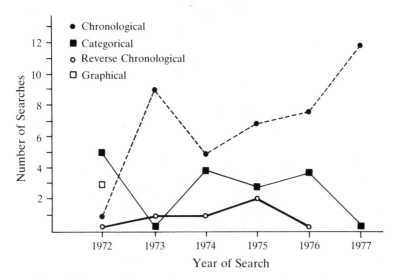

Figure 4.2. Changes in kind of search over 6 years

life. Although graphical representations seem to underlie most of my recall, they are not the final form in which recall was expressed except during the very early periods of this study.

  5. *Unclassified (2.9%).* Two of the 69 searches were unclassified.

A closer examination of kinds of searches shows a systematic change in preference for search method over the course of the 6-year study (see Fig. 4.2). Graphical representations seem to be a special case. Throughout the study graphical representation seemed to organize searches through old memories and appeared implicitly or explicitly as an aid in recalling events more than a couple of years old. In the first months of the study I used graphical or time-line methods both to facilitate and to summarize the results of the searches. Because this method emphasizes regular (semantic) features in memory but omits novel content, it rapidly lost favor and was replaced by categorical summaries. Categorical recall was guided by a series of thematically generated questions: What papers was I writing? What were my friends and I doing? The categories came from the same general classes over the years, although level of abstraction changed over time. Most searches were strictly chronological (forward) within the category, but 30% of all such searches were supplemented by explicit (and successful) chronological searches, as if all available information could not be obtained by a categorical search. Finally, chronological searches began to predominate, and during the last years of the study most recall involved almost exclusively forward chronological searches. Reverse searches (in which I began with present time and moved backward) occurred only four times at widely spaced occasions over the 6-year period.

Free recall procedures became more aversive over the 6-year course of the study, and concurrently the average recall time increased over this period from 13.5 minutes to 55.4 minutes.

Each of the preceding searches involved recall of information up to a year old. What search strategy preferences imply becomes clearer as we look at recall of periods that vary in remoteness. Remember that chronological searches were strongly preferred (for about 5 years) when the search was for information less than a year old. When the 12-year time frame of the Phase 3 study is considered, chronological searches continued to be preferred only in recall of information from recent periods. To be more specific, in Phase 3 (1983) my recall for events from the years 1981 and 1982 involved almost exclusively chronological accounts. Thus, under the conditions of the study, "unaided" chronological searches were possible and *preferred* for at least 2½ years. Recall for the preceding year, 1980, and for all earlier years (done in a random order) was categorical. Curious whether this shift in strategy was obligatory or optional and whether the shift was as stark as it seemed, I attempted chronological recall of the events of 1980 and earlier and found I could not develop an adequate listing of contents without the aid of categories.

You can get a sense for the kind of shift that occurs if you try to remember the events from this morning. Most people can effortlessly access the flow of events and label the items as they "pass." But, as we try to describe the happenings of a week ago, we are forced to access the memories less directly – through our knowledge of habitual occurrences and of the categories of activities appropriate for the time period.

If we look at more remote years, the question may be raised: How does one "find a year"? Protocols for periods recalled 5 to 10 years later are filled with graphical representations that permit me to label and identify years and place landmarks so that I can move more adroitly through these teeming populations. As in other topological representations, the features are not exactly duplicated from time to time. Most include inverted $U$'s representing the passage of academic school years, but the underlying representation is more continuous. Although there are numerous variations in the representations, its basic character has remained unchanged since my teens. Graphical representations alone stopped appearing as the complete protocol because they provide too skimpy a record of recalled events.

Let me focus now on two questions: (1) How dependent are the retrieved contents of memory on the passage of time, and (2) how dependent on the kind of search elected (or required)?

## Contents of memory: recent periods

When a memory should stop being called "recent" may be argued (it depends upon the character of the memory and the exactness with which it must be recalled). Most of the comments regarding the recent periods come from Phase 1 recall and hence involve memories less than 1 year old. The search for recent memories suggested the following:

1. Recall for events in the first year yielded highly accurate and detailed sketches. Indeed, recall protocols for a just-past year were tedious to obtain because of the richness of detail available for episode after episode. Variations in the level of detail in the records cannot be taken too seriously because time constraints force a wealth of available detail to be omitted from all protocols. The data from the recognition–cued recall phases of this study nicely complement these findings. During the first year following their occurrence virtually all events were recalled and dated with good accuracy. Fewer than 1% of the items were forgotten in the first year. Descriptions of unique random events from the file are dated with an average error of less than a week. Dating of the subset of highly salient items that appear in recall is far more accurate.

2. Recent memories can be accessed readily – with virtually any cue. A temporal cue, with no greater flesh, can and does produce very detailed recall. During at least the first year relatively pure chronological recall was obtained. (Data come from all three phases.) In addition, these highly available recent memories may arise "unbidden" in daily life.

3. Viewed globally, the elements that appear in recall protocols were stable for at least a year. (Because the requirement for monthly recall may have created a standard "last year scheme" this stability may be somewhat artifactual.) The same set of items (events or features) are recalled, usually in chronological order. Amalgams occur frequently. One event is tied consistently in recall to other temporally associated events. However, the *contents* are dependent on the specific search method; the use of either categorical recall or reverse chronological order of recall (rather than the preferred – for durations up to 2 years – forward chronological recall) produces dramatic shifts in units accessed. The chronological search, unsurprisingly, was more likely to produce events unrelated to higher order themes. Categorical searches were highly accurate for elements within the categories, but whole categories were sometimes omitted. Another compelling consistency emerged in the 16 categorical searches of 1972–1978. Themes may be roughly classified into

professional/work and social/self-centered. In virtually every recall session during this period, *all* professional/work items were recalled before any social/self-centered items.

### Contents of memory: middle-aged memories

1. Some remarkable shifts took place during the 12 years of the study. It is possible to detect a structuring of the contents that was lacking before. One can see the internal historian (see Greenwald's 1980 discussion of fabrication and the revision of personal history) beginning to exercise its prerogative – rewriting has begun to occur. There are shifts in emphasis and wholesale deletions. Surprisingly, new features appear in recall that reflect a changed appreciation of the importance of an event. For example, meeting a shy scholar 5 years earlier takes on new importance when I begin to date and decide to marry him. The earlier meeting now rewritten or recategorized takes on the character of a landmark or a beacon in a previously unmarked terrain.

2. Chronological search strategies that are speedy, accurate, and complete for memories less than a couple of years old are avoided. Indeed, they are difficult, if not impossible, to perform for these older materials. Categorical searches, with the chronology of the events and episodes within categories still remarkably well fixed, become the norm.

3. During this period the salience of event memories starts becoming crucial. By salience of items I mean such features as their importance, their emotionality, and how often they are rehearsed. The greater the original salience of items, and the greater their continuing relevance to life, the more likely they are to be recalled. However, as I have suggested elsewhere (Linton, 1982), salience is a treacherous concept because item salience changes as our lives' meaning changes. (The observation that many items remain highly salient throughout our life speaks articulately to the stability of our lives rather than of our memories.)

4. Amalgams begin to break down as the "glue" that holds these unrelated events together begins to dissolve. Ordinarily, the less dominant item is completely deleted from recall.

5. Elements and details begin to be lost. Elements do not emerge spontaneously when recall begins; they must be coaxed, inferred, and actively sought. If we use as the frame of reference all of the events ever remembered during the course of the year, we find that at the beginning of the first year 38% of major events are recalled and 30% of the subelements. By the end of the year 30% of the major events still appear but only 18% of the subelements. Although details are available (if with effort) for some events, for others they may not be available even with effort. Events locked into larger units

(extendures) are retained. "Isolated" events have a high probability of being lost, at least with the categorical searches that dominate the quest for old memories.

As features (elements) of events are lost, similar episodes lose their distinctive character and blend together or are lost. This final characteristic of memory is seen more clearly in my recognition–cued recall data. Beginning in the second year and continuing for the remaining 5 years, I forgot about 6% of the items each year (Linton, 1979a). This forgetting had a number of guises.

Perhaps the most ambiguous form of forgetting involves items that (a) must have happened, (b) are logically implied by events that are remembered, or (c) are totally plausible and compelling but cannot be recalled. Other items are lost because superficial descriptions, once adequate, no longer permit me to discriminate between events; often, several events in memory fit a single description. A more complete kind of forgetting occurs when a clearly understandable item does not find a match in memory; I simply "don't recall" the item. A final form, and the most complete form of forgetting, occurs when an item becomes incomprehensible; the description seems to refer to nothing presently in memory. This phenomenon *began* to occur for the first time 3–4 years after the items were written and followed long periods without rehearsal. This change appeared to occur over time, for early tests of such items were fairly typical, with no evidence of item incomprehensibility.

6. A few items, of course, continue to "come unbidden." The interactive nature of memory and personality is manifest by the particular items that persist in reentering consciousness, given the skimpiest of cues.

## What it all means

These memory contents have been viewed in settings comparable to wild animal parks and zoos. Although I am far from the Petri dish, these are relatively domesticated breeds we see here (although enlivened occasionally by a recounting of memories sighted roaming free). What insights may we glean from this examination of memory?

A major concern has been to provide a sense that memory for events and contents can inform us in a way uniquely different from other memory studies about the functioning of the mind and the individual viewed holistically. These event memories are not random excreta but both guide and are shaped by our hierarchically organized knowledge structures. The asides throughout this chapter relating memories to "personality" loosely outline the most obvious classes of relationships.

Implicitly and explicitly, I have argued that we must distinguish between methods that examine what pours out of memory and what can be elicited.

Although these methods lie on a continuum and shade imperceptibly into each other, the end points yield very different views of what a person remembers and a different vision of how the memory works. In a sense we are the memories we access. "Thoughts that come unbidden" may be akin to the free associations used by psychoanalysts and may be a special and potentially rich field for cognitive psychologists to till.

What about stability of contents in recall? At least within a single method, the contents of memory show good stability over time. Changes that occur are attributable to at least three sources and their interactions: (a) changes in the higher order structure of memory, (b) changes in search strategies, and (c) decreases in association among materials. More work must be done to disentangle these intertwined threads.

More specifically, I have detailed some systematic features in my own memory, most of which probably have some generality across individuals. A tendency to prefer positive to negatively toned events pervades the system. The probability of recalling negative items decreases with the passage of time. Over the 12-year course of this study this result is found for recall, not for recognition. Fundamental changes in conceptions about what is important are reflected in the contents of free recall. A shift in emphasis from work-related to self-related items is reflected in the specific contents that are accessed, the order in which contents are accessed, and the rubrics under which access occurs. Extendures are a significant feature of recall, serving as major units of recall, as landmarks, and as cues for more detailed recall. They provide a convenient unit for analysis because unlike events and smaller units they are likely to appear in recall in some form for many years.

The present "conclusions" are only tentative because only a few kinds of searches have been systematically performed and because even a study of a dozen years is relatively brief in the context of a lifetime. Further changes will surely take place as the decades pass. Salaman (1970), who has examined more closely than anyone the changes that take place in memory in old age, argues that one resolves the meaning of childhood memories in old age. Perhaps changes in search methods will continue to interact with the general structure of the mind to permit the sudden renewed access to very ancient memories that Salaman describes.

## References

Bower, G. H. (1981). Mood and memory. *American Psychologist, 36,* 129–148.
Brown, R., & Kulik, J. (1977). Flashbulb memories. *Cognition, 5,* 73–99.
Brown, R., & McNeill, D. (1966). The "tip of the tongue" phenomenon. *Journal of Verbal Learning and Verbal Behavior, 5,* 325–337.

Crovitz, H. F., & Quina-Holland, K. (1976). Proportion of episodic memories from early child-hood by years of age. *Bulletin of the Psychonomic Society, 7,* 61–62.

Greenwald, A. G. (1980). The totalitarian ego: Fabrication and revision of personal history. *American Psychologist, 35,* 603–618.

Lindsay, P. H., & Norman, D. A. (1977). *An Introduction to Psychology* (2nd ed.). New York: Academic Press.

Linton, M. (1975). Memory for real-world events. In D. A. Norman & D. E. Rumelhart (Eds.), *Explorations in cognition* (pp. 376–404). San Francisco: Freeman.

   (1979*a*). Real-world memory after six years: An in vivo study of very long term memory. In M. M. Gruneberg, P. E. Morris, & R. N. Sykes (Eds.), *Practical aspects of memory* (pp. 69–76). London: Academic Press.

   (1979*b*, July). I remember it well. *Psychology Today,* pp. 80–86.

   (1982). Transformations of memory in everyday life. In U. Neisser (Ed.), *Memory observed: Remembering in natural contexts* (77–91). San Francisco: Freeman.

Matlin, M., & Stang, D. (1978). *The Pollyanna principle: Selectivity in language, memory, and thought.* Cambridge, MA: Schenkman.

Neisser, U. (1981). John Dean's memory: A case study. *Cognition, 9,* 1–22.

Norman, D. A. (1981). Categorization of action slips. *Psychological Review, 88,* 1–15.

Salaman, E. (1970). *A collection of moments: A study of involuntary memories.* London: Long-man Group.

Thompson, C. P. (1982). Memory for unique personal events: The roommate study. *Memory and Cognition, 10,* 324–332.

Yarmey, A. D., & Bull, M. P., III. (1978). Where were you when President Kennedy was assassinated? *Bulletin of the Psychonomic Society, 11,* 133–135.

## Part III

# The general organization of autobiographical memory

Some basic observations challenge the researcher trying to understand the structure of autobiographical memory. Autobiographical memory shares properties with all human memory. It is highly organized. It tends to preserve the general gist of events, or series of events, but usually not the details. It is vast, requiring search and decision for retrieval. In addition, autobiographical memory presents problems that memory theorists trying to explain most phenomena can often safely ignore. First, autobiographical memory is memory for a whole lifetime and, as such, memories have much longer times than usual to change, distort, and be reconstructed. Second, this long passage of time is confounded with the development of the rememberer so that a college sophomore may be asked to recall an event encoded by a 6-year-old. Third, autobiographical memory is important affectively. It is the sum of peoples' knowledge of their own lives and as such is the basis for their concept of self.

This section presents diverse approaches to exploring the organization of autobiographical memory. On the one hand, the scope of evidence and theory is widened to include literary criticism of autobiographies, social psychology, personality theory, and development. On the other, the classification of a sample of autobiographical memories is used to specify a model that attempts to define the nebulous term *schema* in enough detail so that even a machine could understand it.

# 5 Nested structure in autobiographical memory

*Ulric Neisser*

The study of any kind of memory should properly begin with a description of the material that is to be remembered. In the case of autobiographical memory that material consists of events that we have personally experienced – or, to put it another way, of our personal experiences of events. But what is an event? How are events experienced? This chapter is an attempt to open a discussion of those issues and of their implications for the study of memory. I shall focus on the fact that the events defined at one level of analysis may themselves be constituents of other, larger events. This "nested" structure appears not only in the events themselves but also in the way they are experienced and remembered. Because different levels of nesting are specified by different kinds of information, they can be perceived and remembered somewhat independently. Recalling an experienced event is a matter not of reviving a single record but of moving appropriately among nested levels of structure.

My own present activity offers a convenient example. What am I doing right now? Obviously, I am writing a chapter for David Rubin's book on autobiographical memory. Just as obviously, I am sitting at my word processor. More concretely, I am sitting on a chair facing a screen that displays what has already been written in small green-on-black letters. I am successively touching the individual keys of the word processor (and looking at them, too, because touch typing is beyond me) in order to produce that display. These actions could be specified in even more detail if there were any reason to do so: There was a moment just now at which I was writing the word *These* to begin this very sentence. For that matter, there was a certain instant at which I was typing the *T* in *These*. That instant is past now. I am now typing other letters and other words, but I am still writing the same chapter.

Although the *T* instant was very recent, I have already forgotten it. I must have struck the *T* – there it is on the screen – but I no longer have any recollection of doing so or even of writing the word *These* in which it was embedded. Such rapid forgetting is quite normal: By now you have probably forgotten reading *These* as completely as I have forgotten writing it (cf. Sachs,

1967). We rarely retain such brief and insignificant events for long. Autobiographical memory is organized in terms of larger units, reflecting the structure of reality at more comprehensive levels.

Although it is true that I am writing a chapter for Rubin's book, that is not all I am writing. This chapter will be the third in a series of articles on the ecological approach to the study of memory (cf. Neisser, 1984, 1985). I am writing *that series,* too, this very afternoon. Striking the *T* in *These* a few minutes ago was a part of writing the series as well as of writing the chapter. I will almost certainly remember writing these articles, which have occupied me intermittently for over a year. The *T* instant vanished from autobiographical memory in a matter of moments, but the simultaneous experience of writing-the-ecological-memory-papers is likely to stay with me for years to come.

These descriptions are intended to be objective, not phenomenological. Unless I am very badly deceived indeed, all the events described so far actually took place, or are taking place. None of them is hypothetical, or imaginary, or even unobservable. Striking a single key and writing a series of papers are both real actions; they differ in comprehensiveness and duration but not in ontological status. We say that key strokes are *molecular* whereas writing words or sentences is (relatively) *molar* (Tolman, 1932); writing a paper or a series of papers counts as more molar still. The more molecular actions are nested in the more molar ones: Typing *T* is nested inside typing *These,* for example. Words are nested in sentences; the words and the sentences themselves are nested in the arguments that I am trying to make. The sentences and arguments are nested in this chapter, the chapter in my projected series of articles, and all of them in a still more extensive activity that might (somewhat pompously) be called "being a cognitive psychologist" or "doing my job." That, too, is presently going on here in my office.

Although the concept of nesting has been introduced here to describe the relations among activities and events, it has many other applications as well. In particular, it plays an essential role in the ecological description of the real environment. J. J. Gibson's account of the nesting of objects is paradigmatic:

Physical reality has structure at all levels of metric size from atoms to galaxies. Within the intermediate band of terrestrial sizes, the environment of animals and men is itself structured at various levels of size. At the level of kilometers, the earth is shaped by mountains and hills. At the level of meters, it is formed by boulders and cliffs and canyons, and also by trees. It is still more finely structured at the level of millimeters by pebbles and crystals and particles of soil, and also by leaves and grass blades and plant cells. All these things are structural units of the terrestrial environment, what we loosely call the forms or shapes of our familiar world.

Now, with respect to these units, an essential point of theory must be emphasized. The smaller units are embedded in the larger units by what I will call *nesting.* For example, canyons are nested within mountains; trees are nested within canyons; leaves are nested within trees; and cells are nested within leaves. There are forms within forms both up and down the scale of size. Units are nested within larger units. Things are components of other things. They would constitute a hierarchy except that this hierarchy is not categorical but full of transitions and overlaps. Hence, for the terrestrial environment, there is no proper unit in terms of which it can be analyzed once and for all. [Gibson, 1979, p. 9]

Not only objects are nested but also places:

A *place* is a location in the environment as contrasted with a point in space. . . . Whereas a point must be located with reference to a coordinate system, a place can be located by its inclusion in a larger place (for example, the fireplace in the cabin by the bend of the river in the Great Plains). Places can be named, but they need not have sharp boundaries. [P. 34]

The nesting of events is very similar to the nesting of places. Events are "located" by inclusion in larger events, just as places are located with reference to larger places. Events, too, can be named and need not have sharp boundaries. Gibson was clear on this point:

Environmental sequences commonly have cycles embedded in larger cycles, that is, *nested* events. Consider the events in speech or music or pantomime or ballet (or in the sexual courting behavior of animals, for that matter). There are some different events and some similar events in the sequence. There will be shorter events that make up longer events and these making up still longer events. All are units of a sort, in the way that syllables, words, phrases, sentences and discourses are units. Units are nested within other units. And the remarkable fact is that both the superordinate and the subordinate events can be perceived. [J. J. Gibson, in Reed & Jones, 1982, p. 208]

An event need not be a continuous temporal unit. Writing-the-ecological-memory-papers has been going on for a year and a half, but it is not the only thing I do. Even the act of writing a single sentence is not always continuous; I interrupted this one at the semicolon to get a cup of coffee. Many activities maintain their identities across interruptions. I may say that it "took me all day" to climb a mountain, for example, when in fact I often stopped climbing to rest. Although my son Joe is certainly attending high school this year, he is not there at this moment: It is Friday evening, and he is at the movies. We often emphasize the coherence of such activities by redefining terms in a way that glosses over interruptions (rest stops can be described as phases of the process of climbing, recreation as a part of going to school), but we are not logically required do so. Many events are intrinsically discontinuous; they are no less real on that account.

It is frequently suggested that events like these have no objective reality – that they are brought into existence only by the way we perceive and talk about them. On that solipsistic assumption, nothing in the world is real until we make it so. To make such an assumption is to confuse selection with invention, flexibility with arbitrariness. The world is rich enough to support an indefinite number of correct descriptions, but not all descriptions are correct.

"Writing a chapter" is only one of many possible descriptions of what I am doing now, but it is certainly true; to say that I was riding a bicycle would be false.

Marigold Linton (Chap. 4) has adopted the term *extendure* for long-lasting events such as these, and I will follow her example. An extendure, then, is a coherent activity or situation in which an individual is involved repeatedly or over a considerable period of time. *Repetitions* are a particularly important class of discontinuous extendures. For example, the many airplane trips I have taken in my life make up an extendure in which the individual trips themselves are nested units. The extendure has invariant properties of its own – all the airplanes had wings and seat belts – but each of the events nested in it was also unique. Because nothing is ever entirely new and nothing is ever exactly repeated, the distinction between repetitions and other types of extendures is not a sharp one. The act of writing this chapter is by no means just a series of repetitions, but it is true that this evening I am working on the chapter *again*.

## Events as experienced

It is a matter of objective fact that I am writing a paper, just as it is a matter of fact that I typed that $T$.[1] But to claim that an event occurred in fact is not the same as claiming that I was actually aware of it. Much happens that I do not notice, and even when I notice something I may not get it right. The difference is critical, because autobiographical memory depends on what was perceived rather than on what really happened. No one can preserve what they have not first acquired. Even as I sit at my word processor, much is passing me by. Perhaps I happened to hit that $T$ key at a special angle, perhaps I have a systematic way of squirming in my chair, perhaps the room is getting warmer, perhaps there is an unnoticed logical inconsistency in my argument. Perhaps, but one proposition is certain: I will not remember anything tomorrow that I did not detect today.

Although that proposition is indeed certain, it is of little use if there is no way to establish what was actually detected. Unfortunately, we are often limited to introspection for that purpose, and it has severe limitations. If perception can occur entirely outside awareness, as has often been suggested, then introspective reports are inadequate ipso facto. Even if unconscious percep-

---

[1] To be sure, "writing a paper" is a meaningful expression only because there are generally accepted ideas about what "papers" are and what is involved in writing them. I have argued elsewhere (Neisser, in press *b*) that most of the concepts of everyday discourse depend for their meaning on what George Lakoff calls "idealized cognitive models." Statements that employ such concepts are no less objective on that account: What they objectively describe is a relation between a state of affairs and a conceptual structure.

tion turns out to be a myth (present evidence is somewhat ambiguous), such reports would still be problematic. Awareness is fleeting and comes in many shades and degrees; introspective reports can be strongly influenced by demand characteristics and experimenter effects. Nevertheless, there is hardly anywhere else to start.

Experienced events, like real ones, have a nested structure. (That is why the description of real events as nested – by no means the only possible description – seems so natural.) I can be *aware* of working on a series of papers, or of writing a chapter for Rubin's book; of making a particular argument, or of typing the word *particular,* or even of striking a single key. To be sure, I am not usually aware of all these things at once. When one of them is uppermost in my thoughts, the others seem to recede from consciousness. As I think about the argument, for example, I am only marginally aware of striking the keys of the word processor. I can focus on the key strokes if I like, but then I will become less aware of the argument. Unattended levels seem to move to the margins of awareness; what remains is just a sense that the presently focal level is linked to others above and below it. Even the most molecular aspects of my actions are experienced as goal-directed, for example, because I still have a sense that they are nested in more molar structures. At the other end of the spectrum, even the most molar units of experience are made subjectively real and tangible by an awareness that more molecular information is easily available – that I could flesh them out with concrete detail at will.

Although there is rarely any reason to attend to more than one of these levels at a time, it is not impossible to do so. Success in such an attempt depends on familiarity and individual skill, as in any other divided-attention task (Hirst, Spelke, Reaves, Caharack, & Neisser, 1980; Spelke, Hirst, & Neisser, 1976). It has often been suggested that simple actions become automatic with practice – indeed "automatic" rings true as a description of the status of the key strokes when I focus on the argument – but awareness can actually move freely in either direction. Higher levels can recede as easily as lower ones: If I focus on the key strokes, I become less aware of more molar units. Sometimes it is impossible to perceive the more extended units, because they have not yet come into existence. In 1983, when I was working on the first article in this series, there was no *series* at all (nor was I planning to write one). Nevertheless, the series exists now, and my recollection of writing it includes the first paper as well as the later ones.

## Levels of information

Events and extendures have nested levels of structure, and so does our experience of them. How does that correspondence come about? This question does not even arise in traditional information-processing theories, because they do not discuss the real environment at all. They simplify matters by assuming that, whatever the world may actually be like, only very molecular information about it is available to perceivers. On this assumption, all the molar aspects of experience are mental constructs; the task of cognitive psychology is to understand the process of construction and its products. It is a popular assumption, which I once accepted myself (Neisser, 1967). Reiser, Black, and Kalamarides (Chap. 7) are in this tradition when they casually postulate the existence of "knowledge structures" that guide retrieval from memory. They see no need to account for the surprising fit between those knowledge structures and the known world itself.

The ecological approach assumes, in contrast, that molar events are often perceived just as directly as molecular ones. The environment is equally real at many different levels of analysis, and events at those different levels are typically specified by different kinds of information. From this point of view, the first task for cognitive psychology must be to describe those information structures in their own right. Although I do not yet know how to carry out that task for the remembered events and extendures that are the subject of this paper, others have already undertaken it in the study of perception. Here are some examples of their findings:

> The sizes of visible objects are specified in part by their occlusions of optical texture gradients (Gibson, 1950).
>
> The coherence of a visible event with the sounds that it produces is specified by structural correspondences between the optic and the acoustic arrays (Spelke, 1976).
>
> The direction in which the observer is moving is specified by the origin point of the optical flow field (Gibson, 1979).
>
> The time remaining before a moving object collides with the observer is specified by Lee's (1980) parameter *tau*, which is given directly in the optical expansion pattern.

The different levels of fact in autobiographical events may also be specified by different kinds of information. On that assumption, the fact that I am writing a paper would be specified by a complex and discontinuous temporal structure, full of consistencies and repetitions as well as of variations from one occasion to the next. The fact that I am writing a particular word, in contrast, would be given by much more localized optical and kinesthetic structures. It is my hypothesis that these several levels of analysis are each represented in memory, leaving more or less independent "traces" behind.

### Nested levels of memory

If different levels of experienced reality are remembered independently, there must be many memory traces indeed. There is a trace of the fact that I am working on this chapter, a different trace of sitting here at the word processor, still other traces of the experiences of writing this sentence, typing this word, striking this key. There are also links between the levels: When one of them becomes active in recall I can locate others that are nested inside it, or in which it is nested. Most recall moves either downward from context or upward from particulars. Direct links at the same level of analysis are relatively rare. Even in the standard cue-word method (Crovitz & Shiffman, 1974), retrieval of a particular event is often mediated by higher order structures. That is why events recalled in this manner tend to cluster in particular seasons of the year (Robinson, Chap. 10) and certain seasons of our lives (Rubin, Wetzler, & Nebes, Chap. 12). Aristotle to the contrary, most associations are not established by simple contiguity or similarity; they are mediated by larger cognitive structures. (The Gestalt psychologists – for example, Kohler, 1947 – insisted long ago that association was just a by-product of perceptual grouping; I am making a similar argument here, with more objectivist assumptions about perception itself.)

Not only the associative links between individual events but also their temporal relations are usually established by reference to embedding structures. That is why we find it so much easier to establish the relative priority of two events when both of them are nested in the same larger unit (Brown, Shevell, & Rips, Chap. 9). Direct awareness of temporal sequence is possible only when the order of events is actually specified by stimulus information (cf. Gibson & Kaushall, 1973).

If memory were perfect, we could move up and down in these nested memory structures as easily as we do in immediate experience. From the memory of writing a paper I could go "downward" to any particular word or sentence that had occurred in it; from remembering a certain turn of phrase I could go "upward" to recall where and when and why I had used it. That kind of total recall is impossible, of course; most of the information at every level has long since been forgotten. But whether we remember the other levels or not, we are still confident of their existence. That confidence makes construction almost as inevitable in memory as it is unnecessary in perception. I can no longer remember making the *T* stroke discussed earlier, for example, but I know that events at that level were once available to me. Therefore, I also know how to make them up: The beginnings of construction in memory are provided by the nested structure of reality itself. I have now forgotten how the sentence beginning with the *T* stroke continued after *These,* but I could probably reconstruct a good deal of it; I would start by working downward from the argument.

Some years ago, I compared constructive activity in memory to the work of a paleontologist who constructs models of prehistoric animals for museum displays: "Out of a few stored bone chips, we remember a dinosaur" (Neisser,

1967, p. 285). That metaphor is too one-sided: It suggests that only the molecular aspects of events are stored whereas molar ones are always constructed. If there is objective information to specify larger units and extendures as well as brief events, construction can go in either direction. Given the feeding habits of the dinosaur, we may be able to reconstruct the shapes of the bones in its foot.

Recall is almost always constructive. No matter how well you remember an event, the information available will not specify all the context that once gave it meaning or all the molecular actions that were nested inside it. If you care to try, you can build on what remains to reconstruct some of what is missing. How much you make up and how much you are content to omit will depend on your situation at the time of recall and on your intentions. Detailed and colorful accounts are effective if you want to impress an audience; less elaboration is appropriate when you are testifying in court. (Some witnesses, especially young children, may not understand the difference between those two situations.) Perhaps the smallest amount of elaboration takes place when you are remembering silently for your own purposes; more appears as soon as you offer an overt account to another person. Any description that spans several levels of analysis probably requires at least a modest amount of constructive activity. As others have observed, that activity is strongly influenced by self-schemata (Brewer, Chap. 3; Barclay, Chap. 6) and by the schematic conventions of narrative itself (Spence, 1982).

## The effect of repetition

The occurrence of two similar or related events creates an extended event that exists in its own right, just as two babies born together are a set of twins and two aces make a pair. Each of the separate events leaves its own trace in memory, but there is also the trace of the pair itself. Suppose, for example, that I am first shown pictures of an automobile accident and then asked leading questions that offer additional or conflicting information. Loftus, Miller, and Burns (1978) suggest that the leading-question event would essentially rewrite the trace of the picture event, so that the latter would no longer exist in its original form. Bekerian and Bowers (1983) suggest, on the contrary, that both traces would remain distinct in memory. The present hypothesis implies that there would be at least *three* traces: one of the picture, one of the leading question, and one of the entire event including both the picture and the question. (I am oversimplifying; there would actually be many more than three.) Which of them will serve as the basis of later recall depends on many different variables. In general, molar traces survive and remain accessible over longer periods of time than molecular ones.

Any sequence that includes many repetitions – many trips, many days of work on a manuscript – has its own invariant properties. As a rule, those properties are more easily available in memory than the individual episodes themselves. This produces what Linton (1982) has called the transition from episodic to semantic memory. The more airplane trips we take, the more we know about flying in general and the less we remember about any particular journey. Sometimes we actually forget all the separate occasions and retain only the invariant properties. More often, however, a few individual events remain accessible. One of them is usually the most recent instance of the class (cf. Brewer, Chap. 3), but a few others may also survive in a kind of splendid isolation.

An isolated memory of this kind can be deceptive. Although it seems to represent only a single episode, we may actually be using it to stand for an entire extendure. I have called such memories *repisodic* (Neisser, 1981) to contrast with Tulving's (1972) terms, "episodic" and "semantic." (Repisodic memories do not fit comfortably on either side of Tulving's dichotomy: They are not purely episodic, but they seem to be.) They could equally well be called "representative" or "symbolic" memories. Freud's concept of "screen memory" (1899/1956) is also relevant here: A screen memory seems to describe only a single and unimportant childhood episode but really represents something deeper. I believe that Brown and Kulik's (1977) "flashbulb memories" are also repisodic in this sense: We remember the moment when we first heard that Kennedy has been shot because it links us to a historic occasion (Neisser, 1982). The same principle probably applies to most of our vivid and well-preserved memories, though their significance is usually personal rather than political (Rubin & Kozin, 1984).

**Conclusion**

My aim in this essay has been to provide the beginnings of an ecological theory of memory. In doing so, I am building on the work of others who have made similar efforts. J. J. Gibson often insisted that there could be no sharp distinction between perceiving and remembering (e.g., 1979, p. 253); Bransford, McCarrell, Franks, and Nitsch (1977) have used ecological concepts explicitly in criticizing traditional interpretations of memory; J. J. Jenkins's (1974) contextualism is certainly compatible with the suggestions made here. These approaches and mine are "ecological" in the sense that they take the temporal structure of the real, to-be-remembered world seriously. On this view, the first theoretical step is not to devise models of hypothetical mental processes but to describe real events themselves in a way that makes theoretical sense.

That description will not come easily. Some aspects of it still seem too difficult to address directly: I have said very little about which combinations of events count as extendures and which do not. It is indeed a fact that I am writing three papers on the ecological approach to memory, but there are an infinite number of other such facts. Do other combinations of papers comprise other extendures? All possible combinations? Does writing this paper combine with other nonwriting activities as well? Which ones? It is a fact that I struck the *T* key in writing *These* above, but I may have scratched my nose as well: Is the nose scratch nested in the chapter too? These are difficult questions, but they do not arise only in the ecological approach. All cognitive theories face essentially the same problem: It arises in the definition of objects as well as of extendures. Its best-known formulation is due to Quine (1960): If we hear a speaker of an unfamiliar language say "gavagai" as a rabbit runs by, how do we know that *gavagai* means "rabbit"? Could it not mean "brief temporal segment of rabbit" or "rabbit parts" or "rabbit next to a tree"? Ecological theories solve Quine's problem in the case of objects by postulating that natural units are specified objectively in the structure of the stimulus array itself and that perceivers are directly tuned to that structure. (How nonecological theories solve it I do not know.) Some similar solution must be found for events if we are ever to understand how they are perceived and remembered.

The recent surge of interest in autobiographical memory has resulted in many valuable empirical findings; it may be time to begin theorizing about them. From the ecological point of view, our first theoretical step must be primarily descriptive. Before we can understand what memory is like, we need an adequate analysis of what is remembered. I have tried to begin that analysis here by describing the nested structure of real events and the correspondingly nested structure of experience. In a somewhat less ecological vein, I have also made suggestions about the format in which event-related information may be stored. I have even postulated the existence of "memory traces," albeit not the kind found in more traditional theories. The traces I have in mind are not copies of events but remnants of directly perceived abstract structures; they are related not by temporal contiguity and association but by being nested within one another. This approach is still very speculative, but it has at least suggested some new ways of thinking about old problems.

## References

Bekerian, D. A., & Bowers, J. M. (1983). Eyewitness testimony: Were we misled? *Journal of Experimental Psychology: Learning, Memory, and Cognition, 9,* 139–145.

Bransford, J. D., McCarrell, N. S., Franks, J. J., & Nitsch, K. E. (1977). Toward unexplaining memory. In R. Shaw & J. Bransford (Eds.), *Perceiving, acting, and knowing: Toward an ecological psychology*. Hillsdale, NJ: Erlbaum.

Brown, R., & Kulik, J. (1977). Flashbulb memories. *Cognition, 5,* 73–99.

Crovitz, H. F., & Schiffman, H. (1974). Frequency of episodic memories as a function of their age. *Bulletin of the Psychonomic Society, 4,* 517–518.

Freud, S. (1956). Screen memories. In *Collected papers of Sigmund Freud* (Vol. 5). London: Hogarth Press. (Original work published 1899)

Gibson, J. J. (1950). *The perception of the visual world*. Boston: Houghton Mifflin.

    (1979). *The ecological approach to visual perception*. Boston: Houghton Mifflin.

Gibson, J. J., & Kaushall, P. (1973). *Reversible and irreversible events* [Film]. State College, PA: Psychological Cinema Register.

Hirst, W., Spelke, E. S., Reaves, C. C., Caharack, G., & Neisser, U. (1980). Dividing attention without alternation or automaticity. *Journal of Experimental Psychology: General, 109,* 98–117.

Jenkins, J. J. (1974). Remember that old theory of memory? Well, forget it! *American Psychologist, 29,* 785–795.

Kohler, W. (1947). *Gestalt psychology*. New York: Liveright.

Lee, D. N. (1980). The optic flow field: The foundation of vision. *Philosophical Transactions of the Royal Society, B 290,* 169–179.

Linton, M. (1982). Transformations of memory in everyday life. In U. Neisser (Ed.), *Memory observed: Remembering in natural contexts* (pp. 77–91). San Francisco: Freeman.

Loftus, E., Miller, D., & Burns, H. (1978). Semantic integration of verbal information into a visual memory. *Journal of Experimental Psychology: Human Learning and Memory, 4,* 19–31.

Neisser, U. (1967). *Cognitive psychology*. New York: Appleton-Century-Crofts.

    (1981). John Dean's memory: A case study. *Cognition, 9,* 1–22.

    (1982). Snapshots or benchmarks? In U. Neisser (Ed.), *Memory observed: Remembering in natural contexts* (pp. 43–48). San Francisco: Freeman.

    (1984). Interpreting Harry Bahrick's discovery: What confers immunity against forgetting? *Journal of Experimental Psychology: General, 113,* 32–35.

    (1985). The role of theory in the ecological study of memory: Comment on Bruce. *Journal of Experimental Psychology: General, 114,* 272–276.

    (in press). From direct perception to conceptual structure. In U. Neisser (Ed.), *Concepts reconsidered: The ecological and intellectual bases of categorization*. Cambridge: Cambridge University Press.

Quine, W. v. O. (1960). *Word and object*. Cambridge, MA: MIT Press.

Reed, E., & Jones, R. (1982). *Reasons for realism: Selected essays of James J. Gibson*. Hillsdale, NJ: Erlbaum.

Rubin, D. C., & Kozin, M. (1984). Vivid memories. *Cognition, 16,* 81–95.

Sachs, J. S. (1967). Recognition memory for syntactic and semantic aspects of connected discourse. *Perception and Psychophysics, 2,* 437–442.

Spelke, E. (1976). Infants' intermodal perception of events. *Cognitive Psychology, 8,* 553–560.

Spelke, E. S., Hirst, W., & Neisser, U. (1976). Skills of divided attention. *Cognition, 4,* 215–230.

Spence, D. P. (1982). *Narrative truth and historical truth: Meaning and interpretation in psychoanalysis*. New York: Norton.

Tolman, E. C. (1932). *Purposive behavior in animals and men*. New York: Appleton-Century-Crofts.

Tulving, E. (1972). Episodic and semantic memory. In E. Tulving & W. Donaldson (Eds.), *Organization of memory* (pp. 381–403). New York: Academic Press.

# 6     Schematization of autobiographical memory

*Craig R. Barclay*

## Introduction

The issues addressed in this chapter reflect concerns about the nature and acquisition of everyday autobiographical memories. One view is that such memories represent life events as those events actually happened; there is little change in what is remembered with the passage of time and as different experiences accumulate – most autobiographical memories have distinct, enduring, and episodic qualities (Tulving, 1972). I assume instead that (*a*) most autobiographical memories are *reconstructions* of past episodic events (Bartlett, 1932), (*b*) these recollections are driven by *self-schemata* (Markus, 1977), and (*c*) such self-schemata are acquired through a *schematization* process of one's memories for routine and often mundane everyday events and activities (Freud, 1914/1960; Piaget & Inhelder, 1973). If most autobiographical memories are reconstructions, then they are not often exact in detail even though these memories are true in the sense of maintaining the integrity and gist of past life events. Although many of the generic properties of one's autobiographical memories may change only gradually or with the occurrence of some socially significant transition, the elaborations of specific events probably vary over time, and those elaborations could be affected by one's current self-knowledge base.

Particularly lucid illustrations of the reconstructive nature of autobiographical memories are given by Mark Twain (1917/1975). He writes:

> I used to remember my brother Henry walking into a fire outdoors when he was a week old. It is remarkable in me to remember a thing like that, and it is still more remarkable that I should cling to the delusion for thirty years that I did remember it – of course it never happened; he would not have been able to walk at that age. [P. 3]

Or,

Appreciation is expressed to Kevin Miller and Henry Wellman for their comments and encouragement and to Kim Marentay for his assistance in preparing this manuscript. The author was supported in part by NICHD Grant HD–07109.

For many years I believed that I remembered helping my grandfather drink his whiskey toddy when I was six weeks old, but I do not tell about that any more now; I am grown old and my memory is not as active as it used to be. When I was younger I could remember anything, whether it had happened or not; but my faculties are decaying now and soon I shall be so I cannot remember anything but the things that never happened. It is sad to go to pieces like this, but we all have to do it. [P. 3]

These examples suggest that memories for some events are confabulations; inaccuracies are revealed through logical analysis. It may be that many other personal memories, not subject to such analyses, are also inaccurate, even though we strongly believe that those memories happened in precisely the way remembered, for example, flashbulb memories (Brown & Kulik, 1977).

Consider another example reported by Neisser (1981) that illustrates other interesting features of this phenomenon. When John Dean's Watergate testimony was compared with tape recordings of conversations in the White House Oval Office, he was quite inaccurate in reporting many details and event sequences. But the tapes supported Dean's description of the intent of the actors in the coverup and the significance of the events surrounding the Watergate incident. Although Dean's story was not strictly accurate, he nonetheless told the truth; his reconstructed scenario was correct in the sense of its veracity.

It seems that, as with Dean's testimony, our autobiographical recollections are based on facts that have been interpreted and fitted into a consistent story or schema. This schema functions to provide consistency between one's life as lived and the abbreviated story told at any given time. In this chapter, I will concentrate on how this story about ourselves might be acquired from routine life events – the focus is on the schematization of autobiographical memories. My proposition is quite simple; what we know about ourselves is gleaned from what we do, think, and feel every day.

This chapter is organized in three sections. A section on background is presented first to provide a context for the notion that everyday memories are schematized and form self-schemata incorporating life themes (Csikszentmihalyi & Beattie, 1979). A selection of ideas from the literary autobiography and psychological literatures is presented. These ideas illustrate differences between what one knows about self at a general, conceptual level and what may be remembered or reconstructed specifically. Next, empirical findings are reported from our own research that are consistent with the view that many autobiographical memories are reconstructive and become schematized as a function of similarity in meaning between what one thinks could or should have happened in the past and what actually occurred. The implications of these findings for understanding certain anomalies in everyday memories are discussed in the last section.

**Background**

*Literary autobiography*

Much of the pertinent work in this area has dealt with autobiography from a
critical perspective, as a literary genre separate from fiction (Olney, 1980;
Spengemann, 1980). Autobiography is defined as one's own story of his or
her life (Olney, 1980). One analogy is that autobiography is a "self-portrait"
(Howarth, 1980); another, preferred metaphor is that an autobiography is an
epic poem, reconstructed using well-formed themes to make sense out of
one's life at any given time (see Lord, 1960). Like the oral poet, the person
recounting his or her life produces a story such that the "moment of compo-
sition is the performance" (Lord, 1960, p. 13). It may be that, at that moment,
the person's current self-knowledge and feelings about self mediate the reconstructive process. In this sense, autobiography is an artifact, not based on
precise recollections but manufactured to best represent one's contemporary
view of self (Mandel, 1980). The essential ingredient of autobiography is that
the meaning of the author's life is portrayed honestly; the morphology of that
portrayal can vary tremendously.

   Howarth (1980) proposes that most autobiographies take one of three
forms. He describes these forms in terms of "autobiographical strategies" –
literary procedures used to tell a story – which include oratory, drama, and
poetry. In oratory, the autobiographer attempts to present an "idealized self,"
thereby offering an ideological message assumed to have significance for the
reader. The theme of the oratorical form provides a formula to live by, "its
purpose is didactic, [the] story is allegorical, seeking to represent in a single
life an idealized pattern of human behavior" (Howarth, 1980, p. 89). The
author employing this strategy crafts an autobiography rich in terms of the
spiritual meaning of life but uses details only figuratively.

   The dramatic form, unlike oratorical autobiography, does not portray the
author as an ideologist. In dramatic autobiographies, life is made up of
events, ordered in time, that can be viewed and appreciated by the reader for
their intrinsic value. No life presented in this way preaches a message; "Instead of dogma, [the authors] cherish idiosyncracy – not merely as a lesson
to others, but also as a performance of their innate skill" (Howarth, 1980, p.
98). Here, authors take the freedom to dramatize their lives while maintaining
constancy in such personal qualities as honesty and virtue. Details of setting
and events are often elaborated with great care to give a realistic impression.
Details are used to aid the reader in discovering the "truth" about an author's
life. Again, it is unnecessary that these details be accurate in any way; they

need only elaborate the reader's knowledge of the author and support the theme of the autobiography.

In the poetic autobiographical form the author neither sermonizes nor acts out life on a stage. The major purpose of the poetic form is to present a life that reflects an ongoing effort to discover self. At any moment, the author is uncertain about the meaning of life; readers must import that information for themselves. The truth value of a poetic autobiography is carried by the author's constant search for meaning in life. The stress is placed on the process of becoming, not on a message about what the author's life was or means for the reader. Descriptive details provide a context and setting for events; they reflect more the autobiographer's imagination than reality.

The integrating strand through each of these autobiographical forms is that what is written must convey precisely and honestly the autobiographer's intentions. The striking difference is the degree of poetic freedom taken to represent the meaning of one's life. Regardless of the particular form, however, the authors' attempts to tell the truth about their lives must convince the reader that the "events" and feelings written about really happened in a manner conceptually near to the way reported. Otherwise, the autobiography as a genre would fall into the category of fiction.

"Truthfulness" in literary autobiography is interesting psychologically because the author may think the information reported is accurate but upon careful analysis may find it is not. Thus, the autobiographer's memory and memory failures are informative and contribute to our understanding of reconstructive memory processes.

A clear example of the role of memory in autobiography was presented by Salaman (1970). She was writing about "involuntary memories," or recollections that became conscious for no apparent reason and triggered other associated memories. Of special interest is Salaman's intuition about the merging of memories with similar perceptual features. She writes:

> One day, while working on some early memories, and living in one of the 1905 Revolution when I was five, I was terribly taken aback. I was looking out of the window, with my eyes on two women running past, just underneath, each frightened in her own way. They had neither hats nor kerchiefs and their hair was bobbed. "The Revolutionaries," Mother said, close behind me: I turned my head to her. To my amazement I realized that the room I was looking at was the sitting-room of the house to which we moved when I was thirteen! I looked again at my other memories and now realize that I was using the background of the later house. Let me say straight away that this house, unlike the houses where we lived between 1908 and 1913, was on the same side of the road as the first, not far from it, and not unlike it to look at. The parlor in both houses had two windows which looked out on the street. [P. 32]

Commonalities in backgrounds from the different houses she lived in became fused to provide the context for these early memories. Her "amazement" was due to the recognition that her memory fooled her into placing events in a context different from their actual settings. The details of the houses were similar and very familiar. Perhaps many autobiographical memories acquire schematic properties in this way. That is, through similarities in certain perceptual or conceptual features the past is reconstructed such that the person adds or takes away information to make a story coherent and believable to themselves and others at some particular time.

*Psychological literature*

What are the psychological mechanisms underlying the seemingly generative and effable nature of autobiography and autobiographical memory? Answers to this question may lie in the cognitive, developmental, social, and personality literatures. Specifically, the work on identity formation, self-schemata, and self-prototypes is directly relevant to an understanding of how one acquires an autobiographical memory system.[1] In each of these literatures, a central construct is proposed as an organizing principle for integrating experiences in the person's life. The formation of that structure certainly is grounded in specific life activities. These daily experiences are not necessarily unique in the sense of changing one's life at the moment they occur. Instead, they are associated with one's daily commerce with the environment, and most life changes seem to occur gradually.

Identity formation is the development of a sense of sameness or consistency about one's self. Erikson (1968) suggests that this awareness of consistency is revised over time in the context of some social reality. Epstein (1973) elaborates this view, arguing that a sense of identity is a self-concept – more precisely, a personal theory about one's self:

It [identity] is a theory that the individual has unwittingly constructed about himself as an experiencing, functioning individual. . . . [The] basic functions [of a self-theory] are to facilitate the maintenance of self-esteem, and to organize the data of experience in a manner that can be coped with effectively. [P. 407]

Self-theories are analogous to formal theories in that they organize self-referenced information and establish expectations for the future. Self-theories embody the assumptions, concepts, and principles about self that are acquired over time. Also, self-theories that serve an effective problem-solving function are characterized by their extensiveness (Epstein, 1973); they are useful for integrating information and finding problem solutions in different situations

---

[1] The concept acquisition literature has been reviewed extensively, especially from a developmental perspective (e.g., Nelson, 1977). Also, autobiographical memory seen from an artificial-intelligence viewpoint is well represented by Reiser (1983). No attempt is made here to duplicate these efforts.

the individual considers personally important. The structure of a self-theory, therefore, influences the processing of autobiographical information. In this regard Marcia (1966, 1976) has proposed that self-theories can be indexed according to an "identity status" taxonomy. The identity status measure is used to differentiate among different types of resolutions a person may make in response to an identity crisis. A crisis is a decision-making period during which a person reexamines and reevaluates basic beliefs and values; a committed individual is personally invested in those beliefs and values in the sense of ego involvement (Berzonsky, 1981; Marcia, 1968). Four resolution modes are possible, given the consideration of whether or not people experience crisis and commitment. These modes are (1) *achievement,* characterized by the formation of a commitment following an identity crisis; (2) *moratorium,* a state in which the individual is in a continued crisis and struggling to achieve a sense of self; (3) *foreclosure,* the status in which the person takes a prescribed social role and maintains values from childhood without experiencing a crisis; and (4) *diffusion,* marked by a lack of both crisis and commitment.

Research has shown that persons in these status categories differ in the way they deal with information and how they approach problems and make decisions. For instance, Marcia (1976) has found that foreclosures consistently score highest, relative to individuals in the other status categories, on measures of authoritarianism, and they also tend to be more rigid when stressed. Foreclosures are also more externally controlled (Adams & Shea, 1979; Marcia, 1980) and unrealistic in their attributions about success and failure on some tasks (Marcia, 1966). In contrast, achievers are relatively open to information, more internally controlled, and less rigid under stress (Adams & Shea, 1979; Berzonsky, 1981; Marcia, 1980).

Self-schemata and self-prototypes share theoretical kinship with self-theories. Markus (1977) states that "Self-schemata are cognitive generalizations about the self, derived from past experience, that organize and guide the processing of self-referenced information contained in the individual's social experiences" (p. 64). Self-schemata are composed of two broad classes of cognitive representations: information abstracted from specific episodic events and more general information derived from exposure to repeatedly occurring events. Markus (1977) argues that self-schemata are constructions based on the processing of past information that come to control attention and memory for self-referenced material in the present. Further, individual differences in self-schemata should be found to the extent that people differ in their everyday experiences and memories for those experiences.

Markus (1977, 1980) has shown that the a priori classification of individuals as being either *dependent* or *independent schematics,* or *aschematics,* is predictive of how frequently and quickly these different groups process descriptive adjectives consistent with their self-conceptions of dependency. Independents, for example, respond more rapidly and to a greater proportion of adjectives like "individualistic" and "assertive" as self-descriptive than do dependents. Individuals classified as independent schematic are also able to recall and report more specific events from their past that are associated with independent rather than dependent behavior. Symmetrical effects were found for the Dependents; the adjectives responded to and events recalled were associated more with dependent than with independent behavior.

Other researchers have proposed that the self can be considered as a cognitive "prototype" (e.g., Kuiper & Derry, 1980; Rogers, 1980; Rogers, Rogers, & Kuiper, 1979). A prototype, according to Rosch (1973, 1978) and her colleagues (Rosch, Mervis, Gray, Johnson, & Boyers-Bream, 1976), is a cognitive construction that incorporates one's knowledge about any given category of information, including the self, and this information is represented in memory. The representation carries the meaning of a given category of knowledge (Cantor, Mischel, & Schwartz, 1982).

Markus and Sentis (1980) and Rogers (1980) have found that information consistent with one's prototypic self-concept is remembered more accurately than inconsistent information (see also Mischel, Ebbesen, & Zeiss, 1976). Rogers, Rogers, and Kuiper (1979) have further demonstrated that "false alarm" rates (i.e., incorrectly identifying new information as experienced in the past) were inflated when individuals were asked to recognize whether or not self-descriptive adjectives were previously presented. The number of false recognitions increased as the new adjectives became more consistent with the person's prototypic view of self.

In sum, the major themes in literary autobiography and the selected works briefly cited on identity, personal theories, self-schemata, and self-prototypes are conceptually alike. That is, autobiographical material may not be correct in detail, although it must maintain the integrity of one's life; and self-concepts help mediate self-referenced information so that what is remembered is compatable with one's existing self-knowledge. Personal memories, however, need not accurately reflect some event or event sequence. It seems that the organizing function of self-knowledge is built up over time through varied exposure to repetitive episodic events.

## Schematization of autobiographical memory

Schematization is the process through which generalizable action structures are acquired (Head, 1921; Oldfield & Zangwill, 1942). These structures represent both the outcomes of actions and the procedural knowledge used to regulate future acts (Neisser, 1976; Piaget & Inhelder, 1973). It is assumed that the contents of one's thoughts are determined by behavioral and mental activities engaged in on a regular basis. Through repeated exposure to similar kinds of activities, common features are noticed that become the focus of one's mental efforts. In this way, information derived from daily activities is represented cognitively. Thus, for autobiographical material, schematization leads to the conceptual organization and storage in memory of everyday self-referenced information.

Most self-referenced information from our daily lives cannot be remembered precisely because of mental capacity limitations. However, schematization allows us to process large amounts of such material through summarizing consistencies and regularities in our experiences. On these assumptions, it is reasonable to argue that autobiographical memories change over time because new events occur and many life experiences become repetitious, making any single event indistinguishable from related happenings (e.g., Linton, 1982). People do not simply forget the details of everyday events, although they could. Instead, when information is remembered, acquired autobiographical self-knowledge drives the reconstruction of plausible, but often inaccurate, elaborations of previous experiences. Memories for most everyday life events are, therefore, transformed, distorted, or forgotten. Moreover, "events" that have not occurred but are conceptually similar to what one expects from prior recurring experiences may be incorrectly identified as happening in the past. Inaccuracies should also increase as time passes because generic aspects of events and activities may become condensed and blended further with continuing exposure to like incidents. In an initial attempt to explore these expectations we (Barclay & Wellman, 1986) examined memory for everyday autobiographical events over 2½ years.

A review of much of the literature on autobiographical memory indicated that although the topic has attracted considerable attention (e.g., Colgrove, 1899; Dudycha & Dudycha, 1941; Galton, 1879; Henri & Henri, 1895) most of the reported data are anecdotal (see also Reed, 1979). Furthermore, in more recent studies, methodologies are often used that do not allow for an assessment of the validity of memory (e.g., Bahrick, Bahrick, & Wittlinger, 1975; Crovitz & Schiffman, 1974; Fitzgerald, 1980). In many of these studies, subjects were presented cue words (e.g., "happy") and told to recall associated life events. Once the events were generated, they were dated. In the typical study, no checks were made to determine if the reported events actually occurred or if the events (assuming they did occur) were dated accurately (exceptions include work by Rubin, 1982, and Thompson, 1982). Studying schematization and reconstructive aspects of such recollections requires veridical records of memorable events. Deviations between what actually happened and what the person claims to have occurred are the measures of interest.

One notable study in which verifiable records of memorable daily events were kept was reported by Linton (1975). A number of her findings are relevant to the present discussion even though the main purpose of her study was to determine when certain events had occurred in her life. In particular, she found little forgetting over the first 20 months of her 6-year longitudinal study. Also, her memory was not predictable from assessments of how emotion-arousing some events seemed at the time recorded. These findings are interesting because, based on both laboratory experiments and some studies using naturally occurring events (e.g., Gold & Neisser, 1980; Thompson, 1982), we would expect a more rapid forgetting rate of such episodic material and higher levels of remembering for events associated with affective cues (e.g., Bower, 1981; Brown & Kulik, 1977).

Of course, Linton's (1975) overall memory performance reflects somewhat her pretest knowledge that the events judged really did occur because she had written them. Her memory could also indicate a response bias to incorrectly identify events that might have occurred because those events were compatible with her general knowledge about what she was likely to be doing at the time the records were made. It was not possible given her purpose and methodology to separate true memory for events from the tendency to verify that all of the records were indeed remembered.

A useful method for differentiating memory from a response bias is to present nonevents or foil items along with records of actual events. In our work, a recognition paradigm was used in which subjects' original records were included among foils. In addition to assessing the contribution of a response bias to overall memory performance, we were able to manipulate selected aspects of the foils in an effort to determine which features of the nonevents lead to false recognitions. Three types of foil items were used: foil evaluations, foil descriptions, and foil others. Foil-evaluation and foil-description items were constructed from the original records reported by our subjects. Foil evaluations were included because it was felt that if people coded information with evaluative or affective cues (e.g., Bower, 1981; Robinson, 1980; Waters & Leeper, 1936) these foils would be correctly rejected at a higher rate than records with changes in descriptive details. The foil evaluations were made by rewriting the subjects' reported emotional reactions or evaluations of events; descriptive details and elaborations of records were changed in creating the foil descriptions. Foil-other items were records of a person not participating in this study but sharing the same types of daily experiences as our subjects. Examples of each of these foil types are presented in Table 6.1.

Daily records were gathered from our subjects during 4 consecutive months of data collection. The original sample consisted of six graduate student volunteers who kept records of three memorable events a day for 5 days each week, excluding weekends. The recorded events were self-selected, and the

Table 6.1. *Examples of record types*

| Original | Foil evaluation | Foil description | Foil other |
|---|---|---|---|
| I went shopping downtown looking for an anniversary present for my parents but couldn't find a thing. I get so frustrated when I can't find what I want. | I went shopping downtown looking for an anniversary present for my parents but couldn't find a thing. I guess I should keep looking tomorrow. | I went shopping downtown. I must have gone to 10 stores before giving up and going home. I get so frustrated when I can't find what I want. | Spent a tiring afternoon in the library searching material for a paper. I must have looked for a dozen journals someone else had already checked out. What a pain. |

*Note:* An original record was used to construct only one foil in a test – either a foil evaluation or a foil description but not both. Original records were sampled without replacement, and none served as both an original and a foil item.

subjects knew they would be tests. Unfortunately, three participants were lost to attrition by the end of the project. Inspection of the data available for these subjects indicated that their lost scores probably did not bias the overall results.

The subjects were encouraged to use a simplified format derived from story grammars in keeping their daily records (e.g., Stein & Goldman, 1979). This format included a context in which the memorable event was set, the event itself, and some emotional and behavioral reaction or evaluation of the event. For instance, *(Context)* "I was driving in my car *(Event)* when the person in front of me hit her brakes. *(Behavioral Reaction)* I had to stop quickly before running into her. *(Emotional Reaction)* I was so scared my heart was racing." It was stressed that the content of the event was most important and should not be sacrificed to meet format restrictions.

Five posttests were given after all of the records were collected. The first four posttests were spaced in time to generate a 1-year longitudinal delay with memory for autobiographical information evaluated at 1-month intervals. In the final analyses these intervals were blocked in four groups of 3 months each. Items were taken from the first data collection period for the long-term posttest to extend the maximum delay interval to 2½ years. At each time of testing, the subjects were presented with a 45-item recognition test.[2] Of the test items, 18 were duplicates of original records; 27 were foils (9 each were foil evaluations, foil descriptions, and foil others). The subjects were in-

---

[2] Temporal ordering and dating of original records were also assessed. These data are not reported here; they are available elsewhere (Barclay & Wellman, 1986).

Table 6.2. *Performance rates in proportions on originals (hits) and foils (false alarms) over 2½ years*

| | Delay interval (months) | | | | |
|---|---|---|---|---|---|
| | 1–3 (*n* = 5) | 4–6 (*n* = 4) | 7–9 (*n* = 3) | 10–12 (*n* = 3) | 30–31 (*n* = 3) |
| Original | .92 | .94 | .95 | .95 | .79 |
| Foil evaluation | .38 | .47 | .62 | .52 | .48 |
| Foil description | .42 | .47 | .47 | .56 | .52 |
| Foil other | .16 | .30 | .17 | .41 | .04 |

structed to affirm as their own memories only items that were exact replicas of original records.

The results of interest are presented in Table 6.2. "Hits" were scored as accurate verifications of original records, and "false alarms" were incorrect recognitions of foil items. Inspection of these data show that recognition of original records was excellent over the initial 12 months and declined to .79 after 2½ years. The error rates for foil-evaluation and foil-description items were significantly greater than those found for original and foil-other items. Also, false alarm rates on foil-evaluation and foil-description items increased over the 1–3-month delay interval only. No evidence was found that the kinds of events reported were coded with affective tags that made the events especially memorable, because error rates between foil-evaluation and foil-description items did not differ. The false alarm rate on foil-other items was quite variable overall. This indicated that at each test the subjects could usually differentiate their own memories from someone else's, although at times with some difficulties.

Clearly, people can recognize events that have occurred in their lives; however, the high false alarm rate suggests that this is not because of direct access to some stored duplicate of original records. If this were the case, then more, if not all, of the foils should have been rejected as nonevents. Instead, recognition of everyday events results from a tendency to identify, as one's own, "memories" similar to what could have happened in the past – the most similar items being originals and the least similar, foil others.

Thus, it seems that the tendency to falsely recognize nonevents should vary directly with the conceptual similarity between nonevents and what one expects to have occurred in one's life. We examined this issue in detail by first pairing all foil-evaluation and foil-description items from the 1-year delay interval with their corresponding original records. Next, independent raters

Table 6.3. *Mean semantic difference ratings for foil evaluation and foil description items as a function of response outcome*

|  | Response outcome | |
| --- | --- | --- |
|  | Correct rejection | False alarm |
| Foil evaluation | 4.39 | 3.82 |
| Foil description | 3.65 | 2.88 |

*Note:* 1 = not semantically different; 7 = very semantically different.

judged the degree to which each foil differed semantically from its associated original. The raters were asked to decide whether or not the foils carried the essential truth value contained in the original records and to ignore changes in syntax. A 7-point scale was used in which a low rating (e.g., 1) indicated greater semantic similarity than a high rating (e.g., 7). These data are summarized in Table 6.3 where it is seen that the mean semantic difference ratings for false alarms was *less* than that found for foil items correctly rejected. False alarms increased as foil items became more conceptually like originals. Apparently, this "semantic similarity effect" accounts, at least in part, for many of the inaccuracies found in people's recognition of everyday autobiographical information.

Further, false alarm rates on foil-evaluation and foil-description items should vary with similarity over time. If autobiographical information is being schematized, then we would expect an interaction between the length of delay and *degree* of semantic similarity of foil items incorrectly identified as one's own memories relative to the original records from which those foils were constructed. Hypothetically, because memory for details deteriorates as typical event characteristics are abstracted, false alarms on conceptually similar nonevents should increase with time, and the rate of this increase should depend on how conceptually similar nonevents are to what actually happened. More specifically, inaccurate identifications of foil-evaluation and foil-description items should be more frequent at shorter delay intervals for foils "high" in semantic similarity than for items "low" in similarity. In addition, as foils become more remote in time, the magnitude of the false recognition difference between high- and low-similarity items should decrease because low-similarity foils remain distinctive from actual events relatively longer than do high-similarity items.

Again, all of the foil-evaluation and foil-description items rated by the independent judges were considered. Foil-evaluation items with mean ratings of ≤ 3.6 were included in the pool of "high"-similarity foils; those with mean

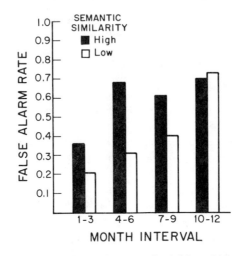

Figure 6.1. False-alarm rates for foil items high and low in semantic similarity over a 1-year delay interval

ratings of $\geq 4.5$ were "low." High-similarity foil-description items had mean ratings of $\leq 2.8$, and low items had means of $\geq 3.8$. The boundaries created by these mean ratings included items in the upper and lower thirds of the similarity rating distributions for both foil-evaluation and foil-description items. No systematic differences were found in the judges' ratings of semantic similarity over delay intervals. However, the judges rated the foil-description items as more similar than foil evaluations. The subjects obviously did not make this same discrimination, because no overall performance differences were found between foil-evaluation and foil-description items (Table 6.2). Subsequently, foil-evaluation and foil-description items were combined and divided into high- and low-similarity groups. False alarm rates for each group were then plotted over month delay. These data are presented in Figure 6.1.

A clear interaction between month delay and semantic similarity is seen here ($\chi^2_{(3)} = 16.40, p < .01$).[3] The false alarm rates for both groups of items were relatively low at the 1–3-month delay interval, although high-similarity items were incorrectly recognized slightly more frequently than low-similarity items. The false alarm rate on high-similarity foils increased substantially at the 4–6-month interval and remained stable over the next 7–12 months; for low-similarity items, the increase over the 4–6, 7–9, and 10–12-month intervals was gradual. After 10–12 months, there were no differences between high- and low-similarity items.

[3] This statistic is reported only as a rough estimate of a Type 1 error. Too few subjects were tested to conduct appropriate analyses.

It is apparent that semantic similarity interacted with temporal delay in expected ways. The probability of incorrectly identifying foils as one's own memories was greater if those items were high in conceptual likeness to actual events than if the items were seen as low in similarity, at least for the first 9-month delay intervals. With time, the false recognition rate increased, and this acceleration was faster for the high- than for the low-similarity items, especially in the early delay intervals; after a year, people were just as likely to make errors on foils regardless of similarity.

Altogether, the evidence supports the claim that the remembering of autobiographical material may at times reflect memories for actual events, but in many instances such memories represent reconstructions of events that could have taken place. Likewise, forgetting autobiographical information could indicate the absence of certain memories; however, it seems that the nonrecognition of actual events occurs because of the merging of episodic memories into more generic "event" categories representing the semantic features of everyday activities. In short, our autobiographical memories are not exact. Details associated with some repetitive daily events seem to be condensed, thereby losing any distinct memorable features. Further, the likelihood of erroneously identifying some event depends on the degree to which the "event" is conceptually related to what could have taken place. The rate at which information associated with everyday events is schematized also seems to depend on how conceptually similar some nonevent is to one's expectations. In general, there are both variances and invariances in what people remember about their daily lives. The relative invariances seem to be in the underlying autobiographical self-knowledge derived from everyday activities; change occurs in the reconstructions of exactly how, and in what ways, some events happened.

## Implications

Memory is a great artist. For every man and for every woman it makes the recollection of his or her life a work of art and an unfaithful record. [Maurois, 1929, pp. 157–158]

The description of autobiographical memory as reconstructive and acquired through a schematization process may apply to many instances of functional anomalies in everyday memories. Any situation resulting in the false recognition of new information as previously experienced may be explained in terms of similarity in surface features and semantic properties between what is remembered and fact. Conversely, failures to remember some specific event would also be due to a similarity effect because actual events merge into and become indistinguishable from generic "events" compatible with what the person thinks could have happened. Consider the following two examples taken from Reed (1979).

In some situations people think they have experienced sensations, physical environments, or activities in the past when they know rationally they have not. The most well-known instance is déjà vu, for example, walking into a restaurant and thinking you have eaten there before but then realizing that you could not have because it is your first visit to the city. In the context of the present discussion, it is likely that déjà vu occurs, in part, because a present situation is perceptually or conceptually related to other frequently occurring sensations or activities that share common characteristics. A feeling of déjà vu is, therefore, not a memory failure in the sense of an inability to recollect the past; instead, such a feeling, though reflecting an inaccuracy in memory, probably results from the identification of elements compatible with one's existing knowledge. Portrayed in this way, déjà vu is a false recognition of information, but information within some domain of possibility given an individual's accumulated self-knowledge. The sensation associated with déjà vu perhaps results from surprise and an awareness that one's memory is fallible.

In another situation people may believe that they have had a novel experience when, in fact, they have not. Cryptomnesia is a memory anomaly in which a person recollects a past experience but does not attribute the remembrance to memory; the experience is treated as if it were a first occurrence. Such situations result in the incorrect rejection of "old" experiences as new. A functional consequence of this phenomenon is, for example, that one may think one has had an original idea even though someone else had suggested it earlier; or, an idea was truly original but forgotten and then rediscovered, with no memory for the initial discovery. Unlike déjà vu, cryptomnesia is a memory failure that is not associated with the false recognition of conceptually similar experiences; however, as with déjà vu, cryptomnesia occurs because the characteristics of a present situation cannot be differentiated from the past. Interestingly, these inabilities to distinguish past from present seemingly differ depending on whether some experience actually occurred; however, underlying both types of memory errors is the same conceptual system constructed from schematized experiences.

Our awareness of memory failures, including knowing about fabricating inaccuracies or failing to acknowledge the source of information, comes about through logical analysis and reminding by others. The sense of surprise at the moment of awareness that memory is in error, though attention-getting, could be misleading. Focusing only on obvious errors would suggest that such errors are atypical of memory in general. However, what appear as functional disorders in memory may represent normative aspects of human cognition. It is not unusual to find that many personal memories include predictable distortions if it is assumed that the remembrance of most everyday occurrences is reconstructive and based on schematized self-knowledge. The frequency of our everyday memory failures is probably greater than we are aware of and, in most cases, not indicative of some pathology.

The clearest implication of the theoretical stance taken here is that there is a discrepancy between what one remembers about everyday autobiographical events and what really happened. This discrepancy could result from similar and repetitious experiences becoming schematized, forming autobiographical self-schemata (Markus, 1977). These self-schemata would represent a view of one's life that may appear to be quite different in content when compared to precise information about actual daily events. It is not the case, however, that the meaning around which autobiographical memory is organized is a complete fabrication of life events. There is a fundamental integrity to one's autobiographical recollections.

It appears that most autobiographical memories are true but inaccurate. What is remembered in particular probably does not reflect the way some event really happened. It could be that none of our autobiographical memories are retrieved as duplicates of actual events; but such "memories" are familiar enough to our expectations that they elicit false identifications. These errors, though, may be mediated by an accurate "self-portrait," because not just any "memory" is acceptable as one's own. The sense of familiarity created by an event is associated with a judgment that the event is true to what most likely occurred and consistent with what should have happened.

## References

Adams, G. R., & Shea, J. A. (1979). The relationship between identity status, locus of control, and ego development. *Journal of Youth and Adolescence, 8,* 81–89.

Bahrick, H. P., Bahrick, P. O., & Wittlinger, R. P. (1975). Fifty years of memory for names and faces: A cross-sectional approach. *Journal of Experimental Psychology: General, 104,* 54–75.

Barclay, C. R., & Wellman, H. M. (1986). Accuracies and inaccuracies in autobiographical memories. *Journal of Memory and Language, 25,* 93–103.

Bartlett, F. C. (1932). *Remembering: A study in experimental and social psychology.* New York: Macmillan.

Berzonsky, M. D. (1981). *Adolescent development.* New York: Macmillan.

Bower, G. H. (1981). Mood and memory. *American Psychologist, 36,* 129–148.

Brown, R., & Kulik, J. (1977). Flashbulb memories. *Cognition, 5,* 73–99.

Cantor, N., Mischel, W., & Schwartz, J. C. (1982). A prototype analysis of psychological situation. *Cognitive Psychology, 14,* 45–77.

Colgrove, F. W. (1899). Individual memories. *American Journal of Psychology, 10,* 228–255.

Crovitz, H. F., & Schiffman, H. (1974). Frequency of episodic memories as a function of their age. *Bulletin of the Psychonomic Society, 4,* 517–518.

Csikszentmihalyi, M., & Beattie, O. V. (1979). Life themes: A theoretical and empirical exploration of their origins and effects. *Journal of Humanistic Psychology, 19,* 45–63.

Dudycha, G. J., & Dudycha, M. M. (1941). Childhood memories: A review of the literature. *Psychological Bulletin, 38,* 668–682.

Epstein, S. (1973). The self-concept revisited, or a theory of a theory. *American Psychologist, 28,* 404–416.

Erikson, E. H. (1968). *Identity: Youth and crisis.* New York: Norton.

Fitzgerald, J. M. (1980). Sampling autobiographical memory reports in adolescents. *Developmental Psychology, 16,* 675–676.

Freud, S. (1914/1960). *The psychopathology of everyday life.* New York: Norton.

Galton, F. (1879). Psychometric experiments. *Brain, 2,* 149–162.

Gold, E., & Neisser, U. (1980). Recollections of kindergarten. *Quarterly Newsletter of the Laboratory of Comparative Human Cognition, 2,* 77–80.

Head, H. (1921). *Studies in neurology (II).* Oxford: Oxford University Press.

Howarth, W. L. (1980). Some principles of autobiography. In J. Olney (Ed.), *Autobiography: Essays theoretical and critical* (pp. 84–114). Princeton: Princeton University Press. (Originally published in *New Literary History, 5,* [1974], 363–381)

Henri, V., & Henri, C. (1895). On our earliest recollections of childhood. *Psychological Review, 2,* 215–216.

Kuiper, N. A., & Derry, P. A. (1980). The self as a cognitive prototype: An application to person perception and depression. In N. Cantor & J. F. Kihlstrom (Eds.), *Personality, cognition and social interaction* (pp. 215–232). Hillsdale, NJ: Erlbaum.

Linton, M. (1975). Memory for real-world events. In D. A. Norman & D. E. Rumelhart (Eds.), *Explorations in cognition* (pp. 376–404). San Francisco: Freeman.

(1982). Transformations of memory in everyday life. In U. Neisser (Ed.), *Memory observed: Remembering in natural contexts* (pp. 77–91). San Francisco: Freeman.

Lord, A. B. (1960). *The singer of tales.* Cambridge, MA: Harvard University Press.

Mandel, B. J. (1980). Full of life now. In J. Olney (Ed.), *Autobiography: Essays theoretical and critical* (pp. 49–72). Princeton: Princeton University Press.

Marcia, J. E. (1966). Development and validation of ego identity status. *Journal of Personality and Social Psychology, 3,* 551–558.

(1968). The case history of a construct: Ego identity status. In W. E. Vinacke (Ed.), *Readings in general psychology* (pp. 325–332). New York: American Books.

(1976). Identity six years after: A follow-up study. *Journal of Youth and Adolescence, 5,* 145–160.

(1980). Identity in adolescence. In J. Adelson (Ed.), *Handbook of adolescent psychology* (pp. 159–187). New York: Wiley.

Markus, H. (1977). Self-schemata and processing information about the self. *Journal of Personality and Social Psychology, 35,* 63–78.

(1980). The self in thought and memory. In D. M. Wegner & R. R. Vallacher (Eds.), *The self in social psychology* (pp. 102–130). New York: Oxford University Press.

Markus, H., & Sentis, K. (1980). The self in social information processing. In J. Suls (Ed.), *Social psychological perspectives on the self* (pp. 41–70). Hillsdale, NJ: Erlbaum.

Maurois, A. (1929). *Aspects of biography.* New York: Appleton.

Mischel, W., Ebbsen, E. B., & Zeiss, A. M. (1976). Determinants of selective memory about self. *Journal of Consulting and Clinical Psychology, 44,* 92–103.

Neisser, U. (1976). *Cognition and reality.* San Francisco: Freeman.

(1981). John Dean's memory: A case study. *Cognition, 9,* 1–22.

Nelson, K. (1977). Cognitive development and the acquisition of concepts. In R. C. Anderson, R. J. Spiro, & W. E. Montague (Eds.), *Schooling and the acquisition of knowledge* (pp. 215–240). Hillsdale, NJ: Erlbaum.

Oldfield, R. C., & Zangwill, O. L. (1942). Head's concept of the schema and its application in contemporary British psychology. *British Journal of Psychology, 32,* 267–286.

Olney, J. (Ed.). (1980). *Autobiography: Essays theoretical and critical.* Princeton: Princeton University Press.

Piaget, J., & Inhelder, B. (1973). *Memory and intelligence.* New York: Basic Books.

Reed, G. (1979). Everyday anomalies of recall and recognition. In J. F. Kihlstrom & F. J. Evans (Eds.), *Functional disorders of memory* (pp. 1–28). Hillsdale, N.J.: Erlbaum.

Reiser, B. J. (1983). *Contexts and indices in autobiographical memory* (Tech. Rep. No. 24). New Haven: Cognitive Science Program, Yale University.

Robinson, J. A. (1980). Affect and retrieval of personal memories. *Motivation and Emotion, 4,* 149–174.

Rogers, T. B. (1980). A model of the self as an aspect of the human information processing system. In N. Cantor & J. H. Kihlstrom (Eds.), *Personality, cognition, and social interaction* (pp. 193–214). Hillsdale, NJ: Erlbaum.

Rogers, T. B., Rogers, P. I., & Kuiper, N. A. (1979). Evidence for the self as a cognition prototype: "The false alarm effect." *Personality and Social Psychology Bulletin, 5,* 53–58.

Rosch, E. (1973). On the internal structure of perceptual and semantic categories. In T. E. Moore (Ed.), *Cognitive development and acquisition of language.* New York: Academic Press.

(1978). Principles of categorization. In T. S. Rosch & B. B. Lloyd (Eds.), *Cognition and categorization* (pp. 29–47). Hillsdale, NJ: Erlbaum.

Rosch, E., Mervis, C., Gray, W., Johnson, D., & Boyes-Braem, P. (1976). Basic objects in natural categories. *Cognitive Psychology, 8,* 382–439.

Rubin, D. C. (1982). On the retention function for autobiographical memory. *Journal of Verbal Learning and Verbal Behavior, 21,* 21–38.

Salaman, E. (1970). *A collection of moments: A study of involuntary memories.* London: Longman Group.

Spengemann, W. C. (1980). *The forms of autobiography.* New Haven: Yale University Press.

Stein, N. L. & Goldman, S. (1979). *Children's knowledge about social situations* (Tech. Rep. No. 147). Urbana: University of Illinois, Center for the Study of Reading.

Thompson, C. P. (1982). Memory for unique personal events: The roommate study. *Memory and Cognition, 10,* 324–332.

Tulving, E. (1972). Episodic and semantic memory. In E. Tulving & W. Donaldson (Eds.), *Organization of memory* (pp. 381–403). New York: Academic Press.

Twain, M. (1917/1975). *The autobiography of Mark Twain.* C. Neider (Ed.). New York: Harper & Row.

Waters, R. H., & Leeper, R. (1936). The relation of affective tone to the retention of experiences of daily life. *Journal of Experimental Psychology, 19,* 203–215.

# 7 Strategic memory search processes

*Brian J. Reiser, John B. Black, and Peter Kalamarides*

Remembering experiences from one's own past is a central cognitive process that is a component in the performance of many behaviors. Much of conversation, for example, consists of two parties conveying experiences relevant to their topic of discussion. Comprehension not only relies on generalizations that have been learned about the world but often entails accessing individual experiences in order to make sense of a story or a real-world event (Schank, 1982). Furthermore, planning actions in order to solve problems often requires accessing past experiences along with general knowledge (Carbonell, 1982; Kolodner, 1983a; Ross, 1984).

Consider, however, the difficulty of retrieving particular individual experiences from memory. This type of retrieval typically involves searching through an enormous data base of stored experiences using an ill-specified description of the experience (or type of experience) targeted for retrieval. To date, most studies of memory have largely addressed the architecture of the memory system. Most memory models, for example, have focused on structural factors affecting the retrieval and accessibility of items in memory, such as the frequency of a target item, the discriminability of targets, the recency of encoding the item, and the strength of associations connecting items. Yet, as memory researchers now turn to studies of more natural and complex retrieval phenomena such as memory for real-world events, characterizations of the architecture of the memory system are unlikely to be sufficient (Neisser, 1978; Reiser, in press).

We have argued that autobiographical retrieval is a *directed search* process, where retrieval strategies are employed to direct and narrow the scope of the search, thereby considering only experiences likely to be relevant (Reiser, 1983, in press). Thus, a model of autobiographical memory retrieval requires

This research was supported by grants from the IBM Corporation and the System Development Foundation. Portions of these analyses were included in a dissertation submitted to Yale University by the first author.

addressing how experiences are organized in memory and characterizing the types of reasoning mechanisms employed to constrain the search. Baddeley and Wilson (Chap. 13) report case studies of brain-damaged patients that provide dramatic examples of what happens when this search process runs wild to yield confabulation and detailed experiences that are only peripherally related to the topic. The success of such a search depends on strategic mechanisms to use information selectively to direct search to paths in memory likely to lead to an item with the target features (Kolodner, 1983*b*, 1984; Reiser, 1983, in press). First, there are usually too many paths in memory associated with the cued concept for an undirected or automatic search to be successful. Even when there are several cued concepts, the intersection of those concepts may not yield a sufficiently narrowed search set. Furthermore, those concepts may not correspond to the features used to describe and discriminate the target experiences in memory. For these reasons, retrieval strategies are employed to elaborate the original query into a more complete description of the target event. To find an event in memory, it is necessary to construct a plausible scenario for that event's occurrence, thus using essentially the same mechanisms necessary to understand the original event. Retrieval is therefore a process of *reunderstanding* the experience (even to the extent of distorting the memory for the experience as discussed in Linton, Chap. 4; Barclay, Chap. 6; and Fitzgerald, Chap. 8). In order to find a particular event in memory, for example, one might pose the questions:

> Why would I have been doing that?
> What might I have been doing when that occurred?
> Who might have been with me when that occurred?
> What would have led to such an event?
> What would have happened following such an event?

Thus, when a college student subject is asked to recall a particular conversation with another student, he or she might consider the most likely type of context for that event, such as a college bar or restaurant. Alternatively, the subject might consider circumstances likely to have led to the conversation and try to find the setting for the event by considering events that may have preceded it.

These types of questions correspond to the types of reasoning we have found in autobiographical memory search, such as strategies based on goals, activity settings, enabling conditions, and consequences of event. In this chapter we will examine the retrieval strategies used to direct search for autobiographical experiences. In the following section we present our model of the organization and retrieval mechanisms in autobiographical memory.

**The context-plus-index model**

In the context-plus-index model, experiences are retrieved from memory by first retrieving the general context in which the event was encoded and then specifying the particular features that uniquely identify and discriminate that event from others in that context (Reiser, 1983; Reiser, Black, & Abelson, 1985). This model of retrieval builds on work by Kolodner (1983b, 1984) and Schank (1982) delineating how individual experiences are connected in memory to knowledge structures. The encoding contexts for experiences consist of the knowledge structures used to drive understanding and planning in the event. For example, experiences at rock concerts would be stored in memory with the Going to Rock Concerts knowledge structure, because the general knowledge represented in that structure was employed when the experience occurred in order to understand the actions of others and to figure out what actions were appropriate in that social situation. Individual concerts that one attended would be associated with that structure in memory, connected by indexes that described how each concert differed from the standard or proto-typical concert stored in the knowledge structure. Thus, "the first time I saw Bruce Springsteen," "the time I saw Simon and Garfunkel in Central Park," and "the Talking Heads concert before my thesis defense" would index or pick out individual experiences stored with the Going to Rock Concerts context.

The context-plus-index model proposes a very rich indexing and organizational scheme for experiences in autobiographical memory. Indeed, examination of autobiographical retrieval exhibits a set of reasoning mechanisms employed to direct search that rely on a rich representation of general world knowledge. It is important, however, to point out that these complex structures are not proposed solely to account for autobiographical memory phenomena. Instead, the organization we are proposing for autobiographical memory is motivated also by considerations of the use of these same knowledge structures for planning and performing actions, comprehension of texts and real-world events, and memory retrieval of general and specific information learned from texts and from real-world experience. For example, the same knowledge structure one uses to figure out what actions to perform in restaurants is used to understand the behavior of others in restaurants and to understand discourse about restaurants. As a consequence of accessing the knowledge structure Eating at Restaurants while actually visiting restaurants, representations of particular restaurant experiences become associated with that knowledge structure in memory. (Studies of these knowledge structures in various memory, comprehension, and reasoning tasks are reported in Galambos, Abelson, & Black, in press.)

In order to retrieve an experience from memory, the first step therefore entails accessing a context likely to have encoded such an experience. In some cases, this context may be stated in a query (e.g., "Remember that concert where . . ."), and in other cases, the context may be accessed based on information related to concepts in the query (e.g., "Have you seen George today?"). Thus, a first use of strategies is to select an appropriate context for search. To return to our college student example, when asked to remember a conversation the subject may begin the search by generating "going out to lunch" or "going out drinking" as possible contexts in which such a conversation might have occurred.

A second use of retrieval strategies occurs when searching within the chosen context. As we have said, in order to retrieve an experience, it is necessary to specify a set of features that discriminate the experience from others in the context. Frequently, the search cue does not contain enough information to make these discriminations, and thus retrieval strategies must be employed to infer plausible features of the target experience. These retrieval mechanisms rely primarily on general information represented in the knowledge structure in order to make these inferences. Thus, the original cue is elaborated to develop a more complete description of the type of experience likely to contain the target features. Partial information that is retrieved at each stage of the search can be used to direct further probes of memory until enough elaborations have been made to discriminate an experience from the others in that context (Kolodner, 1983*b,* 1984; Norman & Bobrow, 1979; Reiser, 1983; Williams & Hollan, 1981). To return again to our college student example, after the subject has narrowed the likely context to conversations in restaurants, he must continue to predict more features in order to find the target conversation. Knowledge about students combined with generalizations contained in the Eating in Restaurants structure (e.g., the preconditions for eating in different classes of restaurants) could be used to direct the search toward Eating in College Hangouts rather than Eating in Fancy New York Restaurants, because the latter is unlikely to be the context for the target lunch experience.

It is important to point out that not all information associated with a knowledge structure context is equally useful for retrieval. In order to effectively predict circumstances that would include an event with the target features, strategies must utilize social knowledge about the causes, motivations, and results of behavior. Directed retrieval is the selective use of associated information in order to determine which paths to follow in memory. In this chapter, we present a study of the strategies used by subjects to retrieve individual experiences from memory. In order to explain why subjects utilize these strategies, it is necessary to relate them to the organization of the memory system.

A retrieval strategy is effective because it uses available information to provide features that are effective retrieval cues. Thus, characterizing the ways
experiences are organized and represented in memory should provide explanations of why these strategies are effective and how they operate.

To investigate the types of strategies used in autobiographical memory, we
examined the verbal protocols of six Yale students who were asked to "think
aloud" as they tried to recall autobiographical experiences matching certain
combinations of cues. The subjects were instructed to mention whatever came
to mind, even if it did not match the presented criteria. There were several
motivations for the choice of cues in this study. First, we were interested in
providing cues that would elicit a wide variety of retrieval strategies. However, we wanted to select cues that most of the subjects would be able to
answer, so we did not select descriptions that were too unusual. Instead, we
developed variations of cues based on several everyday events and common
mental states. The first cue type, activities, referred to stereotypical action
sequences such as visiting a dentist or dining at a restaurant. We chose activities because our previous experiments have suggested that these structures
are central organizing contexts in autobiographical memory (Reiser, Black,
& Abelson, 1985). Furthermore, work on scripts (Bower, Black, & Turner,
1979; Schank & Abelson, 1977) and Memory Organization Packets (particular proposals about how activities are represented in memory; Schank, 1982)
suggests the importance of these structures in comprehension and planning.
Thus, we expect knowledge about these types of events to be useful in constructing features of a target experience. That activities are effective cues for
autobiographical memories is also emphasized by Linton (Chap. 4), Barclay
(Chap. 6), Fitzgerald (Chap. 8), and Robinson (Chap. 10).

The second major cue type included common mental states such as feeling
happy or feeling disappointed. Because such feelings occur in such a wide
variety of circumstances, we expected queries involving these cues to be more
difficult to answer, and thus subjects would be more likely to exhibit explicit
use of retrieval strategies to direct memory search.

We included three additional types of cues to examine the effects of placing
additional constraints on experiences involving activities. An activity-plus-
state cue combined an activity and a mental state (e.g., felt hungry on a train
ride). An activity variant cue referred to a particular subclass of an activity,
such as visiting a public library or going to a birthday party. Finally, activity-
plus-failure cues referred to the failure of a goal in the activity and thus represented somewhat more unusual occurrences. We have found that infrequent
occurrences are more difficult to recall (Reiser, 1983; Reiser & Black, 1983),
and thus such trials are more likely to exhibit retrieval strategies. The full list
of cues is displayed in Table 7.1. Each subject was asked all 20 questions in
a different random order.

Table 7.1. *Stimuli used in protocol study*

| Activity | Mental state |
|---|---|
| Had hair cut | Felt impatient |
| Went to museum | Felt ambitious |
| Went to dentist | Felt happy |
| Went to concert | Felt disappointed |

| Activity variant | Activity + state |
|---|---|
| Went to frightening movie | Felt cold at exam |
| Visited friend in hospital | Felt hungry on train |
| Went to public library | Felt annoyed at laundromat |
| Went to birthday party | Felt relieved at doctor's office |

Activity + goal failure

Didn't have proper identification at bank
Couldn't pay for item while shopping
Didn't get what was ordered in restaurant
Had bad weather during vacation

## Retrieval strategies

In this section we shall review the types of retrieval strategies found in the subjects' verbal protocols. In some cases, these strategies were explicitly mentioned by subjects. More frequently, the protocols exhibited indirect evidence for the use of retrieval strategies in the type of intermediate products mentioned prior to access of an experience or in the characteristics of the remembered experiences. First, subjects often elaborated the original query, describing these new retrieval contexts before they were effective in accessing particular experiences. Second, the redefinition of the query was observable in "false starts," cases where the subject articulated a new category for search but then discovered that the category did not contain a suitable experience. "Near misses" represent a third type of evidence for reformulations of the query. In these cases, the subject remembered an experience that was similar in some respects to the target experience but did not match the presented description. The ways in which the near miss is similar to the target event suggest the type of inferences made during retrieval to modify the query. It is interesting to note that the protocols for the cases in which subjects *fail* to retrieve a matching experience are often the most illuminating of the search processes. When subjects successfully retrieve an experience, they are often able to do so quickly enough that they do not recount the intermediate steps in the inference and retrieval process. Finally, in some cases subjects retrieved

Table 7.2. *Retrieval success and use of strategies (n* = 120 trials)

|  | Successful retrievals | Near misses | Retrieval failures | Trials with strategies |
|---|---|---|---|---|
| Activity | 24 | 0 | 0 | 10 |
| Mental state | 23 | 1 | 0 | 12 |
| Activity variant | 20 | 3 | 1 | 9 |
| Activity + state | 16 | 5 | 3 | 14 |
| Activity + goal failure | 17 | 4 | 3 | 14 |
| Total | 100 | 13 | 7 | 59 |

several experiences that varied along some dimension. For example, in one case a subject retrieved three different experiences matching the cue, each involving a different person. Such cases suggest the general strategy of generating possible values for a particular dimension to direct search to a subclass of the original category. In all these cases, the new contexts suggest the type of reasoning mechanisms used to predict features of the target experience and thus constrain search.

Subjects successfully retrieved experiences on 83% of the trials, retrieved near misses on 11% of the trials, and failed to recall an experience on the remaining 6% of the trials. A total of 48% of the protocols exhibited the use of one or more retrieval strategies. Strategies were found on 40% of the successful retrievals, 71% of the failed retrievals, and 100% of the near misses. As shown in Table 7.2, there was some tendency for more difficult trials to be more likely to exhibit strategies. The two most difficult cue types, activity-plus-state cues and activity-plus-goal-failure cues also exhibited more strategies than the other cue types.

The strategies used to retrieve experiences fall into two classes. First, strategies were employed in order to select a context for search. This involved reformulating or extending the original question to predict plausible scenarios in which an experience of the stated type is likely to occur, in this way generating a candidate memory category to investigate. The second type of strategy involved searching within the chosen category. These retrieval mechanisms inferred additional features to add to the main category in order to further constrain the type of experience sought. We shall address each of these strategy types in turn. The strategies are summarized in Table 7.3.

*Finding a context*

In the majority of cases involving activity queries, the apparent category used for search was the activity stated in the question. For example, of the 12 near

Table 7.3. *Strategies exhibited in protocols*

I.  Finding a context
    A.  Activity-based Search: Search activity mentioned in query
    B.  Find Related Activity
        1.  Employ causal reasoning to predict activity leading to given state
        2.  Use situational definition of concept
II. Searching within a context

*Activity subclass strategies*
    A.  Activity Subclass Selection: Focus search on a subclass of the activity
        1.  Find a specific variant of the activity, such as college eateries
        2.  Find specific instance, such as a particular restaurant, library, or store
    B.  Activity Subclass Enumeration: Use a strategy to enumerate classes of the activity
        so that one can be selected for search

*Accessing external knowledge*
    C.  Participant Selection
    D.  Map Search
    E.  Select Time Era: Find a portion of your life likely to be the setting for the target
        event

*Causal chain reasoning strategies*
    E.  Infer Motivating Goal: Infer reason for performing target event
    F.  Infer Event Cause: Infer event or state that would lead to target event
    G.  Infer Event Results: Infer result of target event

misses on questions involving activities, 10 matched the activity, and only 2 matched the other cue. These cases were activity-plus-state trials where the subject retrieved an experience that matched the state and a related activity (e.g., "feeling cold during a class" vs. "feeling cold during an exam"). There were no cases where a near miss matched the additional constraint (subclass, mental state, or goal failure) without matching the activity. Thus, activities appear to be the principal search contexts used by these search mechanisms, consistent with our previous results (Reiser et al., 1985). We call a focus on the presented activity Activity-based Search and strategies employed to select an event type not contained in the cue Find Related Activity strategies. In Activity-based Search, experiences involving an activity are generated and tested for the additional constraint. Protocol 1 illustrates the selection of the activity "exams" over the state cue "feeling cold" as a category for search. (The strategy for generating experiences with the activity is not explicit in this protocol. In the next section we shall discuss some of the strategies for finding experiences associated with an activity.)

[1] E: Think of a time when you felt cold at an exam.

S: Felt cold at an exam? Um hum, that's a tough one. Uh, I'm trying to remember the exams that I was in. I can't remember ever being cold. I remember, um, I can picture all the times that I sat in exams in lecture halls and things like that, but I can't remember ever being cold. Or it wasn't a conscious thing or it didn't stick in my mind or something. I don't remember.

Activity-based Search can also be seen when a constraint is placed on the activity. Processing typically focuses on finding experiences within the activity that match that constraint, rather than on finding events that match the constraint and then checking them to see if they match the activity. For example, subjects asked to remember an experience where they had bad weather on vacation often remembered incidents on vacation where the weather was good but did not report bad-weather events that did not occur on vacation.

The next protocol exhibits a Find Related Activity strategy to find an activity related to the state in the question.

[2] E: Think of a time when you felt ambitious.

S: What I'm thinking is this could be tough – ambitious is just not my style. I'm sure there must be something.

E: What's going through your mind?

S: I'm trying to think along school lines, because that is where I would be ambitious, like work or something, doing school work. I'm trying to think of exactly what I have done . . . ambitious. Um, I think probably since I can't find anything for school I'd say getting signatures. When I first went to school in the tenth grade I wanted to be class president, so I went and the first day of school . . . I chased people around and got signatures and got in a half a day one hundred and fifty signatures from people I didn't know, and that was relatively ambitious for me.

Here the subject redefined the query by bringing in another knowledge structure on which to focus the search. Specifically, the subject used her knowledge about ambition to consider a variety of circumstances in which she was likely to have experienced that mental state. This process led to thinking about school situations, first focusing on school work and then other school activities, namely, elections. Reasoning about the causes or results of a particular state is a frequent type of Find Related Activity strategy.

In some cases, there is no evidence for "deliberate" reasoning about causes of the mental state. Instead, an activity appears to be available upon accessing the state. For example, one subject queried about feeling impatient replied, "Oh, I'm just impatient in lines," and then continued the search to pin down one particular experience waiting in line for tickets to a concert. Another subject responded to the question about feeling ambitious by saying, "I guess every time I sit down to study for an exam I feel ambitious to get a good grade." When prompted for a particular experience, the subject reported the first exam experience that came to mind. In these cases, the mental states appear to have a *situational definition* for the subject. That is, accessing the mental state brings along with it one or more types of situations in which that state is typically experienced. The description in general terms prior to retrieval of individual experiences is evidence in these protocols for the strategic reformulation of a question about mental states (e.g., ambition) into a question about a type of event (studying for exams). Although mental-state trials were only somewhat more likely than activity trials to exhibit strategies, it is interesting to note that every mental-state trial on which a strategy was observed (50% of the mental-state trials) involved a Find Related Activity strategy. These strategies are similar to the Component to Context Instantiation Strategies in Kolodner's model (Kolodner, 1983*b*, 1984), in which a component of the query (e.g., the time or a participant involved in an event) is used to access a related context to guide search.

## Searching within a context

Another usage of strategies occurs after a context has been selected. It is necessary to select enough features to discriminate an experience from the others stored in that context. This typically requires adding information to the retrieval description, because memory queries usually contain an incomplete specification of the target event.

We observed three basic types of strategies for searching within a chosen context. The first group of strategies involved selecting subclasses or variants of the activity in order to further focus the search. The second group involved focusing on some component of the event such as a participant or the time period of the person's life and accessing knowledge from another knowledge structure in order to direct search within the activity. Finally, the third type of strategy involved reasoning about the prerequisites or results of the target event.

*Selecting and enumerating subclasses of contexts.* The first type of directed search within a context involves considering subclasses of that context to predict which would be likely to be the setting for an experience with the target features. In the next protocol, the subject used knowledge about the named activity to construct a more specific search context within the activity.

[3] E: Think of a time when you went shopping and couldn't pay for the item that you wanted.

S: Um, it happens when I go grocery shopping in Connecticut because I don't have any check-cashing-privilege cards. Like, for example, Pathmark will have a special card that they issue. And so I have to pay with cash and I don't always calculate exactly what's in the carriage. So I'll have to put back, like, yogurt . . . usually, yogurt's what goes. But otherwise I usually pay by check when I'm in Massachusetts, so I don't have to, you know, worry about putting anything back.

> E: Can you think of one particular experience?
>
> S: Uh, yes. Pathmark in East Haven, I often do that.
>
> E: Can you describe one time?
>
> S: Yes, when I was in East Haven, I was – didn't have enough so I had to put back, I think, three yogurts. And the girl was very nice and I thought to myself, "Oh, I should ask for a subtotal next time."

This protocol is a clear example of the type of successive refinement that is often necessary in autobiographical memory search. In this case, the subject considered different types of shopping and apparently decided that shopping experiences in Connecticut were more likely to fit the "couldn't pay for the item" criterion than shopping experiences in Massachusetts. This decision involves figuring out what variety of the activity is most likely to lead to an experience with the desired characteristics. We call this strategy Activity Subclass Selection. It is interesting to note that in this protocol, as in many others, a great deal of general information is available before individual experiences can be accessed. The presence of this information supports the notion that this general information is used to direct the search process. The subject first described a generalized version of the experience, drawn from the prototype stored in the Grocery Shopping in Connecticut structure, and when prompted narrowed it down first to Grocery Shopping at Pathmark and finally to a particular experience involving yogurt.

The type of reasoning used to select among the possible subclasses of an activity can be seen in Protocol 4.

> [4] E: Think of a time when you went to a restaurant and didn't get what you ordered.
>
> S: That's actually never happened. Um, I guess I don't go out often enough to have that happen to me, particularly, but that's never happened.
>
> E: Well, what came to mind?
>
> S: I was just trying to think of any time when such an incident ever happened and I really can't recall one. Um, I was thinking of sort of . . . the first thing I thought of was what is the most likely type of restaurant, you know, the Yorkside, Naples style or the fancier restaurant style, and I was just thinking have I ever had that happen to me and decided no.

Here the subject first made a decision about the type of restaurant most likely to have been the setting for an experience in which his order was not filled properly. He thus discriminated between two subclasses of the restaurant activity, experiences involving the Yorkside and Naples type of restaurant (college eateries in New Haven) and "fancier" restaurants. The causal knowledge represented in the restaurant activity presumably led to the inference that service was more likely to be sloppy in a college eatery than in a fancy restaurant, and thus that subclass of experiences was more likely to contain one with the target attributes. Although this search was not successful, the false start reveals the type of reasoning employed in order to constrain the search after a context has been accessed.

Subclasses of activities can be organized in several ways. In Protocol 3, the subclass of the activity chosen was based first on locations (Connecticut vs. Massachusetts). In Protocol 4, the subclasses were determined by standard varieties of the activity. A subclass of experiences can also be organized according to those events involving a particular instance or exemplar of the activity. Thus, in Protocol 3, the subject finally restricted the search category to Shopping at Pathmark before retrieving an individual experience. Similarly, another subject considered experiences involving a particular restaurant that is "a really hectic place" in order to retrieve an experience where his order was not filled properly. It is important to note that these subclasses are not mutually exclusive. Activities often contain several overlapping organizations of the same experiences. Thus, an experience can usually be accessed by traveling several different paths through contexts and indexes (Kolodner, 1983*b*, 1984; Reiser, 1983).

Selection of subclasses is not always causally motivated. In some cases, the subject simply appears to select the most normative subclass of the activity. Thus, the query will be refined into a more specific query simply by accessing the most accessible subclass of the activity. For example, a subject asked to remember an experience involving bad weather on vacation began by considering one type of vacation: "We usually go to Maine for the summer, so I'm thinking of times we went to Maine."

In some cases, the subject may find it necessary to enumerate several subcategories of the activity and then search the one most likely to contain the target event. The subject may enumerate the subclasses in order to select among them or may enumerate several classes because search fails in one subclass and must be resumed in another subclass. Thus, the Activity Subclass Enumeration strategy accesses several subclasses of the activity so that one can be selected for further focus of the search. Of course, this strategy may be occurring more often than is explicit in our protocols, because some proportion of the Activity Subclass Selection cases may have been preceded by an enumeration of the subclasses that the subject did not bother to report.

[5] E: Think of a time when you went to a public library.

S: Um . . . let's see. The first thing that comes into mind is when I go to the New Haven Public Library. And I actually like that library a lot. And I also remember, I go to school in Oberlin, and I like the public library at Oberlin much better than the college library, because it has a sort of friendlier atmosphere, and there's kids, not all these studious students around. So I remember that public library very well, it was one of my favorite hangouts.

E: Can you think of one particular time?

S: Um . . . one particular time I remember is when I had to pay the overdue fine in pennies because it was the only money I had. It was twenty-eight pennies, I think it was actually thirty pennies but the person let me pay with twenty-eight pennies.

Here the subject first considered several libraries and then when prompted focused on a particular experience in one of those libraries. Similarly, the subject in Protocol 3 appeared to consider shopping in several locations, and the subject in Protocol 4 considered several types of restaurants before selecting one of those subclasses for further search.

What are the methods for enumerating classes of activities? First, general information in the activity can often be used to enumerate several subclasses. We know, for example, that restaurants serve food and that there are different styles of restaurants depending on the type of food (and associated atmosphere) and, further, that each style has associated with it a somewhat different set of preconditions and goals. Thus, this information can be used to select the type of restaurant likely to be the setting for the target event. Another strategy for enumerating classes of activities is to access knowledge outside the activity and use that to generate subclasses. These strategies constitute the second major group of strategies for searching within a context.

*Accessing external knowledge to direct search.* The second group of search strategies for searching within a context involves focusing on a particular component of an experience and then accessing some other source of knowledge in order to direct search within the activity. For example, one can access information about a particular portion of one's life, as defined by a place of residence, school or job status, or personal relationship. These "time eras" can be a useful refinement of the search context because they enable predictions about the types of activities, locations, and other features of an experience (Kolodner, 1984; Reiser, 1983). An example of this strategy, called Select Time Era, can be seen in the following protocol.

[6] E: Think of a time when you went to a birthday party.

S: First of all, I thought of, like, a big birthday party and I couldn't think of any right off so I thought about, oh well, use your birthday party, then I go, wait a minute, I never have birthday parties, I don't remember them that well. So I went back to high school, we always had surprise parties, and one in particular was a surprise party for Michele, this friend of ours. Donna threw it. It was actually a surprise which was amazing because usually you can't keep them a surprise. I think I remember because party is like . . . I always get really drunk at them sometimes, so this one I did get a little wasted at and everyone, it was so great, because everyone sang happy birthday and it was so out of tune that no one cared. It was wonderful.

In this protocol, the subject decided (after a false start) to consider a particular portion of her life (high school) where parties were frequent. In previous studies, we have found subjects often use time eras to categorize experiences they have remembered (Reiser, 1983). Whitten and Leonard (1981) also found subjects using a Cognitive Landmark Identification strategy, where one would refer to landmark events such as moving out of town or changing schools to help organize autobiographical memory search. Similarly, Loftus and Marburger (1983) found that subjects using landmark events were able to make more accurate temporal judgments about their own past experiences. The Select Time Era strategy differs from the other Searching within a Context strategies presented earlier in that the general information utilized by the inference processes was not found within the particular activity being considered. Instead, other knowledge structures (e.g., time eras) were accessed to direct the search within the activity context.

A time era is one type of *larger context*, a larger episode that connects a number of experiences. Other types of larger contexts might be a summer vacation, working on a political campaign, or a series of job interviews. In previous studies, we have found that such larger contexts are frequently used by subjects to categorize experiences they have remembered and that they tend to be repeated across a number of consecutively recalled experiences, supporting the notion that these are useful retrieval contexts (Reiser, 1983).

Another similar method for enumerating and selecting subclasses of activities is a Map Search (Schank, 1982). This strategy involves searching a mental "map" or organization of information. For example, Kolodner reported that people asked to list museums they had visited often appeared to consult a mental map in order to generate candidate cities, which they then tested to see whether they had been the setting for an appropriate experience. Similarly, subjects often appeared to be searching a mental map or time line of courses they had taken, places they had lived, and so on. For example, a subject asked to recall feeling "cold at an exam" reported considering different classes he had taken during the winter in order to try to find an experience matching the cue.

It is also useful to consider people who may have "participated" in the event. The next protocol demonstrates the Participant Selection strategy in an attempt to find an experience within the activity.

[7] E: Think of a time when you went to a birthday party.

S: Um, birthday surprises. [*Pause*] When was the last birthday? I'm trying to think through friends who had a birthday party last. Um, gee, we all have summer birthdays right now and everybody is away, so it's kind of hard to celebrate. Um, Amy's was in November . . . that was nice, it was a real surprise. My roommate, we gave her a surprise party and she kept expecting it to be . . . she knew she was having a party because all her really close friends . . . they gave each person a surprise party. So everyone always knew they were having a surprise party, they were just never sure when it was.

In this protocol the subject considers various friends in order to see whether one of them had a birthday party. Selecting a likely participant is frequently a useful strategy for restricting the search. For example, a subject asked to think of an experience where he felt happy reported trying to "think of a person you're always happy with" and then recalled an experience involving her best friend. Another subject, asked to think of an experience where she felt disappointed, reported thinking about "people [she] had seen over the past two weeks" before recalling a specific experience.

*Causal chain reasoning.* The third major group of strategies for searching within a context involves causal reasoning. In fact, many of the strategies we have discussed have been successful because they enable the prediction of a likely setting for the experience. The Find Related Activity strategy finds activities that result in or are motivated by particular states. A particular subclass of an activity is often selected because that subclass is likely to result in an experience of the type desired. The strategies in this group use another type of causal reasoning, namely, constructing an explicit chain of motivations and events in order to predict results or prerequisites for the target experience. As illustrated in the next protocol, information about goals can be very effective in guiding the search.

[8] E: Think of a time when you went to a public library. [*Pause*] What's going through your mind?

S: That I always go to the library like a mile away from my home in Colorado, and it's hard to think of one particular time so I'm trying to figure out if I can think of like going for one book. And if I can remember doing like one research project, then I could put it together. Well, okay, I remember going to get a book on running, but I didn't have my card so I was talking to a man about running because I had ran up there and it's two miles back. And he was saying, "Oh, well, if you can do it, man." That's as close as I can get to my public library.

Here the subject narrowed the search context "public library" to a particular library in his hometown but was unable at first to think of a particular experience. This refinement of the search context has utilized information encoded within the Going to the Library activity. In order to discriminate among the experiences within that particular library, he focused on reasons that he would have gone to the library. This part of the search process utilized information outside the Going to the Library structure and accessed knowledge about the classes he has had and his hobbies. The search was directed to these structures by using knowledge about the purposes for which one might want a book. In order to isolate a particular experience, he used knowledge contained in these other structures and considered looking for a particular book or a particular research project. This strategy successfully retrieved an experience where he was looking for a book on running but had trouble checking it out. This protocol illustrates a common use of knowledge external to the activity providing the search context, namely, the Infer Motivating Goal strategy. This strategy entails asking the question, "Why would I have performed that activity?" which may lead to the access of other knowledge structures to direct search within the current activity.

The next protocol exhibits another type of reasoning about causes in order to predict the setting for an event.

[9] E: Think of a time when you felt cold at an exam.

S: I was thinking winter first of all, I mean when or what class did I take an exam for in the winter, because I took a semester off and I took the semester off during, like, December and so I'm trying to think, well, I wouldn't have taken any finals in really cold weather so I'm trying to skip through the classes and, um, last semester like January or something where I had any test and I didn't, and so I have to go back even further, and I can't remember taking a test where I was cold. I can just remember taking notes where I was really cold in a philosophy course. Because it was this past winter. I haven't been that cold until this past winter.

In this example, the subject considered the circumstances that would lead to feeling cold during an exam and was thus led to consider the courses she had taken during winter semesters. This type of search strategy, called Infer Event Cause, focuses on causes rather than motivations for a particular state. In this case, the search employed knowledge from a related activity (courses) and knowledge about the state (cold) to construct the search context. This type of reasoning is similar to the Find Related Activity strategy that is used to find an activity that would lead to the type of state described in the query. In both cases a strategy is employed to consider the causes or prerequisites to find a setting for the target event.

The next two near misses demonstrate reasoning about results of actions, illustrating the Infer Event Results strategy.

[10] E: Think of a time when you felt cold at an exam.

S: I never felt cold in an exam, but I can remember when I was taking the GREs I had a headache and that was really annoying.

E: What else could you think of?

S: That I thought, "Oh my gosh, this is interfering with my test taking," and it made me uptight. I was probably . . . I think it was probably nerves and I just couldn't wait for the section to be over because I think at that point we were going to have a break.

[11] E: Think of a time when you went to a bank and didn't have proper identification.

S: Identification . . . they always ask me for identification but I usually have something. Uh, thinking . . . when you said bank . . . I was sort of thinking, well, last time I went to the bank and it was closed and not being . . . and being annoyed that it had closed rather than not having enough money but still not being . . . able to get money out.

The intermediate steps are not explicit in these cases of near misses, but it appears that the subjects predicted a particular type of problem as a result of the feature specified in the question. Each subject found an experience with such a problem, but one that had a cause different from that described in the question. For example, one feature of the target event that may have been predicted in Protocol 10 is "had trouble taking a test," presumably because the cold was distracting. This specification did not access a memory where the cold was at fault but instead found another experience where physical discomfort created a problem in taking a test. Similarly, in Protocol 11 the subject may have searched for an experience where he was unable to withdraw money and found an experience where the bank was closed instead of one where he did not have proper identification.

These near misses demonstrate the type of causal reasoning utilized by the retrieval processes to predict features of the target experience. In both cases, the subjects appear to have inferred the result of the described problem and then searched memory for an experience with that particular result. The reason for transforming the query in this way is that presumably such a problem is a better index for the experience than the circumstances that led to that difficulty.

## Conclusions

We have reviewed a wide range of strategies used to search memory for an experience with a particular set of target characteristics. These strategies demonstrate the type of reasoning used to direct search in autobiographical memory. The strategies are employed to construct a set of circumstances that would be the setting for the target event, considering people's motivations or prior events that would lead to the event, particular variations of events in which the target event would be likely, and possible consequences of the target event. The first step in setting up a scenario entails finding a context to constrain and guide the search. This context may be explicitly provided in the query, but in some cases strategies are required to find a context to begin the search or to redirect a failed search. As we have seen, activities are usually chosen as contexts. These structures contain much information that can be used to elaborate the original query. This includes information about the goals associated with the activity, the type of participants, a sequence of actions that compose the activity, and related activities that often precede or follow the activity. A large variety of strategies are then invoked to guide search within an activity context. A subclass of the activity may be selected that contains some of the preconditions for the target event. Information from other sources may be called upon to enumerate possible subclasses of the activity so that a likely subclass can be selected. Reasoning about the causes, motivations, and likely consequences of the event may be employed to generate additional features of the target experience.

Most of these retrieval strategies employ causal reasoning to find an experience in memory. There are several reasons for this reliance on causal reasoning. The principal reason is that people's representations of events are causally based. Consider the types of mental structures active during the encoding of an experience. Most experiences concern a reaction to a problem or some type of deliberate behavior that is performed to further a set of goals. Thus, the structures accessed in order to act in a particular event are likely to be those knowledge structures containing planning information required to select actions and activities to achieve the desired results. Furthermore, it is typically necessary to understand the actions of the other people involved in a situation by inferring motivations for those actions, and this comprehension relies on the planning knowledge contained in these same structures. Causal explanations appear to be a central component in comprehending both text (Black, 1984; Reiser & Black, 1982) and real-world events (Nisbett & Ross, 1980).

As a consequence of the central role that causal representations play in comprehension, the components of the memory representation for an experience are constructed using causal knowledge and are connected to these planning structures in memory. Thus, the features of experiences that are most relevant will be those that represent the motivations of the people involved, the actions undertaken to achieve those goals, the outcomes of the goals (whether they were achieved, thwarted, or led to new subgoals), and the consequences of the actions for the states of the participants and effects on their future behavior.

A second consideration is the necessity of the knowledge structures to guide the elaboration of the query. The planning structures that serve as contexts in autobiographical memory are rich in predictive power. These structures contain much information useful for predicting likely settings for the event. Clearly, causal reasoning is an effective strategy for constructing a plausible scenario for an event. Information of low causal salience will be of little use for these mechanisms. These aspects do not provide information that can be used by the inference mechanisms to predict other components of the experience. Such low-level details are likely to be peripherally encoded and thus do not provide effective retrieval cues.

In these protocols, we have seen reasoning about several different types of structures in memory. Strategies employed knowledge about activities, goals, people, and time eras. We now briefly review how each of these types of strategies is designed to capitalize on the types of information represented in knowledge structures in order to direct search for an experience.

*Activity-based strategies.* Activities contain much information about the features of experiences. Considering general information in an activity can enable selection of a subclass of experiences likely to be the setting for the target event. Activities also provide access to a rich set of information about motivations for the event, type of actions undertaken to achieve the goals, and participants involved in the event. Each of these types of information may be used to further narrow the focus of the search.

*Goal-based strategies.* Goals are rich sources of information. Considering the goals that could be involved in a target event can aid retrieval in several ways. First, if the activity for the target event is not known (e.g., trying to remember where a particular conversation with someone took place), considering the goals that may be involved with that person or situation can lead to an activity, thus narrowing the search context. Second, if an activity has already been found, considering different ways to fulfill the goals involved can lead to a more specific version of the activity (e.g., "going out for pizza," "going out for Chinese food"). Third, considering a motivating goal for the event may access a connection to a contextualizing episode. Finally, finding a specific goal that may have been involved in the experience enables predictions about many different actions that might have been performed relevant to that goal.

*People-based strategies.* Considering possible participants of an event is another rich source of information. These rules can access goals ("What might I have been trying to accomplish with that person?"), locations ("an old friend from New York"), and subclasses of activities ("going out to eat on Fridays with high school girlfriend"). In general, representations of particular participants may contain much knowledge about the type of activities one may have performed with that person. In addition, these representations may contain several salient landmark events involving that person that may be used to guide search to different *time eras* in one's life to find a target event.

*Time strategies.* Considering the time era in which the event may have occurred can reveal locations and likely participants for an experience. Specifying the time era can also enable inferences about the types of goals and activities for that period of the person's life. For example, if one is trying to answer the question, "When was the last time I saw my old friend Seth?" and the time era for that experience has been inferred (e.g., college in Philadelphia), then that information can be used to generate activities and goals for test: "We used to go drinking in Center City," "We often went to rock concerts together," and so on. Robinson (Chap. 10) also found that time era was an effective organizer of autobiographical memories. Interestingly, Linton (Chap. 4) found that in examining herself she used a time-based strategy for retrieving experiences from the last couple of years but had to switch to an activity-based strategy for older experiences.

In closing, it is important to consider the generality of these reasoning mechanisms. These strategies are used to predict the characteristics of a target event, given certain cues, and thus are useful for searching memory for an experience. As we have argued, however, remembering an experience involves reunderstanding that experience. Thus, memory retrieval mechanisms are also comprehension mechanisms. That is, the same strategies are also used to access relevant features from memory in order to understand an event currently being considered. Similarly, these mechanisms can also be used to answer questions by searching memory for relevant knowledge structures or individual experiences. Thus, these strategies are general mechanisms for reasoning about experiences and the generalizations one has drawn from experience.

We need, however, to add the caveat that we have studied only Yale University students, and this might limit the generality of our findings. For example, Rubin, Wetzler, and Nebes (Chap. 12) discuss how the number of experiences recalled from various amounts of time before the recall is quite different depending on the age of the rememberer – for example, there is a reminiscence effect where memories once poorly remembered are remembered better when one gets older. In our terms, these findings suggest that the memory search strategies employed might vary depending on the age of the rememberer. Thus, studying how memory search strategies vary across the lifespan is an important topic for future research. It is also tempting to speculate that the partial amnesia for childhood experiences (i.e., having a hard time remembering what happened to you before you were 5 or so), discussed by Wetzler and Sweeney (Chap. 11) and Rubin, Wetzler, and Nebes (Chap. 12), occurs because the memory search strategies that our college students employ may not be effective for searching the memory representations constructed by children under the age of 5.

## References

Black, J. B. (1984). Understanding and remembering stories. In J. R. Anderson & S. M. Kosslyn (Eds.), *Tutorials in learning and memory* (pp. 235–255). San Fransisco: Freeman.

Bower, G. H., Black, J. B. & Turner, T. J. (1979). Scripts in memory for text. *Cognitive Psychology, 11,* 177–220.

Carbonell, J. G. (1982). Learning by analogy: Skill acquisition in reactive environments. In R. S. Michalski, J. G. Carbonell, & T. M. Mitchell (Eds.), *Machine learning* (pp. 137–161). Palo Alto, CA: Tioga.

Galambos, J. A., Abelson, R. P, & Black, J. B. (Eds.). (in press). *Knowledge structures.* Hillsdale, NJ: Erlbaum.

Kolodner, J. L. (1983a). Towards an understanding of the role of experience in the evolution from novice to expert. *International Journal of Man-Machine Studies, 19,* 497–518.

(1983b). Reconstructive memory: A computer model. *Cognitive Science, 7,* 281–328.

(1984). *Retrieval and organizational strategies in conceptual memory: A computer model.* Hillsdale, NJ: Erlbaum.

Loftus, E. F., & Marburger, W. (1983). Since the eruption of Mt. St. Helens, has anyone beaten you up? Improving the accuracy of retrospective reports with landmark events. *Memory and Cognition, 11,* 114–120.

Neisser, U. (1978). Memory: What are the important questions? In M. M. Gruneberg, P. E. Morris, & R. N. Sykes (Eds.), *Practical aspects of memory* (pp. 3–24). London: Academic Press.

Nisbett, R., & Ross, L. (1980). *Human inference: Strategies and shortcomings of social judgment.* Englewood Cliffs, NJ: Prentice-Hall.

Norman, D. A., & Bobrow, D. G. (1979). Descriptions: An intermediate stage in memory retrieval. *Cognitive Psychology, 11,* 107–123.

Reiser, B. J. (1983). *Contexts and indices in autobiographical memory.* Doctoral dissertation (Tech. Rep. No. 24). New Haven: Cognitive Science Program, Yale University.

(in press). Knowledge-directed retrieval of autobiographical memories. In J. L. Kolodner & C. K. Riesbeck (Eds.), *Experience and reasoning.* Hillsdale, NJ: Erlbaum.

Reiser, B. J., & Black, J. B. (1982). Processing and structural models of comprehension. *Text, 2,* 225–252.

(1983). The roles of interference and inference in the retrieval of autobiographical memories. *Proceedings of the Fifth Annual Conference of the Cognitive Science Society,* Rochester, NY.

Reiser, B. J., Black, J. B., & Abelson, R. P. (1985). Knowledge structures in the organization and retrieval of autobiographical memories. *Cognitive Psychology.*

Ross, B. H. (1984). Remindings and their effects in learning a cognitive skill. *Cognitive Psychology, 16,* 371–416.

Schank, R. C. (1982). *Dynamic memory: A theory of reminding and learning in computers and people.* Cambridge: Cambridge University Press.

Schank, R. C., & Abelson, R. P. (1977). *Scripts, plans, goals and understanding.* Hillsdale, NJ: Erlbaum.

Whitten, W. B., & Leonard, J. M. (1981). Directed search through autobiographical memory. *Memory and Cognition, 9,* 566–579.

Williams, M. D., & Hollan, J. D. (1981). The process of retrieval from very-long-term memory. *Cognitive Science, 5,* 87–119.

# 8    Autobiographical memory: a developmental perspective

*Joseph M. Fitzgerald*

*A*. I was downtown yesterday. I'm never going again unless I park in a lot. I got a twenty-dollar ticket for parking on the street.

*B*. Yes, those signs are confusing with all the hours and things.

*A*. Yes, I think this spot was safe to park fifteen minutes each day.

*B*. A nice thing happened to me yesterday; a friend called and offered me a free ticket to the opera next week.

*A*. That's great.

This little vignette illustrates the type of memory termed *autobiographical memory*. Having developed an interest in autobiographical memory, I am repeatedly struck by the frequency of spontaneous reports of such memories. Although they are more likely to crop up in such situations as after-dinner conversations than in others, such as the classroom, the recall of specific events from the past is a regular, frequently effortless aspect of daily life. These reports, whether fact or confabulation, provide a rich context for the ongoing flow of human experience. This experience then becomes part of the contents of memory. As the chapters in this volume attest, autobiographical memory promises to become a frequent subject of study in psychology, although such study will not be effortless.

In this chapter, autobiographical memory refers to memories of specific events occurring in an individual's daily experience that are stored without the benefit of conscious memory goal activities on the part of the individual. It is this lack of conscious control that leads us to use the term *involuntary* in characterizing most autobiographical memories. This type of memory stands in contrast to the frequently studied episodic memories for material presented to the individual with the stated purpose of the individual's learning or remembering it (Tulving, 1983). It is also distinct from the study of memory for incidental material, which is presented along with material the individual is asked to study for future recall. As our understanding of autobiographical memory evolves, however, linkages to research on deliberate and incidental memory may become clearer.

122

The remainder of this chapter is organized into three sections. In the first, a review of developmental data is presented that emphasizes what we have learned about conditions influencing the speed with which autobiographical memories are retrieved. In the second section, an argument is presented for accepting a developmental model of autobiographical memory that emphasizes a transactional perspective. The chapter concludes with a discussion of the research questions raised by both the existing literature and the developmental model. In essence, this chapter tries to show that a developmental perspective has already led to the collection of some interesting data, that it provides a theoretically interesting challenge to memory researchers, and that it can lead to a number of interesting research programs.

## Developmental data

Two other chapters in this volume deal with important developmental issues. Rubin, Wetzler, and Nebes (Chap. 12) present a comprehensive review and reanalysis of the correlation between chronological age and the age of memories, effectively arguing for the presence of a reminiscence component in the autobiographical memories of middle-aged and older adults. Wetzler and Sweeney (Chap. 11) present their recent work on childhood amnesia. This brief review will, therefore, concentrate on the response-time variable. In the autobiographical memory task described by Rubin, Wetzler, and Nebes, response time is recorded from the time a prompt is presented until the subject signals that he or she has retrieved a memory to be reported.

Robinson (1976) drew attention to the fact that not all prompts are alike when response time is involved. His study clearly showed that individuals generally respond more slowly to prompts describing *affective* states such as happy and sad than they do to nouns describing objects or verbs describing actions. Robinson suggested that some form of information-processing difference accounted for such differences in response time.

Fitzgerald (1980, 1981) found that adolescents were largely unaffected by prompt type. In fact, junior high school students responded with equal rapidity to affect and object prompts. These adolescents typically report a memory within 5 seconds, regardless of prompt type, whereas college students average about 10 seconds for affect prompts and 6 seconds for nouns.

Fitzgerald and Lawrence (1984) further replicated the difference between junior high and college students. In addition, the predictive values of individual differences variables and characteristics of the prompts were analyzed. The primary finding of this analysis was that differences between prompts were more predictive of response time than were differences between individuals. Specifically, individuals respond more quickly to prompts that are relatively high in rated imagery and meaningfulness (have a high number of associates). This pattern was consistent for age groups ranging from adolescence to late adulthood and for both affect and object prompts. In contrast, individual differences in the ability to form images and verbal fluency were not consistently correlated with response time.

In summary, what we have learned to date from the study of single-word prompts is that words that are low in meaningfulness and imagery are responded to more slowly by individuals of all ages tested and that adults respond to affect prompts more slowly than they do to object prompts. In addressing the slower responses to affect prompts, Rieser, Black, and Abelson (1985) suggest that "experiences are more typically associated with some type of event category than with more abstract categories such as affects." This is a reasonable explanation, similar in general tone to Robinson's original explanation. However, this type of explanation needs to be reconciled with the available developmental data.

Junior high school students typically respond (*a*) as quickly as college students to activity cues, (*b*) faster than college students to affect prompts, and (*c*) with equal speed to both affect and activity cues. Applying Rieser, Black, and Abelson's explanation, one would suggest that events are typically associated with both activities and affective categories in junior high but that somehow, over the adolescent years, affect drops out as an organizing framework. From our meager understanding of adolescent emotional development, this seems improbable.

Another possible explanation is found in the lack of event-age difference between prompt types. The memories are all so recent, and are produced so quickly, that some linkage must be present. This assumption is based on the curvilinear relationship found between response time and event age *in college students* by Robinson (1976) and Rieser, Black, and Abelson (1985). Very recent memories and very old memories are reported more rapidly than the midrange of the event age distribution.

Adolescents report so few memories that correspond to the midrange for college students (6–12 months) that we cannot examine the event-age to response-time correlation. But, given that recent memories tend to be reported rapidly, we can ask why this is so. An imagery-driven explanation might suggest that the image associated with a particular word or phrase is more likely to incorporate features of recent experiences. When memories are tested for their match to the image, more recent memories are more likely to match the current image. Thus, my image for "went to the movies" might include the sensation of air conditioning in the summer but not in the winter. When I form my image of going to the movies in September, it is less likely to match a winter memory because the sensation of walking into a warm building is not part of my current image.

To return to the adolescents' equal recency for affect, action, and object prompts, an imagery hypothesis would suggest that the images of affect for adolescents have a recency bias built into them. What would be the origin of this bias? Do they change their images of *angry, sad,* and *happy* more often than older adolescents and adults? This does seem like a plausible hypothesis for a time of emotional growth. With the attainment of identity and a stable sense of self, what it means to be happy, sad, or angry takes on a more stable definition and allows older memories to "pass the test" of fitting specific retrieval cues. When this stability of definition is compared to the 12-year-old's more fleeting definitions of happiness, anger, and other emotions, the pattern of response-time results makes a great deal of sense.

Clearly, this type of explanation needs much empirical research before it can be accepted. Even more pressing, however, is the need for a theoretical perspective on the development of autobiographical memory processes. Such a perspective must be capable of guiding more than the actuarial aspects of autobiographical memory research, such as the shape of retention functions and predictors of response time. In addition, a developmental model must provide a way for framing questions about the processes of encoding and retrieving the memories. In the following section, a developmental perspective is outlined, which emphasizes the transaction between memories and the development of the individual and his or her cultural context.

## A developmental perspective

Several issues must be addressed by any theory of autobiographical memory. The first of these is the manner in which such memories are represented. Although developmental theories such as Piaget's hypothesize the sequential appearance of different forms of mental representation (Bruner, 1964; Bronckhart & Ventouras-Spycher, 1979; Piaget, 1926), in general artificial intelligence models operate on the premise that human knowledge is represented in the same symbolic fashion at all ages. Thus, Schank and Abelson (1977) describes a system in which knowledge is represented as a series of "conceptualizations" that can be sequentially organized into scripts. They claim that a child as young as 4 months may have "personal scripts" (p. 225).

In contrast, Piaget (1926) theorized that representation undergoes a series of transformations early in life. The earliest forms of thinking are called *fig-urative*. At this level, knowledge is represented as assimilated in perceptual cues. Research on recognition memory in very young infants suggests that they have significant powers of memory (Fagan, 1982; Rovee-Collier, 1980). However, methodologies to test for long-term memories for events with groups this young have not yet been developed.

Toward the end of the first year of life, an ability termed the *symbolic function* emerges. This is the second stage in Piaget's theory of knowledge representation. The symbolic function allows children to form and utilize *signifiers* that are more autonomous from the signified object or event than are perceptual cues. The earliest form of this style of representation is seen in imitation. In one of Piaget's examples, his daughter represents the opening and closing of a matchbox by opening and closing her mouth. This form of representation marks the advent of schematic thinking. Schemata at this early stage are very subjective and idiosyncratic. An observer would have no way of knowing the meaning of the young girl's opening and closing of the mouth unless he had observed the entire interaction. The role of schematic thinking in memory is evident in the capacity for deferred imitation that emerges during the second year. In this type of imitation, children imitate single, isolated acts performed by adults or themselves hours or even days after they are first witnessed.

The highest form of knowledge representation in Piaget's (1926) formulation is termed *semiotic*. This level is marked by the emergence of language, which provides a set of conventional signifiers for a vast array of objects and events. As language skills emerge, the child acquires the ability to report events that occurred in the past, autobiographical memories, but the point at which this ability emerges is not clearly known.

This brief review of Piaget's system makes the point that infants are capable of memory using representational systems other than those associated with the symbolic function and that the symbolic function operates at both prelinguistic and linguistic levels. A similar point could be made by contrasting the iconic, enactive, and symbolic modes of Bruner's system (1964). The implication is that, because memory for stimuli and memory for and imitation of specific events precede the development of symbolic processes, the autobiographical memory system may possess the capacity to operate independently of these processes. Thus, just as individuals learn lists of words without the benefit of mnemonics such as imagery, organization, or rehearsal, they can also code memories for daily experience without benefit of symbolic schemata. What is needed in this area, however, is a methodology that can determine if and/or when episodic memories are formed. Such a method would need to circumvent the traditional reliance on verbal reports of events.

In fact, there may be good reason to lower our reliance on traditional methodologies in considering the nature of autobiographical memory. Psychologists may be too willing to think about memory for events, such as going to a baseball game, in the same fashion as they think about a college sophomore's reading and then recalling a textual description of a baseball game. The Soviet psychologist Zinchenko (1939/1983) noted that memory is always the product of meaningful activity. If an individual is not engaged with the "object," the object will not be remembered. As activities become more highly scripted by the nature of routine and ceremony, knowledge of scripts and ceremonies may aid in the retrieval of autobiographical memories. Bower, Black, and Turner (1979) demonstrated that individuals will falsely claim to recognize actions that are part of a script but were not actually presented in stories that they read. Although these scripts are based on daily activities, is it appropriate to infer that the results of text memory research generalize to the representation and retrieval of all day-to-day memories? Thus, the question is whether reading and studying a story about a trip to the dentist lead to the same memory activities as going to the dentist.

Two sources of differences can be noted. First, there is a contrast between employing deliberate strategies to remember something and the involuntary nature of autobiographical memory. Second, placing a story into text form decontextualizes the experience to a considerable degree. In particular, it removes all physical, sensual cues, as well as many affective cues. Zinchenko (1939/1983) makes the point that human memory is a sensuous human activity. He was quite concerned that models of "logical human memory" were too idealistic. He recognized that involuntary memory occurs in the flow of human activity that serves some need of the person. Such activity may be trivial, but if it engages the person it will be remembered. In fact, his research demonstrated that an action fully realized without memory as its goal is better remembered than a poorly realized action that has memory as its goal.

Zinchenko's conceptualization of memory as a product of activity also provides continuity between studies of autobiographical memory and studies of "flashbulb" memories for personal activities at significant moments in history (Brown & Kulick, 1977). Many people are likely to remember, for example, what they were doing when they heard about John Kennedy's assassination in 1963 because this event involved many activities that fully engaged them, but qualitatively this is no different from a 65-year-old woman who remembers her wedding 40 years ago. Both memories are involuntary memories, and both owe their vividness to the individual's engagement in the activities, cognitive and affective, of the moment.

The reports individuals make of their memories represent a transaction between individuals and their memories (Meacham, 1977). In a transactional viewpoint, the individual can change his memories and his memories can change the person as they provide a part of the context for interpreting experience.

How do such transactions occur? One currently popular view is that memory reports are constructed with the aid of scripts (Schank & Abelson, 1977). Scripts are portrayed as playing a role in both the retrieval of memories and the construction of memories by guiding inferential processes. If I recall that

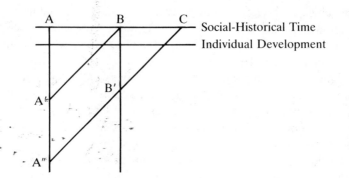

Figure 8.1. A transactional model of memory

a committee meeting was held on a particular day, my report of the meeting may include many inferences about what took place. Thus, I might report that the chairperson called the meeting to order. Upon reading the minutes, however, I may find that the chairperson was late and the meeting was actually called to order by the associate chair. The influence of scripts on memory reports is not questioned here; but perhaps the script model can be enhanced by viewing it as a subset of a more general transactional model.

A developmental perspective on a transactional model is illustrated in Figure 8.1. In this figure the flow of time is from left to right. Three events are represented as *A, B,* and *C.* When event *A* is recalled at *B,* it is recalled as *A'*; when it is recalled at point *C,* it is recalled as A". Riegel (1978) presented this model with only the top line (social-historical time); Figure 8.1 elaborates on his model. To consider events *A, B,* and *C* as occurring not only at three points in social-historical time but also at three points in the development of a particular individual broadens the set of issues raised by the model.

To clearly present the advantages of a transactional approach, a brief description of a nondevelopmental, nontransactional model such as Schank and Abelson's (1977) is needed. In their description of memory, they emphasize that each episode is stored as a "sequence of conceptualizations." A conceptualization is a basic unit of meaning, of which relatively few are needed to represent the much wider set of actions actually described in any language. Examples of conceptualizations include *move, grasp, propel,* and *expel.*

Two of Schank and Abelson's specific claims about memory are central to our discussion. First, they claim that, as an economy measure, when many episodes are similar they are remembered in terms of a "standardized generalized episode which we will call a script" (1977, p. 19). In the recall of a trip to a restaurant, "memory simply lists a pointer (link) to what we call the restaurant script and stores only the items in this particular episode that were significantly different from the standard script as the only items specifically in the description of that episode" (p. 19). Second, they claim that scripts emerge as the result of the comparison of memories for episodes. As similarities are noted between events, the similarities form the structure of the script. Thus, scripts are constructed by the individual. Schank and Abelson hypothesize a series of constructs such as plans, goals, and life themes that provide the knowledge necessary to perform such constructions. What is being emphasized here is that knowledge structures change, and along with them scripts and memories will also change.

Three points in particular must be stressed. First, memory reports derive from transactions between social-historical context and individual development. Scripts such as the now familiar restaurant example develop over time on the basis of experience, but that experience comes through the filter of the individual's previous experience and level of development. Each individual's script will have an idiosyncratic history and idiosyncratic content. These scripts may change over time as a result of either individual change or cultural change. As an example of individual change, consider a 45-year-old woman's script for going to a restaurant, which may include discussing with her husband where to eat. At 60, if this woman were widowed, the script might now include calling a friend to go out with her or simply going alone to a place where she feels comfortable. At the cultural level, tipping the maître d' was customary at many restaurants as recently as the 1960s, but for most diners this custom has gone the way of the hula hoop. As individual and cultural customs changes, scripts change and the inferences found in memory reports might also change.

Developmental changes in other cognitive or social processes also influence both scripts and memory reports. Thus, a 4-year-old child with a low level of role-taking skills may report an incident from a highly egocentric viewpoint. As this child develops the ability to take the perspective of others, his reports of what took place may change. Thus, "Johnny and I were playing and he took my ball. I tried to grab it and he hit me with it" becomes "Johnny and I were playing and he wanted the ball so he took it. I tried to grab it, but I think he got mad and so he hit me with it." The subtle shift in these two reports represents a movement toward recognizing that others have motives for their actions and that these can be inferred from their behavior. In addition to influencing the content of memory reports, this type of development allows individuals to form new scripts, because it gives them a new way to compare memories for events.

The second point to be made is that the symbolic knowledge representation systems known as scripts are a subset of the more general form of representation known as schemata. In their presentation of script theory, Schank and

Abelson (1977) introduce this as a general possibility, and their specific suggestions of goals, plans, and life themes are consistent with this point. But from a developmental view the multiplicity of knowledge representation is not fully captured by their conceptual theory of knowledge. In particular, the role of mental images, inductive, deductive, and social reasoning all merit close attention. In fact, it again seems plausible to suggest that in the report of a specific memory the constructive process may involve multiple knowledge systems transacting with memory. Consider this memory report from an 18-year-old college student in response to the cue word *pleased:*

That reminds me of my sweet-sixteen party. I was very pleased that Daddy gave me a car. My friends all came except Alice, I think she was sick, and then we danced and had cake. And then Dad gave me the keys and I went out in the driveway and the car was there. My friends all died.

This young woman seems to have used not only a script for parties but several other inference-making mechanisms; most notably, social inferences are made through role taking. Her statement about why Alice did not attend is more than simply noting an exception to the script; it is a social inference based upon her understanding of friendship. The same type of social inference is evident in "My friends all died," her way of saying they looked envious or behaved enviously. This particular memory report suggests an interesting contrast. One claim would be that, from a script point of view, when someone receives an extravagant gift friends act as though they are envious, even if they are not. An alternate claim would be that when the young woman reports her memory it is transformed by her current role-taking skills to include inferences she may not actually have made at the time of the party. The distinction between these explanations is fundamentally a question of how general the script notion is, a question requiring further research.

The third point is that schemata are themselves a subset of the more general set of knowledge representation systems. We refer back here to our discussion of the developmental progression noted by Piaget (1926). In particular, the utility of perceptual cues in the process of memory search seems in keeping with the spirit of a unified cognitive system. For example, a person experiences a perceptual event such as a sharp pain and reports that this reminds him of his last trip to the dentist. Is it necessary to invoke the concept of script to explain the retrieval of the memory, the construction of the memory report, neither, or both? This is an empirical question. Developmentalists and cognitive scientists must work together to determine (*a*) if Piaget, Bruner, and others are correct in asserting that multiple ways of knowing are possible, (*b*) if developmentally earlier forms remain effective as later forms develop, and (*c*), if earlier forms do remain effective, how multiple forms of representation interact within a single cognitive system.

## Developmental research

Future research on developmental aspects of autobiographical memory seems likely to be distributed over two broad categories. The first category will consist of research carrying forward the actuarial approach reflected in the few studies that have already been conducted. The second type of research will consist of studies that attempt to modify actuarial methods in order to address questions about developmental changes in the representation of memory.

In the first category, extensions of the type of analysis reported by Rubin, Wetzler, and Nebes (Chap. 12) on the nature of long-term retention functions provide an excellent example of how such data can be analyzed to investigate theoretically exciting issues. If confirmed, the existence of a reminiscence component in the retention functions of middle-aged and older adults can serve as a base line for the clinician working with these populations, to determine, for example, whether a particular individual has an exaggerated tendency to reminisce. More also needs to be learned about possible response-time differences, particularly in the group 75 and above, referred to as the old old.

In younger segments of the lifespan, the actuarial approach can be used to further investigate the childhood amnesia phenomenon. In research with adolescents to date, very few memories have been reported, not only from the preschool era but also from the early school years. In fact, if one analyzes the data available using the techniques suggested by Wetzler & Sweeney (Chap. 11), the "amnesic period" extends beyond the age of 5 or 6 often suggested. However, before any conclusion can be drawn, it is necessary to conduct a series of studies with children in which the instructional set is altered to encourage or require students to search for older memories. By extending such a method downward in age, the actuarial approach may be more sensitive to the phenomena that produce childhood amnesia.

The actuarial type of research might also pursue the relationship between autobiographical memory variables and measures of personality and psychopathology. Such research may occur in both developmental and nondevelopmental contexts. Although early research on early childhood amnesia was dominated by psychoanalytic conceptualizations of repression and other defense mechanisms, as the autobiographical memory literature grows the actuarial approach may fit well with current approaches to personality and psychopathology that emphasize such cognitive constructs as prototypes, self-schemata, and even scripts.

The modification of the actuarial approach to look at developmental changes in the representation of knowledge is more a modification of outlook than a methodological innovation. The work of Rieser and his colleagues represents a nondevelopmental example of such a shift. Their methodological contribution is the introduction of more complex cues, but this change is interesting only because they had laid the theoretical groundwork to make it so.

On the basis of their data, Rieser, Black, and Abelson (1985) argue that the similarity of prompts to the structure of event knowledge facilitates retrieval. They argue that because knowledge is structured according to activities, not actions, presenting activities leads to faster responses than presenting actions ("went to the movies" vs. "looked for a seat"). Their model has great appeal and demonstrated usefulness, but two points need to be kept in mind. The first is that not all events fit into a particular script or activity category (Schank & Abelson, 1977, p. 70). Because individuals can retrieve such memories, models of retrieval must be flexible. Second, autobiographical memories are prompted by a variety of cues, which may present the individual with a *variety* of processing requirements. Research must clarify the extent to which response times are affected by each of these. Thus, Fitzgerald and Lawrence (1984) demonstrated that the imagery value of prompts correlates with response time – the higher the imagery value, the faster the response. It may be easier to form an image of "went to the movies" than of "looked for a seat." Further research that eliminates or controls for differences between categories of complex prompts will allow for the construction of a dynamic model of autobiographical memory.

Rieser, Black, and Abelson (in press) contribute to an emerging consensus that some prompts are better than others when it comes to guiding a memory search, but just what it is that makes them better is still an open question. The complexities of autobiographical memory and knowledge representation require an enduring openness to alternative explanations. Ultimately, the success of the autobiographical memory paradigm is dependent upon the richness of the theoretical framework that grows up around the data. The purpose of this paper is to suggest how a developmental perspective might contribute to that richness by extending the roots of autobiographical memory research into the development of individuals in an ever-changing society.

## References

Bower, G. H., Black, J. B., & Turner, T. J. (1979). Scripts in memory for text. *Cognitive Psychology, 11,* 177–220.

Bronckhart, J. P., & Ventouras-Spycher, M. (1979). The Piagetian concept of representation and the Soviet inspired view of self-regulation. In G. Zivin (Ed.), *The development of self-regulation through private speech* (pp. 99–134). New York: Wiley.

Brown, R., & Kulick, J. (1977). Flashbulb memories. *Cognition, 5,* 73–99.

Bruner, J. (1964). The course of cognitive growth. *American Psychologist, 19,* 1–15.

Cantor, N., & Mischel, W. (1977). Traits as prototypes: Effects on recognition memory. *Journal of Personality and Social Psychology, 35*, 38–48.

Fagan, J. F. (1982). Infant memory. In T. M. Field, A. Huston, H. C. Quay, L. Troll, & G. E. Finley (Eds.), *Review of human development* (pp. 79–92). New York: Wiley.

Fitzgerald, J. M. (1980). Sampling autobiographical memory reports in adolescents. *Developmental Psychology, 16*, 675–676.

(1981). Autobiographical memory reports in adolescence. *Canadian Journal of Psychology, 35*, 69–75.

Fitzgerald, J. M., & Lawrence, R. (1984). Autobiographical memory across the life-span. *Journal of Gerontology, 39*, 692–699.

Meacham, J. (1977). A transactional model of memory. In H. W. Reese & N. Datan (Ed.), *Life-span developmental psychology: Dialectical perspectives on experimental research* (pp. 253–283). New York: Academic Press.

Piaget, J. (1926). *Language and thought of the child*. New York: Harcourt, Brace.

Riegel, K. F. (1978). *Psychology mon amour: A countertext*. Boston: Houghton Mifflin.

Rieser, B. J., Black, J. B., & Abelson, R. P. (1985). Knowledge structures in the organization and retrieval of autobiographical memory. *Cognitive Psychology*.

Robinson, J. A. (1976). Sampling autobiographical memory. *Cognitive Psychology, 8*, 578–595.

Rovee-Collier, C. K., Sullivan, M. W., Enright, M., Lucan, D., & Fagan, J. W. (1980). The reactivation of infant memory. *Science, 208*, 1159–1161.

Rubin, D. C. (1982). On the retention function for autobiographical memory. *Journal of Verbal Learning and Verbal Behavior, 21*, 21–38.

Schank, R. C., & Abelson, R. P. (1977). *Scripts, plans, goals and understanding*. Hillsdale, NJ: Erlbaum.

Tulving, E. (1983). *Elements of episodic memory*. New York: Oxford University Press.

Zinchenko, P. I. (1983). The problem of involuntary memory. *Soviet Psychology, 8*, 55–111. (Reprinted from *Scientific Notes: The Kharkov Pedagogical Institute of Foreign Languages* [1939], *1*, 145–187.)

*Part IV*

# The temporal organization of autobiographical memory

One of the central organizing properties of autobiographical memory is that it occurs along a time line. Events occur before, after, or at about the same time as other events. Events from the same time period tend to appear together in reminiscence and tend to be lost and recovered together in amnesia.

The two chapters in Part IV turn this organizational principle upside down. Instead of time organizing autobiographical memory, autobiographical memory organizes time. Time is not only the ticking of a clock, it is the passage of the events that mark one's life. This latter, personal-social-cultural-event-marked time emerges as the more important for autobiographical memory.

# 9  Public memories and their personal context

*Norman R. Brown, Steven K. Shevell, and Lance J. Rips*

History is an extension of memory.
      M. White (1963)

The reality of these events does not consist in the fact that they occurred but that, first of all, they were remembered, and, second, that they are capable of finding a place in a chronologically ordered sequence.
      H. White (1980)

## Introduction

Every day dozens of noteworthy events are reported in newspapers, on television, and in radio broadcasts. Depending on your reading, viewing, and listening habits, you may be exposed to several different descriptions of the same event over the course of a single day, or you may have to endure hearing the same version repeated a number of times. Further, these events may come up again in conversation and as the topics of magazine articles or film documentaries. The point is that exposure to current events is a common, almost unavoidable part of our daily experience and that information concerning these events, extracted from the media and from our interactions with others, is learned in the context of our own lives.

In this chapter we explore how the knowledge people have of recent history (*public memories*) is linked to their knowledge of their lives (*personal* or *autobiographical memories*). We expect a given public memory to be a blend of facts about the public circumstances in which the event occurred and facts about the personal matrix in which that information was acquired. Put slightly differently, we suppose that a public event is conceived partly as a datum in our broader knowledge of current history, partly as a datum in our knowledge of our own life story. Take, for example, the resignation of former Secretary

We thank Allan Collins and Edward Smith for encouraging us to explore the relation between public and personal histories. We also thank Fred Conrad, Janis Handte, Steen Larsen, and David Rubin for comments on an earlier version of this chapter. This research was supported by a grant from the Spencer Foundation and by NSF Grant SES-8411976.

of State Cyrus Vance. This incident is newsworthy in part because it marked a step in an ongoing crisis in diplomatic affairs. However, such an event also plays an indirect role in our own chronology. We heard about it at a definite point in our personal activities, and it may have had personal effects, say, in our discussions with others. This dual aspect of our awareness of public events is probably most obvious for momentous occasions such as the assassination of John Kennedy (see Neisser's [1982] discussion of historical "benchmarks"), but it may also hold for lesser incidents as well. In the rest of this introduction we consider in more detail the dual nature of memory for public events and then, in the following sections, present some experimental evidence that bears on this issue.

*Public narratives*

Vance's resignation can be seen as a specific act that took place at a particular time (April 21, 1980) and place (Washington, D.C.). Yet our understanding of this event, like our understanding of an episode in a story, depends on our knowledge of the situation that prompted it: Vance's struggle with Brzezinski over the conduct of U.S. foreign policy, Vance's opposition to the rescue mission in Iran, and so on. Media recaps of the resignation prominently mention these antecedents in order to make the event itself intelligible. We will refer to mental concepts of such interconnected historical episodes as *public narratives,* because they partially resemble narrative sequences in fiction: Certain prominent circumstances or conflicts set others in train that are resolved by still other occurrences. The parallel to fiction should not be pushed too far, because there are elements in our concepts of public affairs that are not especially storylike. Events may be produced by large-scale political or economic facts that have little to do with the intentional human acts of fiction. Nevertheless, *narrative* comes close to capturing our sense of historical development when we comprehend why a public event happened.

A number of philosophers of history have also noted the relevance of narratives in explaining public occurrences. Danto (1956) and Gallie (1964), for example, both contend that there is an essential similarity between interpreting historical phenomena and understanding a story. Danto suggests, in particular,

> that *stories* play an important cognitive role in historical inquiry. . . . In a sense, such a story is a loosely articulated "model" of what happened, designating a deployment of events; and insofar as the historian's commitment is to truth, his aim is to draw the model to scale, as it were, so that it reproduces, by some criterion of resemblance, the structure it purports to designate. [1956, p. 21]

The idea that historical explanation is best conceived as a narrative has its detractors (e.g., Mandelbaum, 1967), who point to oversimplifications in its description of the historian's task. But, whatever the merits of this account as a theory of historical method, it does seem a plausible suggestion about people's lay ideas of thematically and causally related sequences of public events. The hostage crisis in Iran, the Grenada invasion, and the Libyan conflict all furnish current examples. (For a similar suggestion with respect to naive physics, see Hayes's [1979] discussion of "histories.")

Rumelhart (1975) and others have developed detailed theories of mental narrative structure in order to predict how people remember and summarize simple stories. We assume that such theories could be adapted or extended to public memories as well, and in the third section of this chapter we offer some evidence that memory search for the properties of an event sometimes recruits information from other events in the same narrative. We note at this point, however, that there is nothing logically necessary about these structures. It is easy to imagine public events organized by their time of occurrence, as are the events in medieval annals or modern appointment books. Alternatively, events might be organized by topic, such as natural disasters or international developments (Kolodner, 1983a, 1983b). Public events present an interesting test case for narrative theories, precisely because public events (unlike fictional episodes) are not created simply to play a part in a story sequence.

*The personal context of the news*

Public narratives locate events in the thematic-causal structures in which they occur; but we experience these events not only against a public backdrop but also within the compass of our own activities. We learned about Vance's resignation in one or more specific media presentations, probably as the result of actions on our part – a decision to buy a newspaper or turn on the television. These personal facts are extrinsic to the event; yet they may be closely linked in our memories of it, in much the way that knowledge of the content of a text passage may be remembered along with its physical position on the page.

There is now ample evidence that extrinsic (or "independent") information is encoded at least some of the time when subjects learn facts in the laboratory (Baddeley, 1982). This evidence derives from two main approaches. One approach seeks to demonstrate that environmental manipulations can influence recall. For example, Smith (1979) and Godden and Baddeley (1975) found that material learned in one setting is better recalled in that setting than in another. Further, Smith (1979) showed that subjects in a new environment who were instructed to recall the original encoding context performed better (recalled more words from a test list) than subjects who were not. Such results indicate that environmental features are encoded in long-term memory and are useful as retrieval cues. The other approach to this problem is more direct.

In a number of studies subjects have been asked to produce some physical aspect of the to-be-remembered items in incidental recall. Aspects that seem to be encoded with the most accuracy and the least effort include location (Mandler, Seegmiller, & Day, 1977; Rothkopf, 1971; Schulman, 1973) and modality (e.g., Light, Stansbury, Rubin, & Linde, 1973). The argument here is that context must have been encoded with the items, because subjects can determine an encoded event's context at the time of recall.

If facts about the learning situation are stored along with the learned substance, we might expect by analogy that memories for public events would include personal details about how the information was acquired. The study of flashbulb memories provides some support for this assumption. According to Brown and Kulik (1977, p. 73), flashbulb memories are "memories for the circumstances in which one first learned of a very surprising and consequential (or emotionally arousing) event." In recent studies of this phenomenon, subjects have been presented with brief descriptions of one or more public events and have been required to recall the personal context in which they first learned about them (Brown & Kulik, 1977; Pillemer, 1984; Winograd & Killinger, 1983; Yarmey & Bull, 1978). The prototypical flashbulb-eliciting event is the assassination of John Kennedy: More than 90% of subjects who were 7 or older at the time are capable of retrieving flashbulb memories for this incident (Brown & Kulik, 1977; Winograd & Killinger, 1983; Yarmey & Bull, 1978). This result is particularly impressive because the studies were performed as long as 16 years after the event took place. However, flashbulb memories are not restricted to the first Kennedy assassination; the assassinations of Martin Luther King and Robert Kennedy, the attempt on Reagan's life, the first Apollo moon landing, and the resignation of Richard Nixon also produce a substantial number of flashbulb memories (Brown & Kulik, 1977; Pillemer, 1984; Winograd & Killinger, 1983).

Flashbulbs are the most obvious places where public narratives and personal chronologies intersect in memory (Neisser, 1982). However, there is little reason to suppose that such cases are limited to extremely important or surprising news. Although people may have more difficulty recalling the circumstances in which they found out about less important public events (e.g., Vance's resignation), it may not be altogether impossible. Moreover, recall itself may not be the most sensitive technique for determining whether this information is available. Our hunch is that many public events produce memory traces of the encoding situation in much the same way as flashbulb items.

*A preview*

Our own approach to the problem of public memories is based on our experience in studying how people determine the dates of public events (Brown,

Rips, & Shevell, 1985). Initial interest in this problem was sparked by the mistakes people make – or the illusions they experience – in deciding when real-world events happened (Baddeley, Lewis, & Nimmo-Smith, 1978; Brown et al., 1985; Linton, 1975; Loftus & Marburger, 1983; Sudman & Bradburn, 1973; Thompson, 1982). As a memory task, this probing for dates is a species of cued recall, for investigators ask subjects to respond with a date to a description of the target event. But research on this problem suggests that dating events is seldom mere retrieval of a prestored calendar date. Rather, the question poses an estimation problem, in which fragmentary evidence from memory is adduced to narrow the possible range of times within which the event occurred. Our contention is that an understanding of this evidence can shed some light on how public events are remembered and how they are integrated with knowledge of surrounding personal facts.

The remaining sections of this chapter describe the results of a series of dating experiments and explore their implications for public and personal memories. The next section discusses the nature of our previous studies and our reasons for viewing dating as estimation. We then report two new experiments that provide some clues about public and personal histories. In the first we asked subjects to think aloud as they dated public events, analyzing transcripts of their performance for evidence of public and personal information. The second experiment, which we call the Period Study, had subjects decide (under reaction-time conditions) whether events happened during intervals that we described to them in either public or autobiographical terms. The results of this experiment suggest that the effects of the descriptions depend on the nature of the target event.

### Event dating, problem solving, and public memories

In a typical dating experiment, subjects are given descriptions of public events and are asked to write down a date (a month and year) for each. The events are taken from major news stories of the preceding years and are described as they might be in a newspaper headline (e.g., "911 die in Jonestown suicides" or "Andrew Young leaves UN post"). If it were true that people commonly store calendar dates for events like these, this task would be a straightforward (though not to say easy) problem, because subjects could locate each event by retrieving its date from long-term memory. However, there are empirical (as well as intuitive) grounds for rejecting the view that subjects usually date events in this way.

Three dating experiments (Underwood, 1977, Exp. 1; Brown et al., 1985, Expts. 1 and 2) give consistent results. The proportion of correct responses (accurate to the month) is very low, ranging from 3% (Brown et al., 1985, Exp. 2) to 12% (Underwood, 1977). Nevertheless, subjects demonstrate that they know a good deal about the ordinal temporal relations among the events. In these studies the rank correlation between mean estimated date and true date ranged from .88 (Brown et al., 1985, Expts. 1 and 2) to .96 (Underwood, 1977). We have replicated this pattern of high correlation between estimated and true date and low "correct" rate in three other unpublished experiments. Taken as a whole, these results suggest that subjects are quite accurate in locating the relative position of important current events but that the retrieval of prestored calendar dates is probably not the source of this accuracy. Explicit and absolute dates are apparently a scarce commodity in long-term memory.

On the surface, these results may seem paradoxical. How can subjects be very accurate in locating current events without knowing when the events took place? A likely solution to this problem lies in the strategies people use to derive a plausible date. Although it is unusual for people to know the exact date on which events occurred, they often have access to a number of potentially informative facts about these events. Some of these facts may allow people to carry out temporal inferences (Collins, 1978) that increase the accuracy of date estimates. These inferences may work by relating the events in question either to each other or to a small set of privileged events that *do* have a specific temporal locus. We can suppose (with Linton, 1975, and Chap. 4) that people maintain a set of "marker events" or "landmarks" that are explicitly dated. In the domain of public events, this set may include the dates for recent presidential terms and for extraordinary events like the bombing of Pearl Harbor or the assassination of John Kennedy. In the autobiographical domain, the set of dated landmarks might be somewhat larger, including dates for events that delineate major periods in a personal chronology. Autobiographical periods could be bounded by events that alter social, educational, occupational, or geographical situations (see Lieury, Aiello, Lepreux, & Mellet, 1980). Information about the span of these periods might also be explicitly stored and readily retrievable.

If this is correct, the dating process may involve a search through memory for explicit landmark facts that have a known (or inferable) relation to the target event (Lieury et al., 1980; Lindsay & Norman, 1975; Linton, 1975). Consider once again the resignation of Cyrus Vance. A subject who knew nothing more than that Vance was Carter's secretary of state would be able to infer that Vance resigned at some point between January 1977 and January 1981. A slightly better informed subject who knew that the resignation took place during the Iranian hostage crisis, and also that the hostage crisis occurred during the latter half of Carter's term, could narrow the range further. This subject could confidently infer that the resignation took place between January 1979 and January 1981.

This dating strategy has some important implicit features. First, dating requires that the subject know the temporal relation between the target event and the landmark. Knowing that Alfred Hitchcock died during April 1980 will not help a person date Vance's resignation unless that person also knows (or can infer) that Vance's resignation took place at about the same time as Hitchcock's death. Second, because the dating task requires subjects to narrow an event's age to a specific month, a single fact (short of the target event's calendar date) often will not provide sufficient information for a precise inference. As a result, subjects may have to retrieve a number of temporally informative facts and perform a number of temporal inferences in order to estimate the date. A final point concerns the role of autobiographical context in the dating process. So far, the examples have been restricted to cases where our fictitious subject retrieves public facts and uses them as a basis for an informed date estimate. However, if autobiographical facts are retrievable, they may also provide useful evidence of an event's age. Indeed, if people maintain fairly detailed personal chronologies, autobiographical facts may be at least as useful as public facts. For example, subjects who can recall where they were when they learned of Vance's resignation can use the knowledge of their own lives to establish the period during which the resignation must have occurred. Robinson (Chap. 10) has shown that the school-year calendar (fall term, winter-spring term, and summer vacation) provides natural boundaries for students' memories, and these divisions may also help subjects to narrow the time of occurrence for an event within a given year.

What emerges from these considerations is an accrual account of the dating process. It seems likely that subjects search memory for an explicit date associated with the target event. But, because it is rare to have access to these dates, subjects engage in range-limiting inference. In doing this, they search for facts that relate the target event to other events that may be dated or datable and for facts that relate the target to temporally bounded periods. Subjects continue retrieving facts and drawing temporal inferences until they find a reasonably precise date for the target event or until they exhaust either the available information or the time allotted for the task. This account is similar to those advanced by Collins (1978) and Lindsay and Norman (1975), and we presuppose it in what follows. The important point is that, if dating requires search for information related to the target event, then we can use the dating task as a means of exploring properties of memory for public events. In the next sections we report two experimental variations on the dating task that were designed to uncover these properties.

## Protocols on dating

In our earlier studies of dating, subjects simply produced a date to a stimulus event, and the date itself was the object of study. However, it is also possible to ask subjects to think aloud as they are making their estimates in the hope that their comments will reveal something of the underlying processes. We undertook such an experiment with three aims in mind. First, we sought direct confirmation that dating can involve inference. Second, we wanted to see whether public events are often stored with retrievable autobiographical information. Third, we hoped the observed patterns of retrieval might indicate the underlying organization of public memories.

*Predictions about dating strategies*

If subjects generally date events using inference, then they should estimate these dates by means of auxiliary facts related to the target, where these auxiliary facts might include other public or personal events. Such strategies contrast with cases in which subjects merely retrieve a date or guess. Thus, we can get a rough idea of the prevalence of inductive strategies by comparing the number of responses in which auxiliary facts are mentioned to those in which no such facts are produced. We need to be cautious in interpreting such results, for it is possible that the mentioned facts are merely rationalizations. Nevertheless, such data can furnish hypotheses about inference strategies that we can later test by more rigorous methods (see, e.g., the experiment reported in the following section of this chapter).

The content of the auxiliary facts is also of interest if we assume that the probability of retrieving a particular type of fact is a function of the strength of its relation to the target event. Thus, if a large proportion of the responses include personal references, this suggests that autobiographical information is frequently related to what people know about historical events. A similar comment applies to mention of public events. If public memories consist of narratives like the hostage crisis, the invasion of Grenada, or the Falklands war, then the link between two current events should be most direct when the events are episodes within the same narrative. This view contrasts with the proposal that public memory is a simple time line and also with the view of public memory as organized according to event category (assassination attempts stored with assassination attempts and natural disasters with natural disasters). If we are correct in assuming that interevent associations tend to be narrative in nature rather than categorical or chronological, then we should find that subjects make more frequent reference to events drawn from the target event's narrative than to any other types of events.

In designing this protocol study, we felt there might be a difference between *political* events, like the resignation of Cyrus Vance, and *nonpolitical* events, like the first Mt. St. Helens eruption. Political events were defined as governmental or military happenings of national or international scope. Nonpolitical

Table 9.1. *Stimulus events used in the protocol study,*
*with their dates*

| | Political events |
|---|---|
| Mar. 1978 | U.S. signs Panama Canal treaty |
| Sep. 1978 | Camp David peace accord signed |
| Oct. 1978 | Congress extends the ERA deadline |
| Oct. 1978 | Sadat and Begin win the Nobel Prize |
| Jan. 1979 | Khomeini overthrows the shah of Iran |
| Jun. 1979 | U.S. and Soviets sign SALT agreement |
| Aug. 1979 | Andrew Young leaves UN post |
| Dec. 1979 | Soviets invade Afghanistan |
| Apr. 1980 | Secretary of State Cyrus Vance resigns |
| Jul. 1980 | U.S. boycotts the Moscow Olympics |
| Sep. 1980 | U.S. sells AWACs to Saudis |
| Sep. 1980 | Iraq initiates Iranian war |
| Jul. 1981 | François Mitterrand becomes French premier |
| Aug. 1981 | U.S. downs two Libyan jets |
| Oct. 1981 | Anwar Sadat assassinated |
| Dec. 1981 | Martial law declared in Poland |
| | Nonpolitical events |
| Apr. 1978 | *Holocaust* aired for the first time |
| Jun. 1978 | Son of Sam convicted |
| Jul. 1978 | First test-tube baby born in England |
| Nov. 1978 | 911 die in Jonestown suicides |
| Mar. 1979 | Three Mile Island accident occurs |
| Jul. 1979 | Skylab falls from orbit |
| Oct. 1979 | Mother Theresa wins Nobel Prize |
| Dec. 1979 | 11 fans die at the Who concert |
| Jan. 1980 | Paul McCartney arrested by Japanese police |
| Mar. 1980 | First Mt. St. Helens eruption occurs |
| Nov. 1980 | 80 die in Las Vegas hotel fire |
| Dec. 1980 | John Lennon murdered by David Chapman |
| Apr. 1981 | First space shuttle launched |
| Jul. 1981 | Prince Charles marries Diana Spencer |
| Jul. 1981 | 125 people die in Kansas City Hyatt disaster |
| Jan. 1982 | AT&T forced to break up |

events were defined in the negative as well-known current events that had no obvious connection to domestic or foreign affairs. Among the nonpolitical events are natural and manmade disasters, crimes, awards, and cultural and scientific firsts. We selected our stimuli so that half were political events and half were nonpolitical events. Table 9.1 contains a complete list of these items. The 32 events spanned a 4-year period, 1978 to 1982, with an approximately equal number of items from each year. The oldest event in the group was about 5 years old at the time of the experiment and the newest a little over a year old. For political and for nonpolitical events, the average date was January 1980. An independent group of pilot subjects had also rated these same events for how much they knew about them. The average knowledge rating on a 0-to-9 scale (0 = no knowledge, 9 = a great deal of knowledge) was 5.3 for the political events and 5.2 for the nonpolitical ones (SE = .98).

We conjectured that political events, by the nature of their content, are likely to be tied into a larger public context, whereas nonpolitical events are not. In particular, many of the political events directly or indirectly involve the president and his administration. Thus, people can determine the approximate time of a political event by knowing the term of the president who was associated with it. One obvious prediction is that people should make more references to presidents and presidential terms when dating political events than when dating nonpolitical events.

In sum, we had four predictions concerning the protocol study. First, subjects should generally mention one or more informative facts in making their date estimates. This would indicate that event dating often involves an inference process like that outlined earlier. Second, if public events are stored with retrievable context, the mentioned facts should include autobiographical details. Third, other public events that subjects mention in the course of dating are likely to be drawn from the same narrative as the target. This result would provide evidence for a narrative organization of events in public memories. Finally, we expected subjects would refer frequently to presidents and presidential administrations when dating political events but not when dating nonpolitical events.

At the beginning of a session in this experiment, subjects were told that the descriptions they would see referred to unique events that happened between January 1976 and the "present" (May 1983) and that they were to respond to each stimulus event with the year and month when it had occurred or, if they could not come up with a precise answer, with a best guess. They were instructed to think aloud as they were deciding and warned that they would be prompted if they fell silent for more than a few seconds. Beyond this prompting, subjects received no feedback on their responses. Each subject received a booklet with the descriptions of the events typed one to a page so that only one event was exposed at a time. The responses to the experimental items were tape-recorded and later transcribed. After completing the protocol phase of the experiment, each subject received a rating form that contained a list of the 32 experimental events in a new random order. Subjects were instructed to indicate how much they knew about each event, using the same rating scale mentioned above. The 15 subjects who participated in this study were recruited from the University of Chicago community and ranged in age from 23 to 30 years old.

## Comparison to earlier results

Before considering the content of the protocols, we need to establish that the dating performance of these subjects is similar to that of subjects who participated in the questionnaire studies cited earlier. Recall that these studies showed strong correlations between objective (true) date and mean subjective date and low frequency of correct (month and year) responses. When equivalent statistics were computed from the date estimates obtained from the protocol subjects, we found a very similar pattern of performance. The correlation between objective date and mean subjective date was large (.83), whereas the percentage of responses (8%) that correctly specified the month and year of the events was well within the range observed in earlier studies. These results indicate that the requirement to verbalize did not interfere with subjects' ability to perform the dating task. Further, this equivalence in performance suggests that the content of the protocols accurately reflects the types of facts and strategies people normally use when dating events.

Two other features of the results deserve mention. First, the type of event (political vs. nonpolitical) did not influence dating accuracy: The average absolute error was 0.97 of a year for political events, and 1.00 year for nonpolitical events ($t < 1$). Second, in agreement with our pilot results, subjects considered nonpolitical events to be about as well known as political events. Mean knowledge rating was 3.8 for the former and 3.5 for the latter ($t < 1$).

## The nature of the protocols

In coding the protocols, each response was first classified as either *justified* or *unjustified*. Justified responses include all those in which the subject made reference to one or more informative facts. If the subject either guessed or simply responded with a date, the response was considered unjustified. Each justified response was then coded for the presence or absence of each of the following five types of information: (*a*) specific temporal facts about the target event (other than the date itself) that could be helpful in approximating the date, (*b*) mentions of presidential terms of office, (*c*) references to public events that are members of the target event's narrative (i.e., events that have an obvious causal relation to the target), (*d*) references to public events that are *not* members of the target event's narrative (i.e., events that are related to the target categorically, chronologically, or in some other way), (*e*) auto-

Table 9.2. *Response categories for protocol study, with examples*

---

*Specific temporal information*
Congress extends the ERA deadline: "That was three years before last June, so it would have been about June of '79."

*Presidential reference*
Andrew Young leaves U.N. post: "It happened near the end of . . . Carter's term, so . . . May of '79."

*Datable public events in same narrative*
Sadat and Begin win the Nobel Prize: "It was a little while after Camp David, which was in '77, I'd say . . . February of '78."

*Datable public events not in same narrative*
Paul McCartney arrested by Japanese police: "Was approximately during the hostage crisis in Iran, because *Saturday Night Live* had this great take-off on it, doing the whole thing of the hostage crisis, day one of Paul McCartney in Japan. . . . So the hostages, what I was saying, the hostages were freed in January of 1981, they'd been in 180 days, approximately, I think, which would have been halfway back to 1980; Paul McCartney was arrested in 1980, then, we'll say, say September 1980."

*Autobiographical reference*
François Mitterrand becomes French premier. "I got in an argument with somebody about Mitterrand, I was in favor of him, and this person wasn't, and I think it was in the spring of, say, April or something, of 1981 that he was elected."

---

biographical references. Examples of these types are given in Table 9.2. All 480 responses were scored for mentions of information from the above categories. As a check on the reliability of the categories, a second judge rescored a sample of 60 responses (4 from each subject). For this sample, the two judges agreed on 92% of the items. There are two important things to note about this coding scheme. First, these categories are not mutually exclusive; a given response may include references that fall into more than one of the categories just described. Second, the categories are not exhaustive because subjects sometimes justified their dates with other sorts of information. Often these justifications were based on facts peculiar to the target event itself. (One subject, e.g., found the date of the wedding of Prince Charles and Diana Spencer by an approximation based on the current age of their son.)

Table 9.3 presents data relevant to the predictions we made earlier. The values in this table are the proportion of responses to political and nonpolitical events that included the types of information discussed above. Our first prediction concerned the general dating strategy people use. We expected subjects to date well-known current events by means of an inductive process rather than by a "retrieve or guess" process. The examples in Table 9.2 demonstrate that subjects use inference strategies; however, they fail to convey

Table 9.3. *Proportion of responses in the protocol study that included retrieval of at least one fact of a given type*

| Response category | Event type | |
|---|---|---|
| | Political | Nonpolitical |
| *Unjustified responses* | .22 | .34 |
| *Justified responses* | | |
| Specific temporal facts | .07 | .08 |
| Presidential term of office | .35 | .04 |
| Datable event from same narrative | .32 | .09 |
| Datable event not in same narrative | .12 | .13 |
| Autobiographical event | .31 | .50 |

just how prevalent these strategies are. We can examine whether inference appears to dominate the dating task by grouping together the unjustified responses with those justified responses that included only specific temporal information, comparing these to the remaining justified responses. Overall, 70% of responses were justified by more than bare temporal information, with 14 of the 15 subjects displaying this dominance ($p < .01$). (All of the confidence levels reported in this section are based on two-tailed sign tests.) This result holds for political and nonpolitical events alike: 77% of the political responses and 64% of the nonpolitical responses were justified by more than strictly temporal facts.

The other three predictions concerned the content of the justified responses. According to the first of these, subjects should frequently mention autobiographical information, and the results clearly indicate this is so. Forty percent of all responses contained at least one autobiographical reference; the autobiographical category is the largest single response category in Table 9.3. This result supports our basic premise that people often store public events with retrievable personal information. This finding is also consistent with the results of Lieury, Aiello, Lepreux, and Mellet (1980), whose subjects reported using autobiographical landmarks in dating public events. Although we made no prediction about whether the political status of an event would influence the amount of recalled autobiographical information, the results hint at such an effect. Subjects made reference to autobiographical facts in 50% of their responses to nonpolitical events but in only 31% of their responses to political events. Although this trend is not significant ($.05 < p < .10$ even in an a priori test), it may provide an important clue to the nature of public memories, and we will therefore return to it later.

We also expected that subjects should make more references to datable events that are members of the target's narrative than to those that are not. This hypothesis, too, was supported by the Table 9.3 data. Subjects mentioned same-narrative events in 20% of the trials and nonnarrative events in 12% ($p < .01$). The results also indicate that an event's political status influences the probability that subjects will retrieve other events from its narrative. Fourteen subjects referred to same-narrative events more frequently when dating political events (average 32%) than when dating nonpolitical events (average 9%).

Finally, we thought that subjects would make more frequent reference to presidential terms when dating political events than when dating nonpolitical ones, and Table 9.3 shows this is correct: Presidential references appeared in 35% of the responses to political events but in only 4% of the responses to the nonpolitical items. Of 15 subjects, 14 displayed the predicted pattern ($p < .01$). This result suggests that presidential administrations provide the historical backdrop for national and international affairs but that this influence does not extend to all aspects of public life.

We can summarize these results by noting an association between the political status of the events and the public or private nature of our subjects' responses. In general, subjects retrieved more public information (i.e., presidential terms and datable public events) than personal information when dating political events but more personal information than public when dating nonpolitical events. For political events, 61% of responses included public facts and 31% autobiographical facts; however, for nonpolitical events, 25% mentioned public facts and 50% autobiographical facts. The combined proportion of public responses to political events and autobiographical responses to nonpolitical events is reliably greater than the combination of autobiographical responses to political events and public responses to nonpolitical ones ($p < .01$). Nevertheless, in spite of these two very different patterns of retrieval, subjects were equally accurate in dating both event types.

## The period study

The findings from the experiment just reported suggest that memory organization for public events may depend on the nature of the events themselves. Political events such as the signing of the SALT agreement or the deposition of the shah of Iran are episodes in a broader historical sequence, and locating these events in time may be partly a matter of determining their place within these public narratives. Of course, nonpolitical public events (e.g., the conviction of Son of Sam or John Lennon's murder) may also participate in longer sequences (the fall of Son of Sam, the story of the Beatles). But these larger units are apparently less salient or at least less helpful in determining the time at which the events happened. Instead, nonpolitical events tend to be dated according to where they fall within the lives of those who have heard about them. They happened "early on in my stay in Japan . . . so I would say nineteen-eighty" or "after I graduated, which was in seventy-nine."

## Public versus personal time intervals

In the present section we explore this distinction between political and non-political events using a technique that may be more sensitive than protocol analysis to the properties of the events' memory organization. According to the ideas just discussed, it should be relatively easy for subjects to determine that a political event occurred during a period or era bounded by other public occurrences and relatively difficult for them to determine if it occurred during a period bounded by personal episodes. By contrast, nonpolitical events should be easier to locate within personally defined than within publicly defined periods. As examples, consider Mitterrand's election and David Chapman's conviction for John Lennon's slaying. The former fits the prototype of a political event and should therefore be easier to locate within a publicly bounded than within a personally bounded interval. The latter is a nonpolitical event and, as such, its time of occurrence should be easier to reckon with respect to personal rather than public periods.

To test this hypothesis, we took advantage of the fact that students who were college seniors at the time of our experiment had enrolled at the university in the fall of 1980. Thus, the interval during which these subjects had been in high school approximately coincided with the Carter administration, whereas their time in college happened during the Reagan administration. This allowed us to ask these subjects whether a given event had occurred during an earlier period (1978–1980) or a later period (1981–1983) that we could describe to them either publicly (Carter's administration vs. Reagan's) or personally (high school years vs. college years). To continue our earlier example, we could ask the subjects on one trial to decide if Mitterrand's election occurred during Carter's term or Reagan's and on another trial to decide if the election occurred while they were in high school or in college. The same two questions can be posed for Chapman's conviction. Our prediction is that subjects will be faster in deciding that Mitterrand was elected while Reagan was president than that Mitterrand was elected while the subjects were in college; however, they should be faster in deciding that Chapman was convicted while they were in college than that he was convicted while Reagan was in office.

We tested this prediction using a standard two-choice reaction-time method. During one of the experimental trials, subjects first saw on a CRT screen a pair of terms that referred to the earlier and the later time period. On personal trials the terms were "high school" and "college," whereas on public trials the terms were "Carter" and "Reagan." One member of the pair was located at the left of the screen and the other on the right. Two seconds after the appearance of these period terms, a description of the target event (e.g., "David Chapman convicted of John Lennon's murder") joined them on the screen. At this point the subjects tried to determine whether the event happened during the earlier or the later interval. To register their choice, they pushed a button on the side corresponding to the position of the appropriate period label. Their reaction times were recorded from the event's presentation until they made their response.

We selected 20 political events and 20 nonpolitical events to serve as stimuli. The events were chosen so that their mean age, word length, word frequency, and rated level of knowledge (as assessed in an independent pilot experiment) were approximately the same for political as for nonpolitical events. Half of the events of each type took place during the earlier period (early 1978 through mid-1980) and half during the more recent period (early 1981 through 1983). A list of these items and their dates is presented in Table 9.4. As noted above, on public-period trials, subjects had to decide whether one of these target events happened during the Carter administration or during the Reagan administration. On personal-period trials subjects had to decide whether the target event happened during their high school years or during their college years. *High school* was defined as the period from the beginning of ninth grade to when the subject entered college. *College* spanned the time the subject entered college to the "present" (March or April of 1984).

A subject saw each event four times during the course of the experiment (once in each of four 40-item blocks). In the first two blocks, presentations were accompanied by periods of one type (public or personal), and in the last two blocks by periods of the other type. Twelve subjects were tested with public periods during the first 80 trials and with personal periods during the last 80 trials. The trials were oppositely ordered (personal first, then public) for a second group of 12 subjects. All subjects received reaction-time and accuracy feedback after every 20 trials.

*Reaction times for political and nonpolitical events*

Figure 9.1 presents the mean correct reaction times for the first half (Blocks 1 and 2) and the second half (Blocks 3 and 4) of this experiment. As is apparent, the pattern of results for the main conditions shifts quite radically

Table 9.4. *Stimulus events for the period study, with their dates*

| | Political events |
|---|---|
| Mar. 1978 | U.S. signs Panama Canal treaty |
| Sep. 1978 | Camp David peace accord signed |
| Feb. 1979 | Ayatollah Khomeini takes over Iran |
| Feb. 1979 | Thatcher first becomes prime minister |
| Jun. 1979 | U.S. and Soviets sign SALT II |
| Aug. 1979 | Andrew Young resigns |
| Nov. 1979 | Iranian "students" take American embassy |
| Dec. 1979 | Soviet Union invades Aghanistan |
| Jan. 1980 | U.S. halts grain sales to Soviets |
| Apr. 1980 | Secretary of State Cyrus Vance resigns post |
| Mar. 1981 | American military advisors arrive in El Salvador |
| Jun. 1981 | François Mitterrand elected premier |
| Aug. 1981 | Sandra O'Connor named to Supreme Court |
| Oct. 1981 | President Anwar Sadat assassinated in Egypt |
| Dec. 1981 | Polish government declares martial law |
| Dec. 1981 | Red Brigade kidnaps General Dozier in Italy |
| Jan. 1982 | Government forces AT&T to divide holdings |
| Apr. 1982 | Argentina captures the Falklands |
| Jun. 1982 | Israeli army invades southern Lebanon |
| Jul. 1982 | George Shultz becomes secretary of state |
| | Nonpolitical events |
| Oct. 1978 | John Paul II becomes pope |
| Nov. 1978 | 911 people die in Jonestown suicides |
| Mar. 1979 | Three Mile Island accident occurs |
| Mar. 1979 | Jane Byrne elected mayor of Chicago |
| May 1979 | 275 die in Chicago DC-10 crash |
| Jul. 1979 | Skylab falls to earth |
| Oct. 1979 | Pope John Paul visits U.S. |
| Nov. 1979 | 11 die at a Who concert |
| Feb. 1980 | John Gacy found guilty of murder |
| Mar. 1980 | First Mt. St. Helens eruption occurs |
| Apr. 1981 | First space shuttle launched |
| May 1981 | Pope John Paul wounded in Rome |
| Jun. 1981 | David Chapman convicted of Lennon's murder |
| Jul. 1981 | Prince Charles marries Diana Spencer |
| Jul. 1981 | 125 die in Kansas City Hyatt disaster |
| Jul. 1981 | Professional baseball players end strike |
| Mar. 1982 | *Chariots of Fire* wins Academy Award |
| Mar. 1982 | John Belushi dies |
| Sep. 1982 | 7 people die in Tylenol murders |
| Dec. 1982 | First artificial heart transplanted successfully |

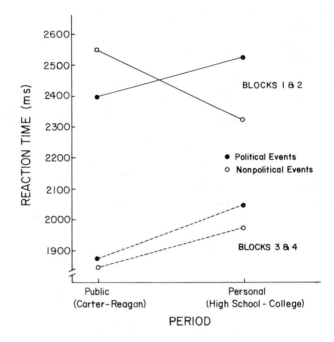

Figure 9.1. Mean reaction time to decide whether a target event occurred during a personally described or a publicly described interval. Filled circles indicate political target events; open circles, nonpolitical events. Solid lines represent data from the first two blocks of trials; broken lines are data from the last two blocks.

across halves. Between Blocks 2 and 3 subjects switched from periods defined in one way (personally or publicly) to periods defined in the opposite way. It seems quite possible that some subjects realized soon after this change that the public periods were coextensive with the personal ones. This would have allowed them to use whichever type of period definition seemed most convenient for the rest of their trials. Because of this distinction between the two parts of the experiment, we consider the results of the two halves separately.

On the basis of the protocol findings, we predicted that subjects would be faster in locating political events with respect to public rather than personal intervals but would be faster in locating nonpolitical events with respect to personal rather than public intervals. Data from the first two blocks of the present experiment bear out this prediction: Reaction times were 107 ms faster when subjects had to decide if a political event happened during the Carter or Reagan administration than when they had to decide if it happened while they were in high school or college. However, reaction times were 220 ms *slower* when the subjects had to place a nonpolitical event as occurring during the Carter or the Reagan period than when they had to place it during their high school or their college years. The interaction between the political status of the events and the personal or public status of the periods was significant when either subjects or events served as the units in an analysis of variance [$F(1,22) = 9.73, p < .01$, in the subject analysis, and $F(1,38) = 4.65, p < .05$, in the events analysis]. This cross-over pattern appeared in both Blocks 1 and 2. Neither the political nature of the events nor the manner in which the periods were defined produced a reliable main effect (all $F$'s < 1). Error rates ran fairly high – 22% overall – and were nearly constant across conditions.

In the second half of the experiment the interaction between political status and period description disappeared almost completely. Figure 9.1 shows that reaction times for political events are again faster when they are compared to presidential terms – a difference of 162 ms. This time, however, nonpolitical events were also 142 ms faster for public periods than for personal ones. The advantage for publicly defined periods is reliable over events [$F(1,38) = 14.36, p < .01$], though not over subjects [$F(1,22) = 2.11, p > .10$]. Lack of significance in the subjects' analysis may be due to variability among subjects as to whether they should make use of the new period labels or convert them back to the labels they had used in the previous two blocks. No other effects were reliable in either analysis of reaction times. The error rate in Blocks 3 and 4 was 20% and, once again, varied only slightly among conditions.

*A tentative explanation*

We take the results from Blocks 1 and 2 to indicate that political events may be more tightly interwoven than nonpolitical events with the public circumstances in which they played a part. Conversely, nonpolitical events may be more firmly anchored than political events in the personal occasions within which they were experienced. The first of these facts is not difficult to explain. Important political events such as the signing of the Camp David accord have clear implications for other national and international happenings. Indeed, any explanation of these events is likely to allude to prior public occurrences and probable consequences, including effects on administration policies. Thus, it is not surprising that subjects in the protocol study often mentioned narratively related events in dating these items. For the same reason, subjects in the period study were relatively quick to identify political events as having taken place during Carter's (or Reagan's) term of office. Nonpolitical events, on the other hand, tend to exist in a more independent fashion. For example, the Jonestown suicides, despite their notoriety, had little impact on other public events of the same period. We would therefore expect them to elicit fewer causally related events in the protocol experiment and to be more difficult to assign to a presidential period.

What is more difficult to understand about these data is the privilege that nonpolitical events enjoy with respect to autobiographical information. One possibility here is that nonpolitical events have greater personal impact than their political counterparts. Political events may be, on the whole, more re- mote than nonpolitical events and less likely to have an effect on people's daily lives. As a result, people may tend to remember the personal circum- stances of nonpolitical events more clearly than those of political events. This would help account for the trend we observed for nonpolitical items to elicit more autobiographical material than political events, as well as for the faster reaction times when subjects classified nonpolitical events as happening while they were in either high school or college (Figure 9.1, Blocks 1 and 2). This account is also consistent with Rubin and Kozin's (1984) finding that "vivid memories" are associated with events that have high-rated personal impor- tance. Of course, it is easy to find counterexamples of political events that have greater personal import than nonpolitical ones. But if our set of stimuli is a fair sample, these cases may be in a minority.

At this stage, obviously, these hypotheses are speculative. The political/ nonpolitical distinction is coarse, with each category covering a wide range of events with distinct attributes. Exactly which of these attributes matters in predicting memory performance is a problem that goes beyond what we can hope to answer here. The main value of the distinction is that it gives us some hints about where to start looking for a deeper theory.

## Conclusion

The research presented in this chapter is a first attempt to understand memo- ries of public events such as the Three Mile Island accident or the deposition of the shah of Iran. The results indicate that the knowledge one stores con- cerning a current event may include facts about the event itself (participants, locations, types of actions), facts relating the event to other events (actions that caused the event, actions resulting from the event), and facts about the event's personal context (how and where the event was learned, with whom the event has been discussed).

We have focused on the link between public and personal memories. Pre- vious studies of flashbulb events suggest that these momentous public inci- dents are stored with personal information. The results of the two studies presented here extend these findings, demonstrating that lesser public memories also have an autobiographical component. However, the relation between public and personal memories is not a simple one. Availability of personal information depends on the content of the remembered event: People are faster to retrieve, and more likely to use, personal information when dating nonpolitical events than when dating political ones.

This research has also demonstrated that the facts recalled to support inductions can provide important hints about a complex knowledge domain. We were able to observe two such clues in the protocols of subjects dating public events. First, subjects retrieved more causally related events when dating political occurrences than when dating nonpolitical ones, suggesting that the political items were more likely to belong to identifiable narratives. Second, we found that subjects mentioned more autobiographical facts when dating nonpolitical than when dating political events, a trend that was confirmed by the reaction-time experiment reported in the last section. These observations strengthen our confidence that inductive judgments highlight organizational properties of very long-term memory and suggest that our research strategy might serve as an entry point for investigating other forms of naturalistic memory.

## References

Baddeley, A. D. (1982). Domains of recollection. *Psychological Review, 89*, 708–729.

Baddeley, A. D., Lewis, V., & Nimmo-Smith, I. (1978). When did you last . . . ? In M. M. Gruneberg, P. E. Morris, & R. N. Sykes (Eds.), *Practical aspects of memory* (pp. 77–83). New York: Academic Press.

Brown, N. R., Rips, L. J., & Shevell, S. K. (1985). Subjective dates of natural events in very-long-term memory. *Cognitive Psychology, 17*, 139–177.

Brown, R., & Kulik, J. (1977). Flashbulb memories. *Cognition, 5*, 73–99.

Collins, A. M. (1978). Fragments of a theory of human plausible reasoning. In D. Waltz (Ed.), *Theoretical issues in natural language processing – 2*, (pp. 194–201). Urbana: University of Illinois.

Danto, A. C. (1956). On explanations in history. *Philosophy of Science, 23*, 15–30.

Gallie, W. B. (1964). *Philosophy and the historical understanding*. New York: Schocken.

Godden, D. R., & Baddeley, A. D. (1975). Context-dependent memory in two natural environments: On land and under water. *British Journal of Psychology, 66*, 325–331.

Hayes, P. J. (1979). The naive physics manifesto. In D. Michie (Ed.), *Expert systems in the micro-electronic age* (pp. 242–270). Edinburgh: Edinburgh University Press.

Kolodner, J. (1983a). Maintaining organization in a dynamic long term memory. *Cognitive Science, 7*, 243–280.

(1983b). Reconstructive memory: A computer model. *Cognitive Science, 7*, 281–328.

Lieury, A., Aiello, B., Lepreux, D., & Mellet, M. (1980). Le rôle des repères dans la récupération et la datation des souvenirs. *L'Année psychologique, 80*, 149–167.

Light, L. L., Stansbury, C., Rubin, C., & Linde, S. (1973). Memory for modality of presentation: Within-modality discrimination. *Memory and Cognition, 1*, 395–400.

Lindsay, P. H., & Norman, D. A. (1975). *Human information processing: An introduction to psychology*. New York: Academic Press.

Linton, M. (1975). Memory for real-world events. In D. A. Norman & D. E. Rumelhart (Eds.), *Explorations in cognition* (pp. 376–404). San Francisco: Freeman.

Loftus, E. F., & Marburger, W. (1983). Since the eruption of Mt. St. Helens, has anyone beaten you up? Improving the accuracy of retrospective reports with landmark events. *Memory and Cognition, 11,* 114–120.

Mandelbaum, M. (1967). A note on history as narrative. *History and Theory, 6,* 413–419.

Mandler, J. M., Seegmiller, D., & Day, J. (1977). On the coding of spatial information. *Memory and Cognition, 5,* 10–16.

Neisser, U. (1982). Snapshot or benchmarks? In U. Neisser (Ed.), *Memory observed: Remembering in natural contexts* (pp. 43–48). San Francisco: Freeman.

Pillemer, D. B. (1984). Flashbulb memories and the assassination attempt on President Reagan. *Cognition, 16,* 63–80.

Rothkopf, E. Z. (1971). Incidental memory for location of information in text. *Journal of Verbal Learning and Verbal Behavior, 10,* 608–613.

Rubin, D. C., & Kozin, M. (1984). Vivid memories. *Cognition, 16,* 81–95.

Rumelhart, D. E. (1975). Notes on a schema for stories. In D. G. Bobrow & A. Collins (Eds.), *Representation and understanding* (pp. 211–236). New York: Academic Press.

Schulman, A. I. (1973). Recognition, memory, and the coding of spatial location. *Memory and Cognition, 1,* 256–260.

Smith, S. M. (1979). Remembering in and out of context. *Journal of Experimental Psychology: Human Learning and Memory, 5,* 342–361.

Sudman, S., & Bradburn, N. M. (1973). Effects of time and memory factors on responses in surveys. *Journal of the American Statistical Association, 68,* 805–815.

Thompson, C. P. (1982). Memory for unique personal events: The roommate study. *Memory and Cognition, 10,* 324–332.

Underwood, B. J. (1977). *Temporal codes in memory.* Hillsdale, NJ: Erlbaum.

White, H. (1980). The value of narrativity in the representation of reality. *Critical Inquiry, 7,* 5–27.

White, M. (1963). The logic of historical narration. In S. Hook (Ed.), *Philosophy and history* (pp. 3–31). New York: New York University Press.

Winograd, E., & Killinger, W. A., Jr. (1983). Relating age at encoding in early childhood to adult recall: Development of flashbulb memories. *Journal of Experimental Psychology: General, 112,* 413–422.

Yarmey, A. D., & Bull, M. P., III. (1978). Where were you when President Kennedy was assassinated? *Bulletin of the Psychonomic Society, 11,* 133–135.

# 10     Temporal reference systems and autobiographical memory

*John A. Robinson*

## Introduction and theoretical orientation

Everyday life is dominated by routines. The flow of action is structured by the recurrent requirements of our society. We work, play, and worship according to timetables that have evolved over centuries and that provide a shared temporal framework for our individual histories. The way we understand time is derived from the social and institutional regulation of action. Although we use clocks and calendars to mark time, we do not experience time as the succession of uniform units of duration. Rather, we experience time as action, and succession as either the repetition of an action or a change from one activity to another. When we have no prescribed activity to perform, as during vacations or in retirement, we may lose track of time or experience a sense of timelessness. Time and action codefine each other, and both are organized through the institutions of society.

Each person engages in a variety of socially regulated activities (e.g., work, schooling, recreation, worship). For convenience I will refer to these various activities as domains of action. I think it is self-evident that participation in a domain of action engenders an appropriate cognitive representation of the temporal pattern associated with it. Viewed as socially prescribed routines, these patterns function as timetables (or schedules or calendars). I shall refer to the cognitive representations of such timetables as *temporal reference systems*. These representations are schemata that codify when and in what order activities occur for a given domain of action. Temporal reference systems play a vital role in cognition. Because our activities conform to timetables, we are able to plan our behavior, coordinate the demands of differing schedules, and make appropriate adjustments when unexpected circumstances disrupt our plans. The expectations that we generate from our temporal reference systems constitute a temporal horizon (Fraisse, 1963). This

I wish to thank John Boles, Ken McNiel, Pak Ng, and Susan Rhodes for helping me collect and analyze the data reported in this essay.

159

horizon is dynamic, reflecting the continually renewed stream of expectations generated by the interplay between planned and completed action. The temporal component of our reality orientation is probably dependent upon our capacity to construct such expectations and to check their validity. I think it likely that temporal reference systems, by virtue of their active role in shaping our expectations and plans, serve as a cognitive background for all conscious thought and perception and impart temporal signs to the processes of consciousness. In this manner temporal information may be automatically encoded, as Hasher and Zacks (1979) have proposed. Temporal reference systems also play a role in remembering. Our knowledge of timetables can guide efforts to recapitulate or reconstruct some episodes as well as our efforts to deduce the times of occurrence for events in the past. Thus, temporal reference systems enable us to maintain a functionally appropriate sense of time, guide our expectations and plans for the future, and provide a framework for reconstructing the past.

Each domain of action has its own timetable, but all domains are organized by reference to a universal temporal period, the year. The differences between domains and their respective timetables arise from the way each differentiates the year into temporal segments and in the ways those segments can be sequenced. Consider the typical year of a farmer, a professional athlete, a clergyman, a student, and a factory worker: The seasons of the athlete are not the same as the seasons the farmer contends with; the liturgical calendar is quite different from the secular school calendar; the factory worker endures an almost undifferentiated year of labor. In spite of these differences there are a number of structuring principles that are the same across domains.

1.  The year is segmented into temporal periods.
2.  Temporal periods are defined in terms of requisite activities, that is, what must be done now, what must be done next, what is to be done later. I propose that temporal periods represent a type of categorization based on modal or typical activities. By analogy to the color spectrum, time is segmented into regions (periods), and each region is defined by the common activity that is performed in that time span. By definition, the boundaries of temporal periods are designated by the initiation or completion of an appropriate activity and a transition to some other type of activity.
3.  The relationship between temporal periods derives from one or more contrastive features. There is always at least one contrast of activity (e.g., work vs. vacation). Additional contrasts may be organized hierarchically. For example, the school year consists of a major contrast between school terms and vacations. Each of the two major activity classes is further differentiated: fall term versus winter–spring term; Christmas–New Year vacation versus summer vacation. Pro-

fessional athletics is organized into the season of competition and the "off season," but the former is further divided into preseason training and postseason tournaments. It is worth noting that, even if the primary activity is continued into the nominally contrasting period, subjectively the temporal period retains its definition. This is recognized by such labels as "summer school," "off-season play," and by wage policies that authorize extra compensation for work on holidays.

4. A year is, by definition, the completion of one cycle of some activity pattern. A functional year need not, however, coincide with the calendar year. For students, a new year functionally begins when school resumes after summer vacation, that is, in August or September rather than in January. I conjecture that, as a general rule, a new annual cycle is felt to begin when the person's principal activity resumes after an interval of contrasting activity. The timing of successive temporal periods within a given domain of action can also vary from one instance to the next. In some domains the timing is largely dependent upon natural processes (e.g., farming, construction); in other domains social or institutional factors regulate the timing of periods.

There are, of course, many details of action and its organization in any domain that are not captured by these structuring principles. Here I wish only to emphasize two general points: First, viewed from the perspective of clock and calendar, time is nominally the same for all members of a society, but experientially time varies across domains of action. Second, there are, nevertheless, some generic principles by which time and action are costructured.

Because temporal reference systems represent domain timetables, they must embody the structural properties of the timetable. Therefore, temporal schemata must, at a minimum, codify the temporal periods and the sequencing of those periods for the domains they represent. I will refer to this proposition as the *structural hypothesis*. I have proposed that the segmentation of time into periods is analogous to a process of categorization. Some investigators (e.g., Rosch, 1975) have concluded that categories are organized around prototypical stimuli, which serve as cognitive reference points for discrimination and classification. Perhaps temporal categories also have reference points. Because it is activity that is categorized, the most salient aspects would be the beginning and ending of an activity class. The activity that initiates or concludes a class and the characteristic intervals of time when those occur may function as temporal reference points. I will refer to this as the *reference points hypothesis*.

The timetable associated with a person's occupation is the predominant source of temporal organization in everyday life, but it is not the only source. All timetables are subject to the overriding interests of society in marking certain events or persons for celebration. Secular and religious holidays punctuate the year at frequent intervals and are regarded as occasions for suspending regular activities. In principle, domain timetables must be integrated with society's celebratory cycle. There are, of course, personal events of recurrent significance (e.g., birthdays, anniversaries) that constitute another celebratory cycle, but they are not typically regarded as legitimate occasions for suspending work or school. Finally, many people are involved in two or more occupations concurrently or in a number of subordinate but regularly scheduled activities, thus multiplying the number of temporal patterns in their lives. Taken together, these varied sources of temporal organization may be said to constitute a person's *temporal frame of reference*. An interesting consequence of the multiplicity of timetables is that the calendar months can vary substantially in salience owing to the varying density of marker events. For example, a month that contains a major holiday and a birthday or anniversary and that coincides with the ending of a temporal period in one's occupational activity is rich in temporal markers. The salience profile for the months will naturally depend upon each person's collection of timetables.

In the remainder of this chapter I will report a series of studies focused on one specific timetable, namely, the school year. I chose it as a place to begin empirical research on timetables for three reasons: It is familiar; it is generic; it has a useful degree of differentiation and organization. It is preferable to begin research on a clear example of a phenomenon before investigating variants or less prototypical cases. Schooling is a nearly universal experience in our society, one that most people experience directly as students and indirectly as parents of students. In fact, a large proportion of the population accommodate their daily lives to the school calendar for three or more decades. The studies to be reported explore the temporal reference system for the school year in a number of ways. Descriptive and experimental methods were used, often in combination. The first two studies were designed to directly assess the structural hypothesis and the reference points hypothesis. The remaining three studies explored the influence of the school-year timetable on remembering. There are two methodological caveats I wish to mention before proceeding. First, as previously noted, the timing of temporal units can vary according to circumstance. In Kentucky, school resumes in late August and ends sometime in May or June depending upon level and district. In other locales those points may occur earlier or later than in ours. The fact does not alter the conceptual analysis, but it does mean that the empirical results could be expected to be somewhat different for other populations. Second, the unit of analysis adopted in these studies is the year and its division into months.

This choice introduced some imprecision into the analyses but seemed preferable to any other I could conceive. The beginning or ending of activity classes does not neatly coincide with the beginning or ending of months. Nevertheless, the regularity and consistency of the results obtained seem to justify my decision. A more serious difficulty is that the Christmas–New Year vacation, which is one of the two major vacation periods of students, could not be isolated without altering the unit of analysis. I decided to accept that limitation because these are basically exploratory studies.

My own understanding of the school year, as a lifelong participant in the schooling process, guided the empirical studies reported in the next section. As I view it, the school-year timetable consists of two major school terms (fall and winter–spring) and two major vacation periods (Christmas–New Year and summer). Various other subdivisions of the school terms are in use depending upon level (e.g., high school vs. college) and locale. But the recess from school at Christmas and in the summer is observed throughout our society. In effect the two major vacations standardize the year into two periods of schooling alternating with lengthy vacations. I regard this as the generic pattern of the school-year timetable. However, for reasons already discussed only three periods – the two school terms and summer vacation – are identified in the following investigations.

**Empirical studies**

*Cognitive status of the school-year timetable*

A technique introduced by DeSoto and Bosley (1962) was adapted to directly test the proposition that the temporal schema for the school year differentiates at least three temporal periods. A free recall learning task was devised using the months of the year as "stimulus" elements and categorizable words as "response" elements. According to my theoretical analysis the three major units of the school-year calendar are subsequences that function as temporal categories. If this is correct, then a list in which the stimulus and response categories are congruent should be easier to learn than a list in which the members of one category overlap the members of the other category. In effect, a congruent list should reduce the problem of association to one of mapping the units of the temporal schema directly into comparable semantic categories. The overlapping or incongruent arrangement should interfere with the mapping and be more difficult to learn.

From 12 semantic categories in the Battig and Montague (1969) norms, 36 words were selected. A sample of the words used in this experiment and their

Table 10.1. *Month–word groupings (Experiment II)*

|        | School-year order | | |
|        | Congruent | Incongruent | Distributed |
|--------|-----------|-------------|-------------|
| Sep    | Wrench    | Accountant  | Wrench      |
| Oct    | Pliers    | Salesman    | Oboe        |
| Nov    | Drill     | Wrench      | Nurse       |
| Dec    | Lathe     | Pliers      | Tuba        |
| Jan    | Oboe      | Drill       | Accountant  |
| Feb    | Tuba      | Lathe       | Pliers      |
| Mar    | Harp      | Oboe        | Organ       |
| Apr    | Cello     | Tuba        | Fireman     |
| May    | Organ     | Harp        | Drill       |
| Jun    | Nurse     | Cello       | Salesman    |
| Jly    | Accountant| Organ       | Lathe       |
| Aug    | Salesman  | Nurse       | Cello       |

|        | Calendar-year order | | |
|        | Congruent | Incongruent | Distributed |
|--------|-----------|-------------|-------------|
| Jan    | Oboe      | Drill       | Accountant  |
| Feb    | Tuba      | Lathe       | Pliers      |
| Mar    | Harp      | Oboe        | Organ       |
| Apr    | Cello     | Tuba        | Fireman     |
| May    | Organ     | Harp        | Drill       |
| Jun    | Nurse     | Cello       | Salesman    |
| Jly    | Accountant| Organ       | Lathe       |
| Aug    | Salesman  | Nurse       | Cello       |
| Sep    | Wrench    | Accountant  | Wrench      |
| Oct    | Pliers    | Salesman    | Oboe        |
| Nov    | Drill     | Wrench      | Nurse       |
| Dec    | Lathe     | Pliers      | Tuba        |

various arrangements is given in Table 10.1. Each month was paired with three words, each from a different semantic category. Thus, each list consisted of 36 month-word pairs. The relationship of congruence or incongruence pertains to the mapping of semantic categories onto the presumed temporal categories. Within categories the specific month-word pairings were arbitrarily determined. In addition to the congruent and incongruent arrangements already described, a third arrangement was included. In this arrangement, words were distributed among the three temporal categories. Because the temporal categories are of unequal size there was necessarily some repetition of semantic categories in two out of three cases. The distributed list minimizes the correspondence of temporal and semantic categories and provides a useful base line for comparing performance on the other two arrangements. The month-word pairs were presented in one of two temporal orders, the calendar-year order (January . . . December) or the school-year order (September . . . August). The combination of presentation orders and structural patterns thus produced a 2 × 3 factorial design for this experiment.

The three words paired with a month were displayed successively (e.g., September–Wrench; September–Velvet; September–Lira). Each pair appeared on the screen of a video monitor for 3 seconds and was immediately replaced by its successor. After the last pair was shown subjects were given 2 minutes to record as many of the words as they could remember. A structured response sheet was provided listing the months (in appropriate order) as columns with three blank lines below each month. Following a warm-up test, subjects were given six study–test trials. The instructions stated that the experiment was examining various ways of organizing time. The subjects were told that there was a pattern underlying the month–word pairs and that they should try to figure it out. Serving as subjects were 108 students, 18 in each of the six conditions of the experiment.

The average number of words correctly recalled and matched with appropriate months is shown in Figures 10.1 and 10.2 for the school-year and calendar-year order, respectively. These recall data were analyzed in a 2 (Order) × 3 (Arrangement) × 6 (Trials) repeated measures analysis of variance. The effect of presentation order was not significant, but the effect of arrangement was highly significant, $F(2,102) = 32.22$, $MS_e = 57.36$, $p < .001$. The effect of trials was also significant, $F(5,510) = 495.31$, $MS_e = 16.61$, $p < .001$, and the order × arrangement interaction was nearly significant ($p < .10$). Using the Neuman–Keuls procedure post-hoc tests showed that performance on the congruent list was significantly better than performance on either the incongruent or distributed lists for both presentation orders. The incongruent and distributed lists did not differ significantly in either presentation order.

A second analysis examined performance in each of the three presumptive temporal categories. The recall data were pooled over trials and aggregated within temporal units to determine correct recall percentage for each temporal category. These data are summarized in Table 10.2. Use of two presentation orders necessarily confounded temporal category and list position, so these results were analyzed separately for calendar-year and school-year groups. The outcome of the analysis, however, was the same for both groups: a significant effect of arrangement [$F(2,51) = 5.82$ and 15.44 for the calendar and school groups, respectively, both $p < .01$]; a significant effect for temporal unit [$F(2,104) = 11.25$ and 23.97, respectively, both $p < .01$]; and a

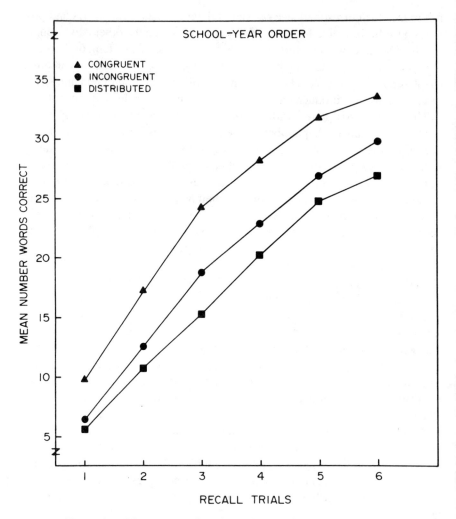

Figure 10.1. Mean number of words recalled per trial in each condition (school-year presentation order)

significant arrangement by unit interaction [$F(4,102) = 2.95$ and $4.29$, respectively, both $p < .05$]. The results of this analysis demonstrate that the advantage of the congruent arrangement affected each of the presumed temporal units or categories. There are some interesting differences in the pattern of performance associated with the two presentation orders. However, because of the confounding of temporal unit, unit size, and list position, these patterns cannot be reliably interpreted.

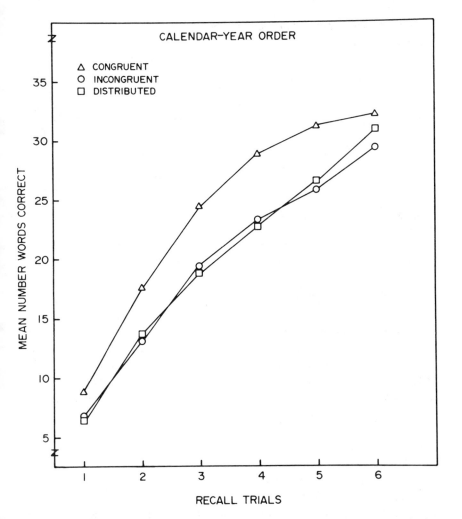

Figure 10.2. Mean number of words recalled per trial in each condition (calendar-year presentation order)

The results of this experiment are consistent with the proposition that the cognitive schema for the school-year timetable functionally differentiates at least three temporal units. That is, the outcome strongly supports the structural hypothesis. Furthermore, the fact that presentation order had no effect on learning indicates that the units of the school-year schema can be identified independently of their calendar sequence.

Table 10.2. *Words correct per temporal unit (mean %)*

|               | Calendar-year order | | |
|               | Congruent | Incongruent | Distributed |
|---------------|-----------|-------------|-------------|
| Winter/spring | 65.68 | 50.98 | 53.21 |
| Summer        | 66.67 | 45.47 | 49.59 |
| Fall          | 67.49 | 66.13 | 61.03 |
|               | School-year order | | |
|               | Congruent | Incongruent | Distributed |
| Fall          | 70.37 | 63.66 | 52.93 |
| Winter/spring | 57.04 | 47.78 | 38.89 |
| Summer        | 79.32 | 51.13 | 56.07 |

## Temporal patterns of affectivity

The organization of the calendar year into alternating terms of school and vacation imposes a succession of short-term goals on students. Each school term culminates in evaluations and is followed by a period of contrasting types of activity. Similarly, each vacation must end and school work resume. These observations imply that there is an affective pattern extending over the calendar year coordinate with and determined by the temporal pattern governing the primary daily activity of schooling. It can be deduced from the structural hypothesis that the affective pattern of a year for students will consist of subpatterns corresponding to the school terms and summer vacation. From the reference points hypothesis it can also be predicted that the months coinciding with beginnings and endings of timetable units should be associated with peak levels of affect.

Two previous studies have demonstrated that changes of affect are systematically associated with the school-year timetable. Osgood, May and Miron (1975) obtained semantic differential ratings of the calendar months from high school and college students. Their results are shown in Figure 10.3. The points have been separated at two intervals to highlight the three primary temporal units of the school year. Anyone involved in schooling will recognize the pattern of ratings: Summer is the most valued time, but endings of school terms represent other peaks of positive affect. The scoop-shaped profile for each school term indicates that beginning school again is a mildly positive time, but the dominant affective gradient is forward-looking toward the end of term. It is also apparent that there is an affective gradient that spans the entire calendar year: The average rating of the fall term is lower than that of

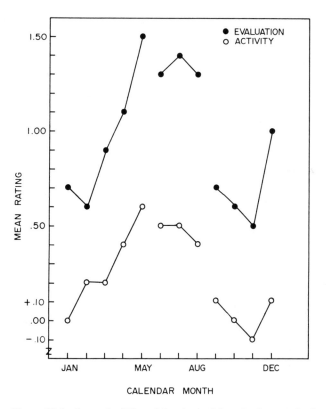

Figure 10.3. Semantic differential ratings of the calendar months (based on data in Osgood, May, & Miron, 1975)

the spring term, and the average of the summer is highest of all. This is easily understood. Not only is May the end of the school year; it represents the completion of a grade, and potentially, a change of status and also the long vacation, the most valued time, which lies ahead.

Nelson (1971) also documented cyclic changes in affectivity across the school year. His results are particularly valuable because they were obtained at a Canadian university operating on the quarter system rather than the semester system. Nelson had subjects evaluate several dimensions of mood at weekly intervals during a term. The results show a profile of changes in positive or negative mood for the sequence of three regular academic terms analogous to that obtained by Osgood, May, and Miron (1975) for the two-semester calendar. Both studies demonstrate that the molar temporal organization of action engenders comparable patterning of affectivity. In short, they mirror each other.

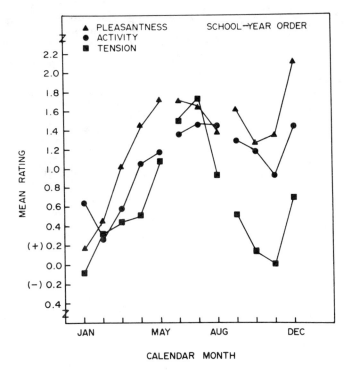

Figure 10.4. Mean composite ratings of the months judged in school-year order

I have replicated the results of Osgood, May, and Miron (1975) using a similar semantic differential methodology. The 12 calendar months were rated on each of nine bipolar adjectival scales by 98 undergraduates. The format of each scale and the rating instructions followed the standard procedure for semantic differential assessments. Each of the nine scales represented one of three dimensions of affectivity as follows: *pleasantness* (pleasant–unpleasant; important–unimportant; interesting–dull); *activity* (fast–slow; short–long, full–empty); *tension* (easy–difficult; flexible–rigid; relaxed–tense). Half of the subjects rated the months in the school-year order (September to August); half rated the months in the calendar-year order (January to December). Scale intervals were assigned scores ranging from + 3 to − 3. The first term of each pair given above was assigned positive values, the second term negative values. Composite scores were generated for each dimension of affectivity by averaging a subject's rating on the three constituent scales. The mean composite ratings of the months obtained in the two rating conditions are shown in Figures 10.4 and 10.5.

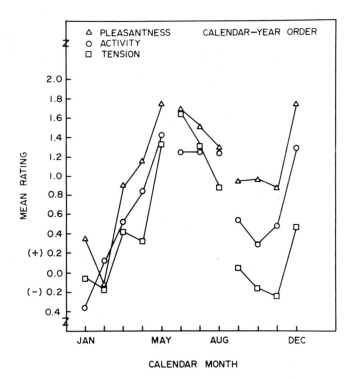

Figure 10.5. Mean composite ratings of the months judged in calendar-year order

The ratings were analyzed in a 2 (Order) × 3 (Scales) × 12 (Months) multivariate repeated measures analysis of variance. There was a significant difference between rating orders, $F(1,96) = 6.83$, $MS_e = 7.23$, $p < .01$. Overall, the school-year order produced somewhat higher ratings than the calendar-year order. However, neither the Order × Scales nor the Order × Month interaction was statistically significant. Thus, the pattern of ratings was the same for both orders. There were statistically significant effects associated with scales (Wilkes lambda = .495, p < .001) and months (lambda = .375, p < .001). The Month × Scale interaction was also significant (lambda = .429, p. < .001).

It is obvious that these results are sustantially the same as those of Osgood, May, and Miron (1975). The only difference is that we did not obtain a stepwise increment in positive affect for successive temporal periods. It is somewhat puzzling to find the steady increase in positive affect for the latter months of the winter–spring term. School demands and concern over evaluation outcomes are steadily increasing during these months, implying that the pattern found for the fall term should obtain. Nelson's (1971) findings are more congruent with common sense in this regard: Negative affect steadily increased across the weeks of each quarter, peaking at the end of the term. However, Nelson's students were reporting their own mood in a temporal context limited to the rating period, whereas our students and Osgood, May, and Miron's evaluated temporal periods in the context of the entire year. Nelson's data may be a truer reflection of experienced mood across the school year, whereas our results and those of Osgood, May, and Miron may reflect generalized perceptions of the school year that incorporate information about concurrent activities and seasonal changes as well as school matters.

The convergent evidence of these studies provides confirmation of the structural hypothesis. Patterned changes in affect clearly reflect the organization of the year into temporal periods corresponding to those that compose the school-year timetable. The evidence for the reference points hypothesis, however, is mixed. The endpoints of school terms do coincide with peak levels of affect (positive or negative), and beginnings are more positive than the following month in a period. But the most prominent and general feature is the forward-oriented gradient of affect increasing during school terms and decreasing during the summer. Endpoints are clearly more salient than beginnings. In a way that is not surprising: They constitute the completion of a period of effort, can entail a change of status, and lead into a period of contrasting activity. Perhaps the change of activity is solely responsible for the moderately elevated affect associated with beginnings. In any case, the reference points hypothesis as initially formulated is too tidy to fit the facts. Finally, it should be noted that the rating pattern obtained when the months were judged in their calendar order was the same as when the months were judged in their functional (school-year) order. To me this signifies that the functional order is the natural one for students.

### The role of the schema in memory retrieval

The next two studies explored the role of the school-year timetable in memory retrieval. The first study explored temporal features in the free recall of life events. We may speculate about the retrieval processes required to perform this simple task. The subject must first generate useful retrieval cues. The school-year schema certainly provides one set of structured cues. These cues are at varying levels of specificity: "School" and "summer" are generic cues that can be translated into more specific cues corresponding to the constituent months. These, in turn, vary in their utility. Some months are associated with recurrent and predictable activities (e.g., birthdays, trips, proms, and graduations), and others are not. Variation in cue specificity may affect the generation of memory reports in two ways: first, in identifying discrete events that the person can assess for remembrances; second, as an associative node that can be used to evoke recollections of temporally contiguous incidents.

Two predictions can be made about performance in the free recall task if we assume that the school-year schema is used to guide memory retrieval. First, the structural hypothesis predicts that memory reports should cluster in recall in groupings coinciding with the major temporal units of the reference system. Second, the reference points hypothesis predicts that certain months are more useful as cues to prompt recollections than other months. Specifically, the months marking the beginning and ending of temporal units should elicit more memory reports than nonreference-point months. This prediction is based on the assumption that reference-point months are associated with specifiable events that, in turn, can be used to evoke other recollections.

Participating in this study were 40 students, 20 in each group. One group engaged in free recall of life events in late November, another group in late April. Because the semesters end in early December and May at the University of Louisville the times chosen were as near to term endpoints as one could practically get and expect to complete the study. Subjects were instructed to report 20 life experiences from the past year or two and were given structured response booklets to record the reports. They were further instructed that the events should be from their own experience rather than public events or the experiences of friends. After recording 20 memories the subjects dated each reported event. They also classified each event according to importance (very important, important, not important) and judged the relative frequency of event rehearsal or mental review in the month after the event and within the past week.

In Figure 10.6 the distribution of reports according to months is shown for both the November and the April groups. The number of reports that were dated as occurring more than 16 months ago was so small (ca. 5%) and irregularly distributed that they were omitted from any data analysis. Also, in order to examine the two groups on comparable temporal units, the data for the 16th month of the April distribution were omitted. Thus, the proportions shown in Figure 10.6 are based on 96% and 94% of the total reports in the November and April groups, respectively. The abscissa of Figure 10.6 identifies calendar months in reverse order beginning with April, that is, the month in which the study was first conducted. This ordering corresponds to the retention interval.

It is quite apparent that the distribution of reports displays the same pattern in both groups and that the discontinuities in the distribution correspond to the temporal units of the school-year calendar. The clustering of memory reports according to the temporal units of the school-year schema was assessed

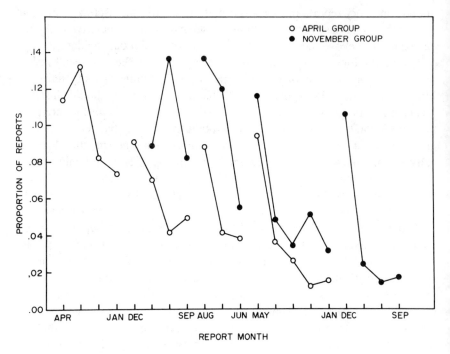

Figure 10.6. Proportion of memory reports per month in unconstrained free recall

by means of the Bousfield and Bousfield (1966) category repetition measure. They also provide a formula for determining whether reports from the same category occur contiguously in recall more often than would be expected by chance. For the two groups combined the mean number of category repetitions was 6.95. This significantly exceeds the mean chance expectation of 4.83, $t(38) = 4.47$, $p < .001$. Thus, the order of reports exhibited organization consistent with the assumption that the temporal units of the school-year schema were actively used in unconstrained memory retrieval.

The memory reports were classified by the subjects as either very important, important, or unimportant. The percentage of reports assigned in each category by the November and April groups, respectively, was: very important, 30.79%, 25.44%; important, 31.67%, 27.78%; unimportant, 37.53%, 46.78%. If variations in the number of reports given per month reflect comparable variations in the relative importance, hence memorability, of events, then we should find a similar pattern of values for both measures. In fact, such a finding would not be surprising because reference-point months are associated with major holidays and other events of personal or social significance, graduation, for example. However, the pattern of importance ratings obtained was not that regular. For the November group the mean importance ratings for reports in two of the temporal segments (summer and winter–spring) mirrored the report frequencies. The rank-order correlation between proportion of reports per month and mean importance was $+.55(df = 15)$, $p < .05$, for the November group. In contrast, there was no correlation between proportion of reports and mean importance (rho $= -.12$) for the April group. I cannot explain this difference between groups, but considering that the pattern of report frequencies is the same in both groups it is fair to conclude that event importance cannot provide a general account of the pattern of event recall.

The relative rehearsal frequency of each report was also judged by respondents. They indicated how often each event was reviewed for a period of time following the event (a week to a month) and during the week preceding the study. The frequency categories used were Very Often, Often, Occasionally, and Not until Now. Subjects were told to use their own experience to interpret the frequency labels. For purposes of scoring the frequency categories were assigned values of 4 (Very Often), 3, 2, and 1 (Not until Now). In both groups subjects reported rehearsing events more often in the period following the event than in the week preceding the study. Rehearsal frequency during the week preceding the study tended to be directly related to the recency of the event. In contrast, rehearsal in the period after an event was relatively stable across the retention period. In other words, as our subjects perceived the situation, they tended to think about events fairly often in their aftermath but progressively less often as time elapsed. The rank-order correlation between mean recent rehearsal and proportion of reports per month was marginally significant for both groups (rho $= .49$ and $.47\ p < .10$), but earlier rehearsal frequency was not correlated with report frequency in either group.

A content analysis of memory reports provided important information about the pattern of event recall. The reports were first sorted into two categories: school-related activities and nonschool-related activities. Both curricular and extracurricular events were included in the school-related category. Thus, athletic events, social activities, exams, graduations, field trips, and so on were all classified as school-related activities. A second classification of the reports divided them into scheduled events and nonscheduled events. Scheduled events are annual or seasonal events associated with predictable times of the year. Thus, birthdays, anniversaries, major holidays and associated activities, the Kentucky Derby, and the state fair, as well as registration and orientation, graduation, and senior prom were all classified as scheduled events. The two types of classification are not mutually exclusive, but they do address somewhat different questions about potential sources of orderliness in the very diverse body of memory reports.

Table 10.3. *Content analysis of memory reports: reports per month classified as school-related activities or as scheduled events (%)*

|       | School-related activities | Scheduled events |
|-------|---------------------------|------------------|
| Sep   | 32.30                     | 5.60             |
| Oct   | 42.60                     | 21.30            |
| Nov   | 27.00                     | 15.30            |
| Dec   | 26.50                     | 55.55            |
| Jan   | 61.00                     | 2.60             |
| Feb   | 35.00                     | 10.60            |
| Mar   | 41.30                     | 17.00            |
| Apr   | 47.30                     | 16.70            |
| May   | 65.00                     | 57.50            |
| Jun   | 12.50                     | 10.00            |
| Jly   | 20.00                     | 28.00            |
| Aug   | 40.00                     | 24.50            |

Initially, the reports were aggregated separately by month and group for classification. The resulting distributions were very similar for the April and November group and for replicated months (e.g., April through January in the April group), so the reports of both groups were pooled for final analysis. These data are summarized in Table 10.3. For the months composing the two school terms, one quarter to two thirds of the reports were of school-related activities with a particularly regular pattern appearing in the winter–spring term. The predominance of school-related activities in the reference-point months of January, May, and August is noteworthy. The analysis of scheduled events identified December and May as peaks with October and July as lesser concentrations. Furthermore, the pattern of scheduled events per month exhibits a progressive increase from beginning to ending of each temporal unit. The relationship between the two classifications varies across the year. For example, in January 61% of the reports related to school, but only 3% qualified as scheduled events, school or otherwise. In December the relationship was reversed: 56% of the reports were of scheduled events – typically holiday activities – but only 27% related to school activities. In May the two classifications converge: Most of the scheduled events were school related, for example, proms, honors assemblies, graduations.

The results of the content analysis clearly indicate that the pattern of event recall was an expression of the subjects' temporal frame of reference, not just a reflection of an isolated temporal reference system. Culturally scheduled

events, school events, and diverse personal experiences were all mingled together in the protocols. The school-year reference system is the major component of students' temporal frame of reference, and the influence of that
system was confirmed by the occurrence of the significant clustering of reports by temporal periods. As with the preceding studies, the reference points
hypothesis was only partially confirmed. More reports were given for months
ending a temporal unit, and those tended to be culturally or scholastically
scheduled events. As before, however, the most reliable pattern feature was a
gradient, in this case of progressive increments in reports from beginning to
end of a temporal period. This suggested that a revision of the reference
points hypothesis may be in order, specifically, that temporal periods are cognitively anchored at their endpoints.

Before accepting this revision I felt it was necessary to rule out an obvious
alternative explanation of the prominence of endpoint events in the protocols.
It could be argued that the scoop-shaped distributions within units are an artifact of the order of memory search. The task favored a backward order of
search. If so, then imposing alternative temporal orders of recall should produce different profiles of report frequencies per month. This reasoning led me
to undertake a more structured exploration of temporally guided retrieval of
personal memories. The months were used as explicit retrieval cues, and subjects were to provide as many memories for each month as they could in a
fixed period of time. The months were presented in either chronological or
random order and in either forward or backward order. The combination of
these arrangements produced a 2 × 2 design for the study. The months were
grouped into three sets of four according to the particular combination desired
(e.g., January, February, March, April; December, July, May, February) and
were displayed on a time line at the top of a page in a response booklet.
Subjects were given 4 minutes per page (i.e., per 4-month block) to generate
and summarize memories of personal experiences that occurred in the specified months. After completing the retrieval phase, subjects dated their recollections. They were asked to provide the month and year for each event.
Furthermore, they were instructed to provide the correct date for any event
that had been initially recalled for an inappropriate month. The study was
conducted in January and introduced as a review of the year that had just
ended. There were 72 students participating in the experiment, 18 in each of
the four conditions.

The mean proportion of memory reports given per month is shown in Figure 10.7 for each of the four retrieval conditions. The data points are again
separated by temporal unit to facilitate inspection and interpretation. There
are some irregularities in the distributions, but the similarity of pattern across
the groups is striking. A multivariate 2 × 2 × 12 repeated measures analysis

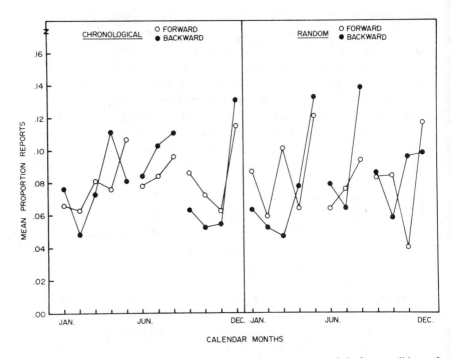

Figure 10.7. Mean proportion of memory reports per month in four conditions of temporally cued recall

of variance was performed on a number of reports per month. Significantly more reports were given in chronological retrieval orders ($\bar{x} = 20.11$) than in random retrieval orders ($\bar{x} = 16.39$), $F(1,68) = 6.34$, $MS_e = 2.95$, $p < .01$. There was no difference between forward and backward retrieval orders in number of reports. There was significant variation in number of reports per month, Wilks lambda $= .421$, $p < .001$, but none of the interactions between retrieval orders and months was significant. In short, the pattern of recall was the same in all four retrieval conditions. The pattern is familiar but is especially clear when the data from all four groups are pooled as is shown in Figure 10.8

All memory reports were classified according to the criteria used in the preceding study to determine the frequency of school-related activities and the frequency of scheduled events for each month. The distribution of reports in these two categories was again very similar across groups, so averages across groups were calculated. In Table 10.4 the mean percentage of reports in each classification is given for each month. It is apparent that these data essentially replicate those of the preceding study. The percentage of school-

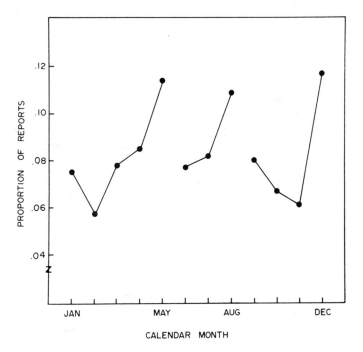

Figure 10.8. Mean proportion of memory reports per month in temporally cued recall (all groups)

Table 10.4. *Reports classified as school-related or as scheduled events (all groups, mean %)*

|  | School-related | Scheduled |
|---|---|---|
| Jan | 26.83 | 32.73 |
| Feb | 29.85 | 23.99 |
| Mar | 33.01 | 19.39 |
| Apr | 37.29 | 31.93 |
| May | 42.00 | 44.52 |
| Jun | 15.08 | 27.32 |
| Jly | 11.25 | 28.79 |
| Aug | 33.21 | 39.49 |
| Sep | 39.73 | 32.12 |
| Oct | 19.92 | 45.54 |
| Nov | 19.87 | 33.91 |
| Dec | 19.82 | 50.75 |

related activities reported increased across months in the winter–spring term and in the summer unit but decreased across months in the fall term. Scheduled events were reported somewhat more often in this study than in the preceding one (33% overall vs. 23%), but the distribution across months was essentially the same. Scheduled events were most frequently reported for May, August, October, and December. The scheduled events reported for May were primarily recollections of graduation and related activities. Those reported for December were typically recollections of holiday activities.

These results and those of the preceding study demonstrate that there is significant and orderly variation in the utility of the different months as temporal cues for memory retrieval. More important, however, is the demonstration that the pattern of event recall is not an artifact of the temporal order of memory search. The results of a content analysis of memory reports indicated that the type and relative frequency of school activities and of scheduled events were similar in all retrieval conditions. This implies that the effectiveness of the month cues in evoking discrete events accounts for the common pattern in the proportional distributions of reports across months. The differences between chronological and random retrieval orders in absolute number of reports may then be due to a second factor, namely, effectiveness of retrieved events in evoking other recollections from the same or contiguous temporal interval.

## The role of temporal reference information in event dating

A final study explored the influence of the school-year schema on memory dating. Common experience indicates that we ascribe dates to remembered events through a process of comparison. That is, we identify some event as a reference point and judge whether a recollected event came before or after the reference event. There are, of course, several other sources of information (e.g., place, season, companion, etc.) that can assist us in narrowing down the possible dates for an event. However, the question I chose to pursue was the influence of contrasting types of temporal reference information on memory dating, namely, a temporal reference schema and a single temporal reference point. The school-year schema provides a structured representation of the entire calendar year and offers a number of temporal reference points and retrieval cues for comparison purposes. One's birthday, on the other hand, constitutes a single reference point but one of high salience and distinctiveness. Both types of reference information are based on stable and recurrent timetables. In theory, use of them might lead to contrasting patterns of inferences about times of occurrence. For example, using a fixed reference point might generate assimilation effects, that is, a tendency to judge events as having occurred nearer to the reference point than was the case. In contrast, use of the school-year frame of reference might generate displacement effects, for example, dating an event that occurred in the fall term as having occurred in the spring term or vice versa.

Initially, I intended to conduct a study of dating accuracy by investigating memory dating of significant public events. I abandoned that plan for two reasons: First, in order to assess the influence of the school-year schema I needed event memories that spanned a number of years of schooling and were reasonably diverse. Significant public events are often disasters of one kind or another and represent a very special class of experiences. Second, students, at least in their high school years, have a very limited interest in news and current events. Consequently, they might not recognize many news events and would rely too heavily on guessing in their reports. A subject should have a reasonable amount of event information available if we are to get a true appraisal of the potential bias associated with the use of temporal reference information in event dating. These considerations led me to a study of the reliability rather than the accuracy of memory dating. The basic approach was to elicit a sample of memories from the high school years and have these dated. These recollections were redated 2 weeks later, using either the school-year structure or a birthday as temporal references. The consistency of event dating and specifically, the number and distribution of discrepancies between the dates given in the two sessions provide evidence about the effect of temporal reference information on memory dating.

A prompt-word technique was used to elicit memories (cf. Robinson, 1976). From the Paivio, Yuille, and Madigan (1968) norms, 31 words were selected that were high in concreteness and, in my judgment, likely to elicit memories from the adolescent years. The 31 words selected sampled several domains of experience: school (*speech, ink*), work (*boss, hammer*), recreation (*cabin, river*), interpersonal relations (*party, kiss*), and so on. Of 30 students participating in the study, 15 were assigned to the school-year condition, 15 to the birthday condition. They were asked to recall an event from their own lives in response to each of the prompt words and were instructed to focus their recall efforts on their adolescent years (i.e., ca. 12–18). The task was self-paced. Subjects dated each remembrance by specifying a month and year. They returned 2 weeks later and were given their memory summaries to redate. A structured response sheet was provided for this purpose. In the birthday condition subjects had to check whether they believed an event occurred either before or after their birthday and then give month and year for the remembrance. In the school-year condition subjects made two judgments before giving an event date: whether the event occurred during a school term and which one (fall or spring); whether the event occurred during a variation period and which one (Christmas or summer).

The event dates obtained under these two temporal sets were converted to

Table 10.5. *Summary of comparisons of birthday and school-year dating conditions*

|  | School year | | Birthday | |
|---|---|---|---|---|
|  | Mean | SD | Mean | SD |
| Event date (mos.): first dating | 53.26 | 14.68 | 50.79 | 20.17 |
| Event date: second dating | 52.99 | 15.40 | 51.12 | 18.04 |
| Dating consistency (Pearson correlation) | .66 | .23 | .84 | .11 |
| Date discrepancy (mos.): directional value | −0.60 | 6.54 | +0.38 | 6.24 |
| Date discrepancy: absolute value | 12.14 | 7.00 | 9.05 | 6.29 |
| Percentage unchanged dates | 19.60 | 11.16 | 28.65 | 18.96 |
| Percentage monthly only changed | 23.68 | 8.70 | 29.32 | 14.96 |
| Percentage year only changed | 21.11 | 8.13 | 12.69 | 7.09 |
| Percentage month and year changed | 36.19 | 12.65 | 29.55 | 18.19 |

numerical scores by counting backward from the month of the study. The average of each subject's dates was calculated in order to compare the temporal distributions of memories in the two groups. The mean of those average dates was 53.26 months for the school group and 50.79 for the birthday group. Thus, subjects succeeded in focusing recall on the specified period, and the two groups generated comparable time samples of memories. The product–moment correlation between the dates given in each session was calculated separately for each subject. The average correlation was +.66 for the school group and +.84 for the birthday group. The difference between groups in dating consistency was statistically significant, $t(28) = 2.78, p <$ .01. Thus, subjects in the birthday condition were significantly more consistent in event dating than those in the school-year condition. These reliability coefficients are lower than those reported in previous studies of autobiographical memory (Robinson, 1976; Rubin, 1982), but only the school-year group's is substantially lower. As subsequent analyses wil indicate, the reduction in dating reliability in the school condition can be attributed to the systematic displacement effects induced by the use of the school-year calendar in redating memory reports.

The dating discrepancies obtained in this study were analyzed in several ways. The results of these various analyses are summarized in Table 10.5. The average discrepancy (in months) between dates was tabulated for each subject, both as an absolute value and in terms of the directional value. Positively signed discrepancies indicate that an older date was given the second time; negatively signed discrepancies indicate that a more recent date was given the second time. The within-group variability on these two measures was so large that the differences between group means were not statistically significant in either case. However, the number of subjects with negative versus positive mean discrepancy scores was quite different between groups. In the birthday group 11 means were positive, 4 were negative; exactly the opposite distribution occurred in the school-year group. This contrast in distribution was statistically significant: The chi square corrected for continuity was 4.80, $p < .05$.

Another distributional analysis categorized dates according to the frequency and type of discrepancy. Four scores were calculated for each subject: percentage of reports given the same date on both occasions, percentage different in month only, percentage different in year only, and percentage different in both month and year. Of these four measures only one was significantly different between groups. The percentage of year-only discrepancies in the school-year group was significantly greater than the birthday group, Mann-Whitney $U = 38$, $p < .01$. Put somewhat differently, when only one temporal element was changed at the second dating it was more likely to be the month in the birthday group but equally likely to be month or year in the school-year condition. To summarize, the school-year group was less consistent in event dating, changed the year of dates more often, and had a greater proportion of negative average discrepancy scores than the birthday group.

The proposal that assimilation effects might occur when a fixed temporal reference point is used was assessed in the following way. Each subject's birth month was used as the standard. The interval between each report and a subject's birth month was then computed without regard for year of occurrence. Intervals were assigned according to the calendar-year sequence. For example, for a subject born in May a report dated February would be 3 months away from the birth month whereas a report dated October would be 5 months away. In this manner the first and second date given for every report were assigned a distance-from-birthday value. If birth month exerts any bias on dating consistency we should observe a regression of distance scores for the second dating toward the birth month. By subtracting the two distance scores we can determine how often second dates were nearer to or farther away from the birth month. The assimilation hypothesis requires a preponderance of negative distance scores. This did not occur. Rather, the distribution of scores was symmetrical, indicating that no assimilation effect occurred in redating.

To assess displacement effects requires a different type of analysis. Displacement is defined in relation to the pattern of temporal organization used as a reference system and consists of exchanges between structural units. For example, the event initially dated in October and subsequently dated in March represents an exchange between school terms. As a first step in this analysis, confusion matrices were prepared to determine how often each month for the

Table 10.6. *Consistency of month dates*

|  | Proportion month unchanged | |
| --- | --- | --- |
|  | School year | Birthday |
| Jan | .14 | .47 |
| Feb | .11 | .33 |
| Mar | .17 | .15 |
| Apr | .39 | .42 |
| May | .31 | .37 |
| Winter/spring term average | (.23) | (.35) |
| Jun | .51 | .42 |
| Jly | .50 | .41 |
| Aug | .32 | .42 |
| Summer average | (.44) | (.42) |
| Sep | .18 | .39 |
| Oct | .34 | .58 |
| Nov | .32 | .40 |
| Dec | .32 | .52 |
| Fall term average | (.29) | (.47) |

first report date was changed to every other month in the second report date. Again, this was done without regard for year of occurrence. To determine whether there was a difference in consistency across months, the proportion of reports given the same month on both occasions was computed. These data are summarized in Table 10.6. There are two interesting features in these data aside from the evident differences between groups. First, in the school-year condition the least consistent months were those at the beginning of the two school terms. In fact, the pattern of consistency for the winter–spring term mirrors those obtained with other tasks in this series of studies. Second, when average consistency per unit is compared, contrasting trends can be observed for the two groups. Average consistency increased from the beginning to the end of the year in the birthday condition. In the school-year condition average consistency was equally low for the two school terms and considerably higher for the summer unit. It is not clear why increasing consistency over the year should occur in the birthday condition, but the outcomes in the school-year condition are readily understood as expressions of the temporal schema in use.

The consistency analysis implies but does not demonstrate the occurrence of displacement. To confirm its occurrence requires evidence that inconsistencies were more likely to involve exchanges between temporal units. In par-

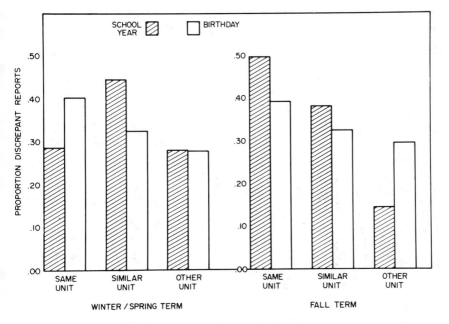

Figure 10.9. Distribution of date discrepancies by school term, structural unit, and dating condition

ticular, it requires evidence of exchanges between appropriate, that is, similar, structural units. An event initially dated in October and subsequenty dated in July is an exchange but one between structurally contrasting temporal units, namely, a school term and a nonschool term. If the second date given was March, the exchange would be between structurally similar units, that is, school terms. For each month, discrepant dates were categorized as being in the same structural unit, in a structurally similar unit, or in a structurally contrasting unit. The proportion of discrepancies in each category is shown in Figure 10.9, separated by school term. For the birthday condition the distribution pattern was the same for both terms: Discrepancies were dated in the same structural unit about 40% of the time, in a similar unit about 33% of the time, and in the summer about 18% of the time. The symmetry of this pattern contrasts with the distribution obtained in the school-year condition. Two features of the school-year group's data are noteworthy. First, for events initially dated in the months of the fall term, more of the discrepancies are assigned to the same or cognate unit and fewer to the summer unit than was the case for the birthday group. Second, for events initially dated in months of the winter–spring term discrepant dates were most often allocated to the other school term with approximately equal proportions in the same unit and in the summer. Both of these features help explain the overall tendency toward forward telescoping of dates already noted for the school-year group. More importantly, both provide evidence, though of different kinds, for temporal displacement. The winter–spring pattern is clear enough – dates are assigned to the structurally cognate unit more often than to any other temporal unit. For the fall term it is the contrast between groups that is informative: Twice as many discrepancies were assigned summer dates by the birthday group as by the school-year group. This implies that the structural contrast of school versus vacation was actively influencing inferences about dates in one group but not in the other.

Not shown in Figure 10.9 is the analysis of the distribution of discrepancies associated with events initially dated in a summer month. The results of that analysis also indicated a contrast between the two groups. For the birthday group discrepancies were again symmetrically distributed: 43% were assigned dates in the same temporal unit (the summer), whereas 31% were given dates in the winter–spring term and 26% were given fall-term dates. The school-year group assigned 48% of the discrepant dates to the same unit (summer) but assigned winter–spring dates in 16% of cases and fall dates in 36% of cases. One way of assessing the statistical significance of these distributions of discrepancies is to compare them with a distribution based on the assumption that discrepancies are equally likely to be in the same, similar, or other temporal unit. For example, if the first event date was in the winter–spring term, there are 4 other months in that term that could be discrepancies, 4 additional months in the similar unit (fall), and 3 in the structurally contrasting unit (summer). If discrepancies are distributed according to equal likelihood, then in the case of this example we would expect 36% to be in the same unit, 36% in the similar unit, and 27% in the other. Analogous computations can be done for each of the other temporal units. By this measure the discrepancies obtained in the school-year condition exceeded expectation by a range of $+23\%$ to $-13\%$ whereas the discrepancies obtained in the birthday condition exceeded expectation by a range of $+12\%$ to $-3\%$.

In summary, the distributional analysis of discrepancies has shown two regularities in the redating pattern of the school-year group: a bias toward forward telescoping of months (fall to winter–spring; summer to fall) and a predominance of exchanges between school terms. In contrast, no evidence of a directional bias or of assimilation to the reference month was found for the birthday group. Loftus and Marburger (1983) have also found that when people use a securely dated reference event the extent of telescoping is reduced. The reduction in dating reliability associated with use of the school-year timetable may seem paradoxical because it provides multiple reference points that should help a person to narrow the choice of dates for recollected

events. I surmise, however, that the two reference strategies lead the rememberer to assess different kinds of information about events and their relationships to other events. As noted previously, there are many clues to time of
occurrence. If a reference strategy predisposes one to attend to some clues
and ignore others, then we could expect conflicting inferences about times of
occurrence to arise. That these "errors" are systematic, hence to some extent
predictable from the strategy in use, is important information.

## Conclusions

Considered in toto, the empirical studies reported here have produced a very
consistent portrait of the temporal reference system for the school-year timetable. Of the two formal hypotheses that guided that research, one, the structural hypothesis, was regularly confirmed, whereas the other, the reference
points hypothesis, requires revision. As initially formulated, the reference
points hypothesis proposed that the beginning and ending intervals of temporal periods are functionally distinctive and, I presumed, equally so. The
evidence of several studies consistently indicated, however, that endings are
the most salient intervals of temporal periods. Beginnings are marked as they
must be, but present evidence strongly suggests that temporal periods are
cognitively anchored by their endpoints. In retrospect, trying to assess the
reference points hypothesis has turned out to be a bit like trying to separate
the dancer from the dance.

The functional analysis of temporal patterning in domains of action advocated in this essay is conceptually nearer to sociological and anthropological
perspectives on time than the traditional psychological perspective. Temporal
reference systems are the cognitive representations of what Lauer (1980) calls
*social time*. Lauer notes that many pretechnological societies use social activities to mark time. He further argues that clock time has been integrated with
but has not replaced social time in technological societies. I think that his
conclusions about the relationship between social and technological methods
of time reckoning should be heeded by cognitive psychologists:

The extent to which social time of any society or any group is dominated by clock
time is a matter of empirical investigation. Social time is not to be equated with clock
time, but clock time may be an important component of the social time of a people.
Although clock time is mechanical, it is invested with social meanings. Even though
it may be dominant, the varying units of clock time will have differing meanings to
people. Finally, while clock time may be defined independently of social life (if we
look at it as a purely physical phenomenon), social time has no reality that is independent of or external to social processes. [Lauer, 1980, pp. 26–27]

If it is true that we develop temporal reference systems to codify the temporal patterns of our everyday activities, then it is highly probable that those
schemata are actively involved in the temporal organization of memory. As

Tulving (1972) reminded us, temporality is one of the defining features of episodic or autobiographical memories. Tulving also noted that the specification of temporal information in memory need not be in terms of clock and calendar but could be based on other forms of organization. Temporal reference systems are prime candidates for such forms of organization.

## References

Battig, W. F., & Montague, W. E. (1969). Category norms for verbal items in 56 categories: A replication and extension of the Connecticut norms. *Journal of Experimental Psychology Monograph, 80*(3, Pt. 2).

Bousfield, A. K., & Bousfield, W. A. (1966). Measurement of clustering and of sequential constancies in repeated free recall. *Psychological Reports, 19,* 935–942.

DeSoto, C. B., & Bosley, J. J. (1962). The cognitive structure of a social structure. *Journal of Abnormal and Social Psychology, 64,* 303–307.

Fraisse, P. (1963). *The psychology of time.* New York: Harper & Row.

Hasher, L., & Zacks, R. T. (1979). Automatic and effortful processes in memory. *Journal of Experimental Psychology: General, 108,* 356–388.

Lauer, R. H. (1980). *Temporal man: The meaning and uses of social time.* New York: Praeger.

Loftus, E. F., & Marburger, W. (1983). Since the eruption of Mt. St. Helens, has anyone beaten you up? Improving the accuracy of retrospective reports with landmark events. *Memory and Cognition, 11,* 114–120.

Nelson, T. M. (1971). Student mood during a full academic year. *Journal of Psychosomatic Research, 15,* 113–122.

Osgood, C. E., May, W. H., & Miron, M. S. (1975). *Cross-cultural universals of affective meaning.* Urbana: University of Illinois Press.

Paivio, A., Yuille, J. C., & Madigan, S. A. (1968). Concreteness, imagery, and meaningfulness values for 925 nouns. *Journal of Experimental Psychology Monograph Supplement, 76*(1, Pt. 2).

Robinson, J. A. (1976). Sampling autobiographical memory. *Cognitive Psychology, 8,* 578–595.

Rosch, E. (1975). Cognitive reference points. *Cognitive Psychology, 7,* 532–547.

Rubin, D. C. (1982). On the retention function for autobiographical memory. *Journal of Verbal Learning and Verbal Behavior, 21,* 21–38.

Tulving, E. (1972). Episodic and semantic memory. In E. Tulving & W. Donaldson (Eds.), *Organization of memory* (pp. 381–403). New York: Academic Press.

*Part V*

# Temporal distributions of autobiographical memories

Crovitz and Schiffman began their 1974 seminal paper, "Frequency of episodic memories as a function of their age," by stating, "It would be desirable to expose by listing the full storage of episodic memory. Such a list should include the age of each memory as referred to the present" (*Bulletin of the Psychonomic Society, 4,* 517). The two chapters in Part V analyze data in which subjects recorded the first memories that came to mind for such a list. Although there was little control of what the subjects chose to recall, subjects of similar ages responded in remarkably similar ways. Their recollections quantitatively demonstrate two phenomena of autobiographical memory that have been discussed qualitatively for some time both experimentally and anecdotally: childhood amnesia and reminiscence. In these chapters, the general existence and form of the phenomena are confirmed, but the quantitative descriptions of the phenomena challenge existing theories.

# 11 Childhood amnesia: an empirical demonstration

*Scott E. Wetzler and John A. Sweeney*

Long before Freud introduced the notion of childhood amnesia, literary figures including Rousseau and Tolstoy had testified to the paucity of early memories (Salaman, 1970). Nevertheless, Freud's (1916/1953*b*, Vol. 16, p. 326) observation of a unique form of forgetting "which veils our earliest youth from us and makes us strangers to it" was probably the first description published in conjunction with an elaborate theoretical explanation. Freud noted that from the ages of 6 to 8 and younger there are few memories, if any at all. Those early memories that do exist are considered "screen memories" in Freud's theory, hiding an emotionally significant event behind the guise of triviality. "A person's earliest childhood memories seem frequently to have preserved what is indifferent and unimportant, whereas (frequently, though certainly not universally) no trace is found in an adult's memory of impressions dating from that time which are important, impressive and rich in affect" (1901/1953*a*, Vol. 6, p. 43). Memory gaps and distortions constitute an important data base for Freud's inferences about infantile sexuality and the mechanism of repression (Kline, 1972), and childhood amnesia has been implicated in the etiology of numerous psychopathological conditions (Freud, 1901/1953*a;* Krohn, 1978). Consequently, childhood memories, their absence or their distortion, deserve investigation from a clinical and experimental standpoint. In addition, if an amnesia were proven to exist, then theories of long-term memory would need to be modified to encompass this phenomenon.

Considering the widespread speculations surrounding childhood amnesia, there is surprisingly little evidential support demonstrating the existence of the phenomenon. Clinical anecdotes are typically offered, but a controlled demonstration of this unique kind of forgetting has been lacking. In particular, a precise definition of childhood amnesia that differentiates it from normal forgetting is sorely needed.

Partial support was provided by NIA Grant AG04278.

191

Ordinary usage of the term *childhood amnesia* suggests a phenomenon in which the adult exhibits deficient recall (not an absolute amnesia) of autobiographical episodic (Tulving, 1972) memories for the childhood years (age 7 and below). A demonstration of childhood amnesia must show deficient recall over the childhood years that is independent of the age at retrieval (current age) and length of the retention interval (time since childhood). That is, adults from 20 to 70 show similar degrees of childhood amnesia, and the memory impairment is greater than what one would expect to find according to simple decay theory (recall decreases as a function of the time since the event).

The usual memory experiment confounds three factors: age at learning, age at retrieval, and the length of the retention interval. When any one of these factors is held constant, the other two may not be independently defined. For example, over a constant retention interval (i.e., 15 years) a 20-year-old subject may have fewer memories (from when he was 5 years old) than a 50-year-old subject has (from when he was 35 years old). But the subject's age at learning has been confounded with his age at retrieval. Therefore, it is impossible to determine whether the deficient recall is due to the age-at-learning factor (childhood amnesia) or to the age-at-retrieval factor (older people always recall more events than younger people).

A comparable problem exists when the age at retrieval is held constant. Then, age at learning is confounded with the length of the retention interval. Because we already know that memories decrease as a function of the length of the retention interval, simple comparisons of the quantity of recent and remote memories are trivial. In a 20-year-old subject, one would expect to find greater recall for the past year than for 15 years ago (when he was 5 years old). This finding cannot demonstrate childhood amnesia.

The ideal childhood amnesia research strategy controls the age at retrieval, varies the age at learning, and defines an expected recall criterion as a result of normal forgetting (the length of the retention interval). Without a base line of expected normal forgetting it is impossible to determine whether or not recall is impaired beyond that base line. Accelerated forgetting over the childhood years would suggest the presence of childhood amnesia. Research designs demonstrating that information from childhood may or may not be retained do not define such a criterion, and therefore they do not disprove or prove the existence of childhood amnesia.

Normal forgetting refers to the constant and homogeneous process of forgetting across all periods of the lifespan. This principle of forgetting can ideally define an expected recall criterion for any period of life. If a person is exposed to 100 events a year, for example, and he forgets 5 events from each year per year, then when he is 20 he will recall 50 events from age 10 (10 years ago) and 75 events from age 15 (5 years ago). Figure 11.1 shows

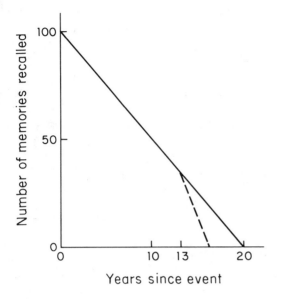

Figure 11.1. The hypothetical distribution of memories across the lifetime of a 20-year-old subject. Solid line represents a linear function of normal forgetting; broken line represents the accelerated forgetting due to childhood amnesia.

the hypothetical distribution of memories recalled over the lifetime of a 20-year-old.

This simple linear function defines a forgetting criterion over the lifespan. Were there evidence that the number of memories recalled from ages 7 and below (13 or more years since the event) is beneath the criterion expected by normal forgetting, then the existence of childhood amnesia would be demonstrated. There would be an accelerated forgetting over those years. In fact, subjects of all retrieval ages should show an accelerated forgetting at a fixed inflexion point. This illustration uses a linear decay model for simplicity of presentation. Actual normal forgetting would of course follow a more complex function (Rubin, 1982; Wickelgren, 1974), but this will be dealt with later.

Although this chapter will concentrate on the quantitative criterion defined by normal forgetting, qualitative criteria are also applicable. If, for example, episodic memories typically display a range of affective experiences, then an absence of equivalent affective experiences from childhood would suggest a unique form of censorship. In other words, if Freud's (1901/1953a) observation that childhood memories are more bland than adult memories is correct, then a certain kind of qualitative amnesia would exist. Another qualitative criterion might be the sequence of memories. For example, the quantity of childhood memories may not be deficient, but the ability to place memories in sequential order might be impaired in comparison to the sequential ordering of memories from adulthood (as suggested by Henri & Henri, 1898). Both these questions, however, are formally identical to the quantitative measure just presented. Instead of measuring the total number of memories, one would measure the affective quality or sequential order of memories and then compare these to predetermined expectancy functions. Thus, these problems reduce to the quantitative one and can be considered in the same way we discuss the quantity of memories here.

In sum, childhood amnesia is here defined as the accelerated forgetting over and above normal forgetting that affects all retention intervals homogeneously.

## Research on childhood amnesia

Historically, evidence supporting and criticizing the childhood amnesia construct has been taken from studies that describe the quantity and quality of early memories as well as from studies that determine the parameters of infantile learning in both humans and animals (Crovitz & Harvey, 1979; Spear, 1979; Waldfogel, 1948). The relevance to the understanding of childhood amnesia of the vast research on early memories and infantile learning is currently unclear. One frequently presented argument against the existence of childhood amnesia has been that, because many affectively rich memories from childhood are retained, the amnesia concept is untenable. However, childhood amnesia has been considered as deficient recall below some expected criterion, not as an absolute amnesia. Arguments for the existence of childhood amnesia are not likely to find support if they claim that a pure childhood amnesia exists. Without establishing quantitative or qualitative criteria with which information retained since childhood may be compared, it is impossible to evaluate existing literature to draw a conclusion about the amnesia question.

The qualitative characteristics of early memories have been examined since Adler (1931) recommended that clinical psychologists use them as simple, nonintrusive assessment instruments. He suggested that patients are often willing to discuss these memories because they take them as "mere facts," not as a mirror into the unconscious (like responses on the Rorschach and Thematic Apperception tests). Adler's suggestion stimulated a line of research into the content of early memories. Investigators have correlated personality type with memory reports classified according to a variety of systems (see Olson, 1979, for a review). Other studies described the age, frequency, stability, and veridicality of early memories for a range of subject populations using many different methods (see Dudycha & Dudycha, 1941, for a review of the early work). These descriptive studies testify to the compelling, affective nature of early memories (although one cannot determine whether the affect is a retroactive elaboration or an accurate representation of the affect experienced during the event), but they cannot resolve the amnesia question without a criterion – that is, a quantitative or qualitative measure defining features of memory from which childhood memories may be shown to deviate.

Similarly, the importance of studies of the quantity of early memories is unclear. Waldfogel's (1948) groundbreaking paper and subsequent follow-up work by Crovitz and his group (Crovitz & Harvey, 1979; Crovitz, Harvey, & McKee, 1980; Crovitz & Quina-Holland, 1976) were intended to address the childhood amnesia issue. However, they did not compare the frequency of early memories with the frequency of memories from other points in the lifespan. Instead, these researchers generated group frequency distributions only for early memories using four different methods: exhaustive free recall over 170 minutes (Waldfogel, 1948), exhaustive free recall over 12 hours (Crovitz & Harvey, 1979), cued recall with simple noun prompts (Crovitz & Quina-Holland, 1976), and cued recall with simple noun prompts of high and low descriptive value (Crovitz, Harvey, & McKee, 1980). In each case the same frequency distribution for early memories was generated. This function is quite robust. Waldfogel (1948) described it as an ogive with a shape similar to composite curves of intellectual and linguistic development. His post-hoc interpretation suggested an encoding deficit in young children, arguing that young children are not intelligent enough to encode information for later retrieval; as they develop the necessary cognitive abilities, more events are encoded. Although this frequency distribution and Waldfogel's interpretation discuss the successful retrieval of early memories, they do not speak to deficiencies in retrieval because the expected criterion is not defined.

The research on human (Burtt, 1941; Levy, 1960; Lindquist, 1945; Rovee-Collier, Sullivan, Enright, Lucas, & Fagan, 1980) and animal (see Campbell & Coulter, 1976, for a review) infantile learning has begun to define the parameters for the retention of information into adulthood. Rovee-Collier, Sullivan, Enright, Lucas, and Fagen (1980) developed a clever learning paradigm in which extremely young subjects can retain learning over substantial intervals. Other human (Levy, 1960; Lindquist, 1945) and animal (Spear, 1979) studies indicate that the younger the age at learning, the shorter the retention interval must be for the effects of learning to be demonstrated. In theory, with short retention intervals and distributed practice, material from infancy may be recalled in adulthood (see Burtt, 1941, for an interesting longitudinal test). However, research on infantile human and animal subjects has not tested autobiographical episodic memory. And, although one may show that information can be retained under certain circumstances, one still requires a criterion measure in order to prove that recall is impaired.

The only empirical work that offers a criterion measure for the recall of information over extremely long intervals comes from the laboratory (Wickelgren, 1974) and from lifespan autobiographical memory studies (Crovitz & Schiffman, 1974; Rubin, 1982). Wickelgren's research on forced-choice recognition tasks has generated a single-trace fragility function that describes the quantity of forgetting over extended decay intervals. The autobiographical memory research has generated a power function that describes the distribution of memories across the lifespan. Its naturalistic methodology makes the autobiographical memory research more relevant to the study of childhood amnesia than laboratory research.

Crovitz's (1970) method of collecting autobiographical memories derives from Galton's "free associative" walks along the Pall Mall. Subjects are presented with semantic prompts and asked to write down the first autobiographical episodic memories that come to mind. The memories are subsequently dated by the subject.[1] This technique generates a group frequency distribution of memories, which describes the relative accessibility of memories across an individual's lifetime. The frequency of memories retrieved within each time marker is plotted against the time since the event. As Rubin (1982) notes, for subjects under the age of 30 this method of collecting autobiographical memory data produces a power function regression equation with an extremely high correlation coefficient (.975), an association that has been replicated by all of the researchers who considered it (Crovitz & Schiffman, 1974; Franklin & Holding, 1977; Robinson, 1976, as reanalyzed by Rubin, 1982; Rubin, 1980, 1982, Expts. 1 & 2; and see Rubin, Wetzler, & Nebes, Chap. 12, for older subjects). Rubin argues that because the curve-fitting approach is necessarily post-hoc it is possible to generate multiple functions (e.g., Wickelgren's [1974] single-trace fragility function). Nonetheless, the power function seems to offer an extremely accurate description of the relative distribution of memories across the lifespan, and therefore it also represents the criterion of normal forgetting across the lifespan.

If this normal forgetting function can account for the distribution of memories over the childhood years, then no additional forgetting mechanism need be invoked. However, if the number of childhood memories is smaller than that predicted by the normal forgetting function, then there is an accelerated forgetting over the childhood years, and support for the existence of childhood amnesia would be provided.

[1]Rubin (1982) discusses the ramifications of various dating procedures.

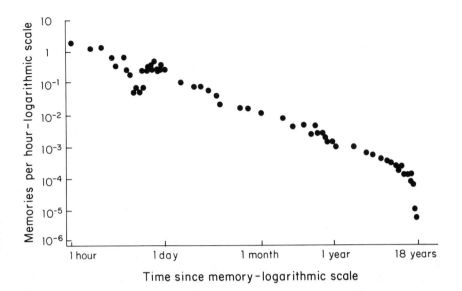

Figure 11.2. The mean number of memories per hour reported from the subjects' lives as a function of the age of those memories. Each point represents the frequency of memories reported for each time marker specified. The regression equation, log (mems/hour) = −.8 (log hours ago) + .3, is based on memories from age 8 (10 years since the event) until the present and extrapolated over the childhood years. From Rubin (1982)

Autobiographical memory data collected by Rubin, (1982, Expt. 1) provide an ideal sample with which to test the childhood amnesia problem. We generated the power function on the basis of all memories from age 8 until the present. Using this function as the normal forgetting criterion, we extrapolated to the earlier childhood years and compared the actual and expected number of memories from birth through age 6 (because age 7 is the inflexion point, it was excluded). By comparing the actual number of memories reported over this period with the expected number of memories on the basis of the extrapolation, it was possible to observe the presence of childhood amnesia.

Figure 11.2 represents Rubin's data plot with a power function derived from the points from age 8 to the present and extrapolated over the childhood years. Each point represents the frequency of memories within a time marker. The time markers consist of each English-language common time delimitation that spans the range of 1 hour to 18 years ago. These include 61 points referring to time markers, such as 23 hours, 6 days, 3 weeks, 11 months, and 18 years. The frequency of memories is the number of reported memories for each time marker divided by the width of the time marker in hours. Thus, we have 61 time markers representing a total of 4,855 memories. A $t$ test was performed to compare each subject's actual number of childhood memories (for ages 6 and below) with the sum of the expected number of childhood memories for these ages generated by the power function extrapolation. There was a significant deficit of childhood memories ($t = 10.19$, $df = 47$, $p < .001$). An inspection of the data points indicates that this difference is due mostly to the two points representing the number of memories from 16 and 17 years ago (or ages 1 and 2 for 18-year-old subjects). These two points along with an implied point of zero frequency for 18 years ago definitely indicate an accelerated forgetting for the childhood years.

Visual inspection of other autobiographical memory data (Crovitz & Schiffman, 1974; Rubin, 1982, Expt. 2) corroborate this finding of deficient recall over the childhood years. Rubin's (1982, Expt. 2) data point representing ages 0 through 5 is well below the power function, and Crovitz & Schiffman's (1974) two data points representing ages 2 and 3 are also well below the power function.

Three experiments (Crovitz & Schiffman, 1974; Rubin, 1982, Expts. 1 & 2) in which undergraduates retrieved autobiographical episodic memories across the lifespan have generated a power function regression equation that defines normal homogeneous forgetting. In each experiment the actual number of childhood memories (for ages 6 and below) is less than the expected number of childhood memories as defined by this criterion. Therefore, childhood amnesia does exist.

The exact age where the childhood amnesia phenomenon may begin to be observed is difficult to evaluate from these lifespan autobiographical memory functions because few points represent the childhood years. By focusing directly on the childhood years, it may be possible to determine exactly where childhood amnesia begins. With this goal in mind, the studies of the frequency of early memories (Crovitz & Harvey, 1979; Crovitz, Harvey, & McKee, 1980; Crovitz & Quina-Holland, 1976; Waldfogel, 1948) are relevant as a means to highlight certain descriptive features, not as evidence that the amnesia exists. As was mentioned above, all four papers, using different methods for collecting autobiographical memories from the childhood years, generated identical frequency distributions. The correlations between these functions were extremely high (all $r$'s above .985) and significant beyond the .001 level.

Figure 11.3 represents Waldfogel's (1948) frequency data as a specimen. Visual inspection indicates that the accelerated forgetting seems to occur after the point at age 5. That childhood amnesia begins below age 5 is in contrast with Freud's (1916/1953b) belief that it begins below ages 6 to 8.

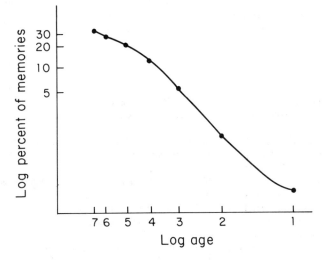

Figure 11.3. The distribution of early childhood memories. The accelerated decline seems to begin below age 5. From Waldfogel (1948)

## Conclusion

Until now the literature on childhood amnesia has been a confusing array of anecdotal evidence and ingenious theoretical speculation, with insufficient attention given to serious attempts to operationally define or demonstrate its existence. Data on the relative distribution of autobiographical memories across the lifespan were analyzed by comparing the number of childhood memories with the expected number of childhood memories based on normal retention and forgetting processes. There were fewer memories than expected for the ages below 5. Consequently, the childhood amnesia construct is useful for that age range.

Future research on this topic must verify the power function as the criterion for normal retention and forgetting for subjects of different ages and comparable acceleration of forgetting over the childhood years in each case. Further corroboration that the decline begins at age 5 is necessary as well. This line of research would help clarify the parameters of childhood amnesia and their changes over the lifespan.

Once childhood amnesia has been well defined and demonstrated, theoretical explanations need to be identified and differentiated. There are three plausible cognitive mechanisms to account for childhood amnesia: encoding deficit, encoding specificity, and retrieval failure (Wetzler & Sweeney, in press). At present, it is unclear to what degree each mechanism is important and how they may be interrelated. The clinical implications of childhood amnesia in different patient populations and on psychotherapeutic technique also need further investigation (Wetzler & Sweeney, in press).

## References

Adler, A. (1931). *What life should mean to you.* Boston: Little, Brown.

Burtt, H. (1941). An experimental study of early childhood memory: Final report. *Journal of Genetic Psychology, 58,* 435–439.

Campbell, B., & Coulter, X. (1976). The ontogenesis of learning and memory. In M. Rosenzweig & E. Bennett (Eds.), *Neural mechanisms of learning and memory* (pp. 209–235). Cambridge MA: MIT Press.

Crovitz, H. F. (1970). *Galton's walk: Methods for the analysis of thinking, intelligence, and creativity.* New York: Harper & Row.

Crovitz, H. F., & Harvey, M. T. (1979). Early childhood amnesia: A quantitative study with implications for the study of retrograde amnesia after brain injury. *Cortex, 15* 331–335.

Crovitz, H. F., Harvey, M. T., & McKee, D. C. (1980). Selecting retrieval cues for early-childhood amnesia: Implications for the study of shrinking retrograde amnesia. *Cortex, 16,* 305–310.

Crovitz, H. F., & Quina-Holland, K. (1976). Proportion of episodic memories from early childhood by years of age. *Bulletin of the Psychonomic Society, 7,* 61–62.

Crovitz, H. F., & Schiffman, H. (1974). Frequency of episodic memories as a function of their age. *Bulletin of the Psychonomic Society, 4,* 517–518.

Dudycha, G. J., & Dudycha, M. M. (1941). Childhood memories: A review of the literature. *Psychological Bulletin, 38,* 668–682.

Franklin, H., & Holding, D. (1977). Personal memories at different ages. *Quarterly Journal of Experimental Psychology, 29,* 527–532.

Freud, S. (1953a). The psychopathology of everyday life. In J. Strachey (Ed.), *The standard edition of the complete psychological works of Sigmund Freud* (Vol. 6). London: Hogarth Press. (Original work published 1901)

(1953b). Introductory lectures on psychoanalysis. In J. Strachey (Ed.), *The standard edition of the complete psychological works of Sigmund Freud* (Vols. 15–16). London: Hogarth Press. (Original work published 1916–17)

Henry, V., & Henri, C. (1898). Earliest recollections. *Popular Science Monthly, 53,* 108–115.

Kline, P. (1972). *Fact and fantasy in Freudian theory.* New York: Plenum.

Krohn, A. (1978). *Hysteria: The elusive neurosis.* New York: International Universities Press.

Levy, D. (1960). The infant's earliest memory of inoculation: A contribution to public health procedures. *Journal of Genetic Psychology, 96,* 3–46.

Lindquist, N. (1945). Some notes on development of memory during the first years of life. *ACTA Paediatric (Stockholm), 31,* 592–598.

Olson, H. (Ed.). (1979). *Early recollections.* Springfield, IL: Thomas.

Robinson, J. A. (1976). Sampling autobiographical memory. *Cognitive Psychology, 8,* 578–595.

Rovee-Collier, C. K., Sullivan, M. W., Enright, M., Lucas, D., & Fagen, J. W. (1980). The reactivation of infant memory. *Science, 108,* 1159–1161.

Rubin, D. C. (1980). 51 properties of 125 words: A unit analysis of verbal behavior. *Journal of Verbal Learning and Verbal Behavior, 19,* 736–755.

(1982). On the retention function for autobiographical memory. *Journal of Verbal Learning and Verbal Behavior, 21,* 21–38.

Salaman, E. (1970). *A collection of moments: A study of involuntary memories*. New York: St. Martin's Press.

Spear, N. (1979). Experimental analysis of infantile amnesia. In J. Kihlstrom & F. Evans (Eds.), *Functional disorders of memory* (pp. 75–102). Hillsdale, NJ: Erlbaum.

Tulving, E. (1972). Episodic and semantic memory. In E. Tulving & W. Donaldson (Eds.), *Organization of memory* (pp. 381–403). New York: Academic Press.

Waldfogel, S. (1948). The Frequency and affective character of childhood memories. *Psychological Monographs, 62*.

Wetzler, S., & Sweeney, J. (in press) Childhood amnesia: A cognitive psychological conceptualization. *Journal of the American Psychoanalytic Association*.

Wickelgren, W. A. (1974). Single-trace fragility theory of memory dynamics. *Memory and Cognition, 2*, 775–780.

# 12    Autobiographical memory across the lifespan

*David C. Rubin, Scott E. Wetzler, and Robert D. Nebes*

## Introduction

Autobiographical memory is a topic that inherently involves a lifespan approach. The development of autobiographical memory in the individual raises issues starting with childhood amnesia and progressing to reminiscence and life review. This chapter analyzes the results of studies from several different laboratories. Together, these studies cover the adult lifespan. In all cases, the data are the dates of autobiographical memories that have been cued by words. In all cases, the dependent measure is the distribution of the memories across the individual's lifespan.

The structure of the chapter is as follows. First, the cuing method used to elicit memories is described. Next, the data obtained with college students are examined in terms of a laboratory retention function. Possible extentions of this retention function to older subjects are then considered before existing studies that use subjects of various ages are reviewed. Reanalysis of the data from these studies suggests that sampling as well as retention determines the relative accessibility of autobiographical memories of older subjects. Individuals begin to reminisce when they reach middle age; they recall a disproportionate number of memories from their early lives. These findings, which are consistent over several studies, lead to a model of autobiographical memory involving three components: retention, reminiscence, and childhood amnesia.

## The method and its interpretation

The procedure used in this chapter is one of the simplest and oldest in experimental psychology. It was first introduced by Galton (1879) and was revived

We are especially indebted to Drs. Cohen, Fitzgerald, Franklin, Holding, Lawrence, Squire, and Zola-Morgan for making their data available to us. We wish to thank Herb Crovitz, Joe Fitzgerald, Davis Howes, and Gregory Lockhead for their comments on the manuscript. Support for the research was provided by NSF Grant BNS-8101116 and by NIA Grant AG04278.

202

more recently by Crovitz and Schiffman (1974). A subject is presented with a word and requested to provide the first discrete autobiographical memory that comes to mind. After a series of such associations, the subject is asked to date the episode described in each memory. The dates can be expressed either in terms of the standard, colloquial time markers of English, such as 10 minutes or 3 years ago (Crovitz & Schiffman, 1974), or in terms of calendar dates (Robinson, 1976). The test–retest reliability of the dating procedure is quite good (McCormack, 1979; Robinson, 1976), and, at least for diary keepers with whom verification is possible, the dating is also quite accurate (Rubin, 1982).

In principle, the data analysis is as simple as the procedure, although in practice a few technical details arise (see Rubin, 1982, for a more complete discussion). To begin the analysis, a histogram is formed with respect to the age of the memories. The bins of the histogram can have a variety of forms, including decades (Zola-Morgan, Cohen, & Squire, 1983), 10 to 20 equal intervals on a logarithmic time scale (Fitzgerald & Lawrence, 1984), the standard, colloquial time markers of English (e.g., 1 hour, 2 hours, . . . 23 hours; 1 day, 2 days, . . . 6 days; 1 week, . . . 1 month, . . . 1 year, . . . ; Crovitz & Schiffman, 1974), or even bins chosen post-hoc to contain equal numbers of memories (Rubin, 1982). For any system, each bin provides the quantitative analysis with two values: (*a*) the number of memories per unit time in the bin and (*b*) a measure of the average age of the memories in the bin.

Assume that individuals encode an equal number of autobiographical memories each day of their lives, except for the period covered by childhood amnesia. For any of the histogram systems, a plot of memories per hour encoded as a function of hours ago is then a horizontal straight line, and a plot of the observed memory per hour values as a function of hours ago is a retention function indicating how many of the encoded memories were actually observed. That is, the histograms provide a picture of the relative ease of recall of autobiographical memories across the lifespan.

## A robust finding in studies using college students

Crovitz and Schiffman (1974) obtained 1,745 dated memories by asking 98 undergraduates to record autobiographical memories evoked by each of 20 high-imagery, high-meaningfulness, high-frequency nouns. Crovitz and Schiffman then formed a histogram using the 60 standard, colloquial time markers of English ranging from 1 hour ago to 17 years ago. The memories per hour could be described by a power function of the hours ago. In particular, memories per hour $= at^{-b}$, where $a$ and $b$ are positive constants and $t$ is time. Their results were plotted on log-log paper producing a straight line of the form log(memories per hour) $= -b\log t + \log a$. The data fit the function surprisingly well with a correlation well over .9. As is common with power functions (Stevens, 1975), only the theoretically relevant slope parameter, $b$, is reported here. This is not a loss of information as $a$ is completely determined by $b$ and the number of dated memories obtained. Crovitz and Schiffman obtained a slope parameter, $b$, of .78.

Robinson (1976) cued 24 undergraduates with 16 object words, 16 activity words, and 16 affect words. These data were reanalyzed (Rubin, 1982) using a histogram with the following eight intervals, which are of approximately equal size on a logarithmic scale: 1, 2 to 3, 4 to 7, 8 to 15, 16 to 31, 32 to 63, 64 to 127, and 128 to 216 months ago. The power function provided a good fit to the object, activity, and affect cues ($r$'s of .973, .990, and .978, respectively) with slope parameters of .73, .83, and 1.18, respectively. The first two slopes were in reasonable agreement with Crovitz and Schiffman's value of .78 for nouns, and the steeper slope for affect words agreed with Robinson's report of more recent memories for affect cues.

Struck by this regularity, Rubin (1982) attempted to replicate the power law fit in two experiments. In the first experiment, 48 undergraduates were each cued by 125 nouns. The dating and histogram procedure followed that of Crovitz and Schiffman. The 4,855 dated memories that were obtained were mapped onto a 60-bin histogram. The fit to the power function was quite good ($r = .974$), and the slope parameter of .82 was in reasonable agreement with the previously obtained values. These data are shown in Wetzler and Sweeney (Chap. 11, Fig. 11.2).

In the second experiment, as in the free recall procedure described by Linton (Chap. 4), no cue words were given. Each of 84 undergraduates was asked to list 50 memories and later to provide a calendar date for each memory. The resulting 4,169 dated memories were rank-ordered by reported age and collapsed into a histogram. The histogram had 48 bins, each containing 85 successively dated memories, and 1 bin containing the 89 remaining oldest memories. The median memory in each bin was used to indicate the average age of memories in the bin. The amount of time that passed between the youngest and the oldest memory in the bin was used to calculate the memory per hour value. Although the procedure and analysis of data differed in many ways from the three previously reported studies, the results were similar. The power function provided a good fit ($r = .972$), and the slope parameter of .76 was in good agreement with Crovitz and Schiffman's .78 value, Robinson's object and activity values of .73 and .83, and Rubin's first experiment value of .82.

Two experiments were then performed to rule out possible explanations based on artifacts. To insure that the power function was not obtained by summing nonpower function distributions from individual words, an experiment was run in which 212 subjects each provided dated memories to five cue words. Analyses were performed for each word individually. Similarly, to insure that the power function was not obtained by summing nonpower function distributions from individual subjects, an experiment was run in which 7 subjects each provided approximately 280 dated memories. Analyses were performed for each subject individually. Although there was variability in the slope parameter among individual words and individual subjects, the fits to power function were quite good: better than .97 for each of the five words and, with the exception of one subject whose data resulted in a .748 correlation, better than .92 for each of the individual subjects.

More recently, Rubin, Groth, and Goldsmith (1984) have shown that the power function provides a good fit to the data even when olfactory cues are used as stimuli instead of words.

The experiments reviewed provide strong support for the claim that a robust, nonartifactual regularity exists in the distribution of autobiographical memories across the lifespan of college students. In particular, the same function was fit to data from several laboratories and from different procedures, with correlations above .95. Moreover, this function also fits laboratory retention data, thereby offering support to the retention function interpretation given earlier.

In a series of experiments, Wickelgren (1972, 1974, 1975) demonstrated that linear, exponential, and logarithmic decay functions fail to provide a good fit to laboratory retention functions, whereas the power function and several other functions that correlate highly with the power function do. The same results were found with the autobiographical memory data; that is, functions that fit laboratory retention data also fit the autobiographical memory data, and functions that fail to fit laboratory retention data also fail to fit the autobiographical memory data. This correspondence supports the claim that the distributions of autobiographical memories obtained by using the cuing method with college students are actually retention functions.

To summarize, the distribution of autobiographical memories obtained from undergraduates is quite regular across a wide range of conditions and can be easily interpreted, both theoretically and empirically, as a retention function.

## Possible age effects

Because subjects have more memories than they can report in the autobiographical memory task, they must always sample from among their accessible memories. Although one can argue that this is also true in most standard laboratory experiments (Rubin, 1982), the proportion of accessible memories reported in the autobiographical memory task is much smaller than in most other laboratory experiments. Because many nonrecalled memories are not lost but could be recalled if requested, the observed function is really a remembering function rather than a forgetting function.

Sampling must be considered in explaining the distribution of autobiographical memories, but sampling alone is not enough. If we assume that autobiographical memories, like all episodic memories, become harder to recall as time passes, then retention, as described in the previous section, must also be considered. The simplest hypothesis to make about retention in autobiographical memory is that it is identical to retention in other episodic memory tasks (e.g., Wickelgren, 1972, 1975). For all data reported in the literature for college students, this hypothesis fits extremely well, so well in fact that only the simplest assumption need be made about sampling. The uniform sampling hypothesis states that people sample randomly with equal probability from among their accessible memories, with differences in the accessibility of memories reflecting the effects of retention.

The problem facing us is that we observe one empirical distribution that is the result of two theoretical functions, a retention and a sampling function, and we have no simple empirical way to separate the two theoretical functions. This was not a serious problem with the data from college students because we could successfully use the standard ploy of assuming that the function we did not wish to consider, the sampling function, existed but was random. In fact, there was no need to mention sampling at all in describing the college student data. If systematic deviations are noted, however, we must decide whether they are due to deviations from our expected retention function or deviations from a random, uniform sampling function. Here we will attribute all deviations to sampling, a choice supported from considerations of both retention and sampling.

In the case of retention, there is a lack of evidence that retention, as opposed to encoding or retrieval, is affected by age (Hulicka, 1967; Hulicka & Weiss, 1965; Wickelgren, 1975). In addition, the standard view of retention is that of a monotonically decreasing function, but nonmonotonic functions will be needed to describe some of the data to be presented here. Examining sampling, we find that people often sample different periods of autobiographical memory, either because they were asked by the experimenter to produce memories from different periods of their lives (Chew, 1979; Crovitz & Harvey, 1979; Crovitz & Quina-Holland, 1976) or because different prompts led them to do so (Rubin, 1980, 1982; Rubin, Groth, & Goldsmith, 1984). More central to this paper than these experimental effects on sampling, however, is the suggestion that changes in sampling occur normally with changes in age (Butler, 1964; Costa & Kastenbaum, 1967; Salaman, 1970).

Given the results obtained with college students, what results should we expect with older adults? In terms of parsimony, we might expect a power function, possibly with systematic variation in the parameters. From general folklore, as well as some existing data, we might expect to see reminiscence suggested by an increase in memories from the subjects' early lives, that is, a nonmonotonically decreasing function. These two classes of possibilities will be considered. Each will describe an aspect of the data to be presented, and both are needed for the model to be proposed.

Assume that the power function is a good description of the data over the lifespan of older, as well as younger, adults. Further, assume for convenience that each subject provides us with the same number of memories, 100. When the slope parameter, $b$, is not equal to 1, integrating the power function yields $(a/(1 - b)) t^{1-b} + c$. Evaluating this function at the limits of 1 and $L$ hours ago, where $L$ is the number of hours in the subject's life up to the time of the experiment, yields $(a/(1 - b)) (L^{1-b} - 1)$. As this integral should account for all 100 memories that a subject produces, we obtain the equation $100 = (a/(1 - b)) (L^{1-b} - 1)$, which, because $L$ is known, can be solved for either $a$, the number of memories per hour at 1 hour ago, or $b$, the power function slope parameter.

At least three possible age changes in $b$ seem empirically and theoretically plausible. If the power function is really a retention function, with only uniform sampling present, then one would expect the rate of loss of memories with time to be the same for subjects of all ages (Hulicka, 1967; Hulicka & Weiss, 1965; Wickelgren, 1975). The first alternative then would have $b$ constant. In order to keep the total number of memories evoked equal to 100, $a$ would have to be smaller for older subjects.

A second alternative would be that subjects at all ages sample an equal number of memories from the recent past, in particular from 1 hour ago. For this alternative $a$ would be constant and $b$ would necessarily increase with the age of the subjects in order to keep the total number of memories constant; that is, as the subjects become older there would have to be relatively more recent memories recalled.

A third alternative would be that subjects tend to sample so that the power function is in terms of the proportion of each subject's lifetime, rather than in terms of absolute time. As a particular example, assume that the ratio of memories from 1 hour ago to the memories from an age equal to the lifetime of the subject, $L$, is the same independent of the age of the subject. The ratio of memories from 1 hour ago to a lifetime ago is $a1^{-b}/aL^{-b}$, or $L^b$. For an 18-year-old providing 100 memories with a slope of .76, the power function would be $1.44\ t^{-.76}$. In order to have the same value of $L^b$, an 80-year-old would need the function $.44\ t^{-.68}$. Thus, $a$ and $b$ would both decrease.

Throughout these discussions we have assumed that each subject produces a small, finite number of memories, 100. This is necessitated by the method that asks for a sample rather than an exhaustive listing of all memories. Thus, our quantitative analyses all refer to the relative proportion of memories remembered from various periods of life and not to the total amount of memories that could be remembered. For instance, we say that if the slope of the power function, $b$, is the same for all ages, then older subjects must recall relatively fewer memories from 1 hour ago than younger subjects do (i.e., $a$ must decrease as the subjects' age increases). This does not imply that older people can recall fewer memories from 1 hour ago; rather, it says only that in relation to memories drawn from throughout their lives older people will have fewer memories from 1 hour ago. It would not be surprising to find that in absolute terms older people have the same number of memories from 1 hour ago as younger people do and a greater number of total accessible memories. Unfortunately, this possibility cannot be tested by the current method.

In review, for the first alternative, a retention function with a uniform sampling of memories from among those accessible, $b$ stays constant as the age of the subject increases. For the other two sampling strategies considered, $b$ either increases or decreases as the age of the subject increases.

In addition to the class of power functions of various parameters, a second possibility, reminiscence, will be considered. All that is implied by the term *reminiscence* is an increase in early memories above what would be expected by a monotonically decreasing retention function. Empirical evidence exists even for this limited definition. In a paper to be discussed later, McCormack (1979) noted a $U$-shaped function for autobiographical memory in older adults, and Franklin and Holding (1977) noted that, although the power law function provided a reasonable fit to the autobiographical memories they collected from older adults, there was evidence of bimodal distributions with increases in the number of memories at the earlier years of their subjects' lives.

Reminiscence, although usually lacking the kind of explicit quantitative definition provided here (Romaniuk, 1981), has been a topic of great interest in aging (Butler, 1964; Costa & Kastenbaum, 1967; Havighurst & Glasser, 1972), personality (Erikson, 1950; Jung, 1934), and literature (Salaman, 1970). Moreover, recent sociobiological approaches to memory and aging make similar predictions about reminiscence (Mergler & Goldstein, 1983). Of practical interest, people who have electroconvulsive shock therapy (Zola-Morgan et al., 1983; Weiner, 1984), Korsakoff's syndrome (Butters & Cermak, Chap. 14), closed-head injury (Crovitz, Chap. 15), or other forms of amnesia (Baddeley & Wilson, Chap. 13) are often reported to have better memory for older than for more recent events (Ribot, 1882).

Having indicated some possible distributions of autobiographical memories for older adults, we can turn to the data.

Table 12.1. *Studies to be reanalyzed*

| | Nominal age | | | | | | | Subjects per age | Cued words per subject | Memories cued per age |
|---|---|---|---|---|---|---|---|---|---|---|
| | 12 | 20 | 30 | 40 | 50 | 60 | 70 | | | |
| Fitzgerald & Lawrence | × | × | | | × | | × | 30 | 40 | 1,200 |
| Franklin & Holding | | | × | × | × | × | × | 20 | 50 | 1,000 |
| Rubin, Wetzler, & Nebes | | × | | | | | × | 20 | 20 | 400 |
| Zola-Morgan, Cohen, & Squire | | | | | × | | | 25 | 10 | 250 |

## Observed age effects

When working in an area where relatively few studies have been published and where, therefore, the effects of variation in methods have not been studied parametrically, it is especially useful to compare results across laboratories. When an unexpected finding occurs, it is reassuring to see it occur several times in slightly different contexts. For these reasons we have sought to re-analyze existing data in addition to collecting our own. We owe more than a footnote to the researchers who allowed their data to be reanalyzed here.

During the last decade, several researchers have performed studies using subjects older than college undergraduates. Table 12.1 presents the four studies available to us. The nominal age of the subjects listed in Table 12.1 was close to the mean age of the group. The actual range of ages in each group was usually 10 to 15 years. All of these studies used the cuing method described. Fitzgerald and Lawrence (1984) presented their subjects with 20 object and 20 affect words. The memories evoked by these two types of cues were analyzed separately. Zola-Morgan, Cohen, and Squire (1983) studied autobiographical memory in amnesics. The data analyzed here are from their three control groups, which had mean ages of approximately 50. The first group consisted of 10 patients who had received bilateral electroconvulsive therapy for relief of depressive illness 3 to 5 months before the experiment; the second group consisted of 8 patients who were to receive right unilateral electroconvulsive therapy for relief of depressive illness 1 to 2 days following the experiment; and the third group consisted of 7 alcoholics. The fact that Zola-Morgan, Cohen, and Squire's subjects were not typical 50-year-olds allows a preliminary comparison to other subject populations. Because of the limited amount of data in each of their three groups, only the combined data are displayed here. However, as can be seen in Zola-Morgan, Cohen, and

Squire's figure 2, the combined data are representative of each group considered separately.

As the data we collected are not described elsewhere, more detail is provided for them. Twenty Duke undergraduates (mean age 19.6 years; range of 18 to 22 years) and 20 older, community-dwelling subjects (mean age 71.2 years; range of 68 to 76 years) took part in the experiment, which was run in R.D.N.'s laboratory during February and March of 1978. Following Crovitz and Schiffman's study (1974), the 20 stimulus words all had Thorndike–Lorge (1944) frequencies of A or AA and imagery and meaningfulness ratings above 6 in the Paivio, Yuille, and Madigan (1968) norms. Of the 20 stimulus words (*avenue, baby, board, cat, dawn, coin, cotton, fire, flag, flower, friend, market, mountain, nail, picture, steam, storm, sugar, ticket,* and *window*), only the word *baby* seems to be associated with clear periods in the lifespan from which it might evoke memories.

The subjects, who were tested individually, were instructed to provide a specific autobiographical memory for each stimulus word. The subjects read each word aloud and then verbally reported the memory it evoked. After all 20 words were presented, the subjects were asked to date each memory as accurately as possible either in terms of their own life such as "It was on my sixth birthday," in terms like "five years ago," or with the actual date. The stimulus words, and when necessary the descriptions of the memories they evoked, were provided for the dating. In order to simplify the dating, all memories less than 1 day old were allowed to be dated as "today."

In addition to the 20-year-olds already reviewed, the ages most available for detailed study, according to Table 12.1, are 50- and 70-year-olds. Figures 12.1 and 12.2 present the data from the 50- and 70-year-old age groups, respectively. For all groups of subjects, the most recent year of life contained between one third and two thirds of all the memories obtained. These recent memories have been excluded from the linear plots of Figures 12.1 and 12.2 in order to prevent the large number of recent memories from condensing the vertical scales. However, these recent memories, which clearly indicate that none of the age groups was living in the past, are examined in detail later, using a logarithmic scale. In addition to examining the 50- and 70-year-old subjects' data separately, the data from the two studies that contain several age groups (the Franklin & Holding and the Fitzgerald & Lawrence studies) are plotted in the same fashion in Figures 12.3 and 12.4.

Figures 12.1 through 12.4 clearly show nonmonotonically decreasing functions for subjects over 40 with the increase in memories occurring at the time when the subjects were approximately 10 to 30 years old. Before examining this finding in more detail, two aspects of the figures themselves should be noted. First, the vertical axes are labeled in terms of the number of memories

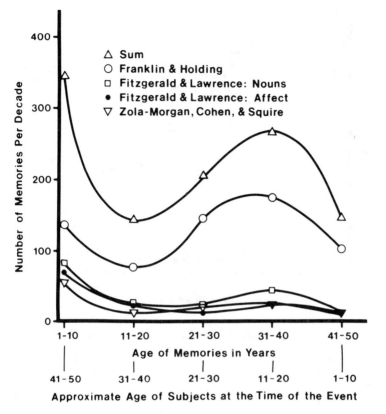

Figure 12.1. The bottom four curves are data from the individual studies that used 50-year-old subjects. The top curve is the sum of the lower four curves. The 1–10-year point from the Zola-Morgan, Cohen, and Squire study actually contains memories from 0 to 10 years.

that fall in each decade, indicating the amount of data being presented. For instance, Figures 12.1 and 12.2 contain a total of 1,104 and 1,373 data points, respectively. All of these data points are combined to produce the summed curves. Second, the horizontal axis is labeled in terms of decades. Although this may seem like a gross division of time, it should be pointed out that the nominal 50- and 70-year-olds actually spanned a range of ages slightly larger than a decade, which makes a finer analysis at the early years of life problematic.

Several observations can be made from the figures presented. First, and of fundamental importance, is the finding that the data from all the different laboratories and conditions show the same basic patterns. The effects found,

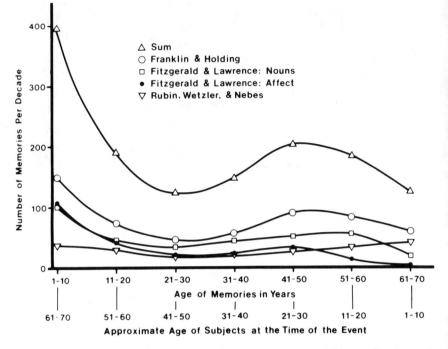

Figure 12.2. The bottom four curves are data from the individual studies that used 70-year-old subjects. The top curve is the sum of the lower four curves.

therefore, can be assumed to be quite robust. Second, reminiscence was not present in subjects younger than age 30. This finding is also supported by detailed analyses of the younger subjects' data. The third observation is that by age 50 there is reminiscence, which is as pronounced as it is with 60- and 70-year-old subjects. In fact, Franklin and Holding's 50-year-olds showed more reminiscence than any other group. From the existing data it is difficult to decide whether 40-year-olds demonstrate reminiscence. Figure 12.3 indicates that the 50-, 60-, and 70-year-olds in Franklin and Holding's study all showed reminiscence in the 10–30-year-old range. This reminiscence was defined, in large part, by a lack of memories from when the subjects were 30 to 40 years old. However, the 30–40-year-old period is the most recent decade for the 40-year-olds and as such should not be expected to show a lack of memories. This in itself may prevent a nonmonotonic function, even if reminiscence is present. Moreover, when the 40-year-olds' data are divided into 5-year instead of 10-year periods, there is some evidence of reminiscence, as

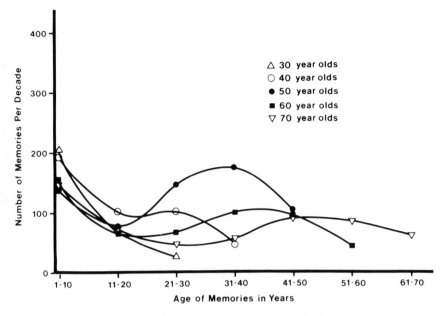

Figure 12.3. The five age groups from Franklin and Holding

can be seen in Franklin and Holding's figure 1. At present, the safest conclusion seems to be that there exists some transition between 35- and 45-year-olds, an age where, according to some theories, life review is supposed to begin (Romaniuk, 1981).

The fourth main observation is that the reminiscence consists of memories from when the subjects were about 10 to about 30 years old, rather than from a given retention interval, such as 40 years ago. The period of reminiscence cannot be specified with more precision because of the wide age range of the subjects in each nominal age group. Although the data for the 70-year-olds may have a period of reminiscence that extends further into adulthood than the 50-year-olds, comparison of the 50-, 60-, and 70-year-olds' data makes it clear that reminiscence can best be described in terms of the age of the subject at the time of the memory rather than in terms of the age of the memory itself.

McCormack's (1979) study, for which data were not available for reanalysis, provided somewhat different results than any of the studies analyzed here. Although the general shape of the four-point functions given by McCormack is like those of Figures 12.1 through 12.4, the reminiscence effect is much larger. McCormack's analyses showed that age differences could not

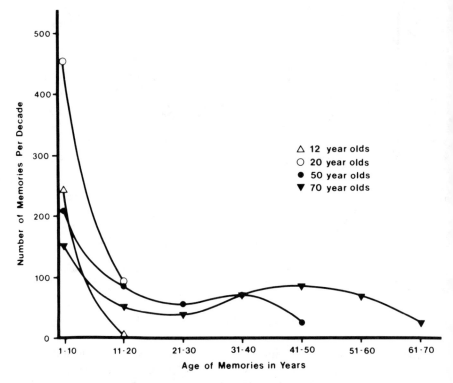

Figure 12.4. The four age groups from Fitzgerald and Lawrence

have caused the larger reminiscence effect. However, the relatively large number of early memories that were obtained could be due to any of the following five procedures not present in the studies reanalyzed here. First, McCormack's words were chosen specifically because they were expected to elicit memories with ease. Such words tend to evoke older memories in college students (Rubin, 1980). Second, subjects dated each memory after it was given, not after the entire set of memories was given. Assuming older memories require more landmarks in order to be dated, this procedure allows for differential priming of older memories (Ireland & Holding, 1981). Third, successive dating, when combined with the oral recording of memories and dates used by McCormack, allows for a greater influence of experimenter expectations on dating. Fourth, in two of McCormack's three experiments subjects may have been removed because they had two thirds of their memories in one quarter of their life. This would most likely be their most recent quarter, thereby increasing the relative number of early memories retained (Ireland &

Table 12.2. *Slope parameters and correlations for recent memories*

|  | Subjects' age | Time period | Number of bins | b | r |
|---|---|---|---|---|---|
| Franklin & Holding | 30 | 1 hr | 61 | .88 | .982 |
|  | 40 | to 20 yrs |  | .88 | .984 |
|  | 50 |  |  | .88 | .977 |
|  | 60 |  |  | .93 | .986 |
|  | 70 |  |  | .93 | .981 |
| Fitzgerald & Lawrence | 12 | 0 days | 12 | 1.05 | .975 |
| (noun cues) | 20 | to 10.6 yrs |  | .83 | .990 |
|  | 50 |  |  | 1.07 | .993 |
|  | 70 |  |  | .94 | .973 |
| Fitzgerald & Lawrence | 12 |  |  | 1.02 | .978 |
| (affect cues) | 20 |  |  | .90 | .990 |
|  | 50 |  |  | 1.02 | .994 |
|  | 70 |  |  | 1.00 | .980 |
| Rubin, Wetzler, & Nebes | 20 | 1 hr | 10 | .93 | .991 |
|  | 70 | to 20 yrs |  | .96 | .991 |

Holding, 1981). Fifth, institutionalized adults were used in two of three experiments.

Before proposing a model to account for the findings, it is necessary to examine the distribution of recent autobiographical memories from subjects of various ages. For this purpose, the power function analyses performed on the data from college sophomores earlier in this chapter were repeated for the most recent 10 to 20 years of all subjects' lives. For the adolescents of the Fitzgerald and Lawrence study, or the college students reported earlier, this period was their entire life, whereas for the older subjects it was only a portion of their life. Table 12.2 presents the results of this analysis. Figure 12.5 presents our data as a sample of a plot on log-log paper.

The particular time period and number of bins used in Table 12.2 for each study depended on the amount and the form of data available. Two basic results should be noticed. First, for the recent portion of all subjects' lives, the power function provides a very good fit, with all correlations above .97. Second, although the slope parameter, *b*, varies from study to study, it does not vary in a systematic way within each study; that is, the rate of loss of memories over the most recent years of subjects' lives is not a clear function of age. To return to the arguments made earlier in this chapter, although the power function may not provide a good fit for the entire lifespan of subjects

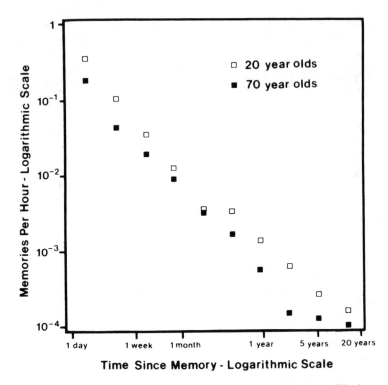

Figure 12.5. Log-log plot of the most recent 20 years of the Rubin, Wetzler, and Nebes data

over 30, it does provide a good fit for the most recent 20 years of all subjects' lives. Moreover, the slope parameter does not vary systematically, thus favoring a retention function interpretation of the power function rather than either of the other two possibilities that were entertained.

A brief technical note is in order: The power function would actually provide a fairly good fit even if older subjects' entire lifespans were included. This is because equal ratios, rather than equal intervals, occupy equal space on the logarithmic scale used to calculate the correlations. Thus, the distance between 1 hour and 4 hours is the same as the distance between 1 month and 4 months or between 20 years and 80 years. In this way, the reminiscence portion of the curve is compressed and given little weight. As a concrete example, Fitzgerald and Lawrence (1984) divided the lives of their 70-year-olds into 15 bins of nearly equal length on a logarithmic scale. The first 12 bins are included in Table 12.2 and cover 10.6 years of the 70-year-olds' lives. The last 3 bins cover the remaining years. In fact, the last bin alone covers over a third of the subjects' lives. This compression of time is not necessarily bad. For instance, the most recent month of a person's life should count more in a retention function than a month that occurred 26 years ago because more memories come from the more recent month and because more of a loss occurs over the period of the more recent month. Nonetheless, the time compression afforded by a logarithmic scale can hide effects occurring in the early years of the subjects' lives in a way a linear scale cannot. Used together, the logarithmic and linear scales provide a more complete description of the data.

## A model

A model to describe adequately the distribution of autobiographical memories across the lifespan must contain at least three components. The first component is a retention function, which is needed to account for the monotonically decreasing function that all subjects exhibit for the most recent 20 years of their lives. The retention component, which provides a base line against which reminiscence can be defined, has been fairly well studied in younger subjects (Crovitz & Schiffman, 1974; Rubin, 1982), as well as in the older subjects presented here. A power function, with a slope parameter that may change with the experimental procedure but not with the age of the subjects tested, has been proposed for the retention function. Although other functions are possible, the power function provides as adequate a fit as any two-parameter function (Rubin, 1982).

The second component will be dealt with only briefly here because it is the subject of Chapter 11. Evidence of childhood amnesia can be observed in all the data collected, at least to the extent that there are fewer memories recorded from the first few years of life than would be expected from most continuous functions. It is possible to fit the data of college students with three parameter functions that pass smoothly through the entire lifespan, including the first few years of life (Rubin, 1982). In fact, when presenting only college students' data in an earlier section of this paper, the power function provided an adequate description of the entire distribution of autobiographical memories. Attempts to avoid including a separate childhood amnesia component, however, become forced when subjects of differing ages are examined in a single study. Using the notation introduced earlier, the retention component is a function of the interval between the experiment and the event remembered, that is, "time ago" or $t$. The childhood amnesia component, however, is a function of the interval between birth and the event remembered, that is, the age of the subject minus "time ago" or $L - t$.

The third component is reminiscence. Because little theory exists that can

RUBIN, WETZLER, AND NEBES

be used to limit its quantitative form, reminiscence will be defined, for the present, by subtraction. The reminiscence component is what is needed in addition to the two other components in order to produce the overall empirical results obtained. Using this minimal definition, we know empirically that the reminiscence component, like childhood amnesia, plays its major role at a period defined by the age of the subject at the time of the remembered event, not by "time ago." In particular, reminiscence occurs at $L - t = 10$ to $30$ years. Moreover, we know that reminiscence occurs only if $L$ is greater than about 35 to 45 years; and, once $L$ is greater than 45 years, it makes little difference how great $L$ is.

For the sake of simplicity, the reminiscence component will be tentatively assumed to be a monotonically increasing function. Other forms of the reminiscence component are, of course, possible. The data presented here are from groups of subjects whose actual ages span 10 to 15 years. Studies using groups of subjects with smaller age ranges are needed in order to specify the nature of the function in more detail.

Quantitatively, combining the three components can be done by multiplication, as is shown in Figure 12.6. Theoretically, the three components correspond to (a) retention as conceived of in the laboratory, that is, a differential probability of recalling memories as a function of their age; (b) either a lack of encoding or an inability to retrieve early memories, as detailed in Wetzler and Sweeney (Chapter 11); and (c) a differential sampling of retained memories that occurs in subjects over a certain age. Causes of this differential sampling are suggested in the existing literature on reminiscence and life review (Butler, 1964; Costa & Kastenbaum, 1967; Erikson, 1950; Havighurst & Glasser, 1972; Jung, 1934; Mergler & Goldstein, 1983; Romaniuk, 1981; Salaman, 1970). Empirical support for various theories can come, in part, from the distribution of memories across the lifespan, but before such speculations are made it seems most reasonable to await a detailed analysis of the memories that constitute the reminiscence component in the procedures used here.

Based on the data already collected, the differential sampling explanation for reminiscence is favored over three other alternatives. The first alternative, a differential encoding explanation, is unlikely because the 12-, 20-, and 30-year-olds have monotonically decreasing functions which, as shown in Table 12.2, closely match the functions that older subjects have for their most recent 20 years of life. Thus, younger subjects do not show evidence of encoding information differentially at ages 10 to 30 when, under a differential encoding hypothesis, they would have to in order to provide more memories for later recall. The second alternative, a differential encoding hypothesis based on memorable events happening in certain calendar years (e.g., an increase in

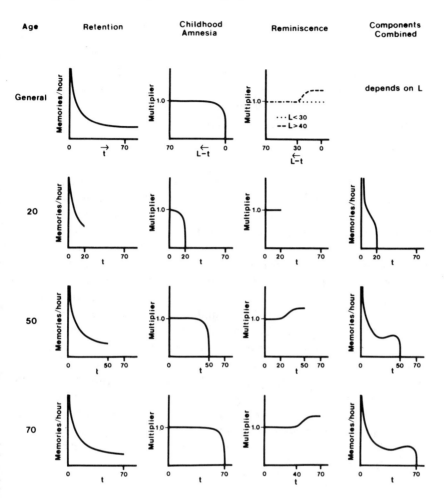

Figure 12.6. A graphic representation of the proposed model

memories for the period around World War II), is unlikely because the periods of reminiscence of different age groups fall on different calendar years. The third alternative for the reminiscence component is to assume that some property of the memory trace increases with time, becoming noticeable after about 30 years. A mathematical model that assumes that memory traces have decreasing strength but increasing resistance as a function of time (Wickelgren, 1972) can adequately account for the college students' data (Rubin, 1982). A different formulation of similar assumptions might also be able to account for memories of older subjects as well. One advantage of an increasing resistance explanation is that it would be consistent with the way most researchers view retrograde amnesia as well as memory loss in senility: Older memories are somehow more resistant to loss. The observation that the period of reminiscence is primarily a function of the age of the subject at the time of encoding rather than a function of the age of the memory, however, argues against the increasing resistance explanation. It is not the age of the memory that matters but the age of the subject at the time of the memory.

## Conclusions

The distribution of autobiographical memories across the lifespan is orderly across laboratories and across changes in experimental conditions. The distribution can be characterized by a combination of a simple retention component for the most recent 20 to 30 years of a subject's life; a childhood amnesia component for the earliest years; and, if and only if the subject is older than about 35, a reminiscence component for the subject's youth. The first component can be specified in quantitative detail. The second and third components can be specified in form, with more detailed descriptions possible as additional data are collected within the framework presented here.

The methods and quantitative rigor of cognitive psychology provided the techniques used to probe the distribution of autobiographical memories. The theories of cognitive psychology provided satisfying explanations for two of the components needed: retention and childhood amnesia. However, the third component, reminiscence, may require an expansion of standard cognitive models. It was clear that such a broadening of horizons would be needed as cognitive psychology matured (Neisser, 1967). Maintaining quantitative and methodological rigor while accomplishing this broadening presents the greatest challenge to future work.

## References

Butler, R. N. (1964). The life review: An interpretation of reminiscence in the aged. In R. Kastenbaum (Ed.), *New thoughts on old age* (pp. 265–280). New York: Springer.

Chew, B. R. (1979). *Probing for remote and recent autobiographical memories.* Paper presented at the 87th annual meeting of the American Psychological Association, New York.

Costa, P., & Kastenbaum, R. (1967). Some aspects of memories and ambitions in centenarians. *Journal of Genetic Psychology, 110,* 3–16.

Crovitz, H. F., & Harvey, M. T. (1979). Early childhood amnesia: A quantitative study with implications for the study of retrograde amnesia after brain injury. *Cortex, 15,* 331–335.

Crovitz, H. F., & Quina-Holland, K. (1976). Proportion of episodic memories from early childhood by years of age. *Bulletin of the Psychonomic Society, 7,* 61–62.

Crovitz, H. F., & Schiffman, H. (1974). Frequency of episodic memories as a function of their age. *Bulletin of the Psychonomic Society, 4,* 517–518.

Erikson, E. (1950). *Childhood and society.* New York: Norton.

Fitzgerald, J. M., & Lawrence, R. (1984). Autobiographical memory across the life-span. *Journal of Gerontology, 39,* 692–699.

Franklin, H. C., & Holding, D. H. (1977). Personal memories at different ages. *Quarterly Journal of Experimental Psychology, 29,* 527–532.

Galton, F. (1879). Psychometric experiments. *Brain, 2,* 149–162.

Havighurst, R. J., & Glasser, R. (1972). An exploratory study of reminiscence. *Journal of Gerontology, 27,* 245–253.

Hulicka, I. M. (1967). Age differences in retention as a function of interference. *Journal of Gerontology, 22,* 180–184.

Hulicka, I. M., & Weiss, R. L. (1965). Age differences in retention as a function of learning. *Journal of Consulting Psychology, 29,* 125–129.

Ireland, C. S., & Holding, D. H. (1981, April). *The age of memories.* Paper presented at the meeting of the Southern Society for Philosophy and Psychology, Louisville, KY.

Jung, C. G. (1934). *Modern man in search of a soul.* New York: Harcourt, Brace.

McCormack, P. D. (1979). Autobiographical memory in the aged. *Canadian Journal of Psychology, 33,* 118–124.

Mergler, N. L., & Goldstein, M. D. (1983). Why are there old people? Senescence as biological and cultural preparedness for the transmission of information. *Human Development, 26,* 72–90.

Neisser, U. (1967). *Cognitive psychology.* New York: Appleton-Century-Crofts.

Paivio, A., Yuille, J. C., & Madigan, S. A. (1968). Concreteness, imagery, and meaningfulness values for 925 nouns. *Journal of Experimental Psychology Monograph Supplement, 76*(1, Pt. 2).

Ribot, T. (1882). *Diseases of memory: An essay in the positive psychology* (W. H. Smith, Trans.). New York: Appleton.

Robinson, J. A. (1976). Sampling autobiographical memory. *Cognitive Psychology, 8,* 578–595.

Romaniuk, M. (1981). Reminiscence and the second half of life. *Experimental Aging Research, 7,* 315–336.

Rubin, D. C. (1980). 51 properties of 125 words: A unit analysis of verbal behavior. *Journal of Verbal Learning and Verbal Behavior, 19,* 736–755.

(1982). On the retention function for autobiographical memory. *Journal of Verbal Learning and Verbal Behavior, 21,* 21–38.

Rubin, D. C., Groth, E., & Goldsmith, D. J. (1984). Olfactory cuing of autobiographical memory. *American Journal of Psychology, 97,* 493–505.

Salaman, E. (1970). *A collection of moments: A study of involuntary memories.* New York: St. Martin's Press.

Stevens, S. S. (1975). *Psychophysics: Introduction to its perceptual, neural, and social prospects.* New York: Wiley.

Thorndike, E. L., & Lorge, I. (1944). *The teacher's word book of 30,000 words.* New York: Teachers College Press, Columbia University.

Weiner, R. D. (1984). Does electroconvulsive therapy cause brain damage? *Behavioral and Brain Sciences, 7,* 1–22.

Wickelgren, W. A. (1972). Trace resistance and the decay of long-term memory. *Journal of Mathematical Psychology, 9,* 418–455.

(1974). Single-trace fragility theory of memory dynamics. *Memory and Cognition, 2,* 775–780.

(1975). Age and storage dynamics in continuous recognition memory. *Developmental Psychology, 11,* 165–169.

Zola-Morgan, S., Cohen, N. J., & Squire, L. R. (1983). Recall of remote episodic memory in amnesia. *Neuropsychologia, 21,* 487–500.

*Part VI*

# Failures of autobiographical memory

---

Children and, as Baddeley and Wilson (Chap. 13), point out, psychologists often study things by seeing how they break. In this section, clinically diagnosed deficits in autobiographical memory are used to support and challenge existing theories of the memory of unimpaired adults. By describing in detail the behavior of a small number of individuals, issues of veridicality, the functional role of autobiographical memory, and the theoretical status of the concept of autobiographical memory are raised in a vivid manner.

# 13    Amnesia, autobiographical memory, and confabulation

*Alan Baddeley and Barbara Wilson*

One approach to the understanding of normal cognitive function is to investigate its breakdown following brain damage. In the area of memory this has proved a very profitable strategy; typically, concepts and techniques developed in the psychological laboratory have been used to analyze memory deficits in the clinic, and this in turn has frequently led to further development and modification of the initial model of normal memory. This chapter is concerned with the early stages of an attempt to approach autobiographical memory within this tradition. Because the study of autobiographical memory in normal subjects is still at a very early stage of development, conclusions are likely to be tentative. We shall be concentrating, however, on a phenomenon that we believe to be sufficiently striking and unequivocal to allow some conclusions, even though our data on normal control subjects are still sparse. We believe that our results, although preliminary, raise interesting questions both for the understanding of normal autobiographical memory and for its breakdown in amnesic patients.

We shall begin by describing our current technique for investigating autobiographical memory, together with its application to a range of patients, most of whom were suffering from long-term memory problems. After a general overview of the autobiographical memory performance of these patients, we shall concentrate on four patients with frontal lobe damage, two of whom show clear evidence of confabulation. These latter patients will be described in more detail, an explanation of their autobiographical memory defect will be proposed, and its implications for autobiographical memory in normal subjects will be discussed.

## Autobiographical memory and amnesia

Our involvement in the study of autobiographical memory stems from an attempt to test the claim of Tulving (1983) that semantic memory and episodic memory involve functionally separate memory systems. In particular, we

225

were concerned to investigate the claim that amnesic patients show normal semantic but defective episodic memory, a topic that is also discussed by Butters and Cermak (Chap. 14). We studied two densely amnesic patients who were unusual in having little or no intellectual impairment other than amnesia. We found their semantic memory performance to be normal, whether measured in terms of vocabulary score, speed of sentence verification, or capacity for generating items from semantic categories. At the same time both patients had clear deficits of episodic memory as reflected in their performance on standard laboratory learning tasks, such as free recall or paired-associate learning, and as reflected in everyday life. At a superficial level, therefore, their performance appeared to support Tulving's distinction. It occurred to us at this point in the study, however, that other potentially important variables differed between the semantic and episodic tasks we had studied (Baddeley, 1984). In particular, whereas episodic memory was typically measured by new learning, semantic memory measures were based on learning that had occurred many years ago, a point that had been made independently by Zola-Morgan, Cohen, and Squire (1983).

We, like Zola-Morgan, Cohen, and Squire, decided to explore the issue further by attempting to study the capacity of our subjects to recall specific personal episodes from their autobiographical memory. If semantic memory is intact but episodic memory grossly disrupted, one might expect to observe substantially impoverished autobiographical memory. On the other hand, if the crucial factor in preservation of memory is time of learning, then one might expect amnesic patients to show normal autobiographical memory, at least for episodes experienced many years before the onset of their illness. Unbeknown to us at the time, two other groups were asking the same question. Cermak and O'Connor (1983) investigated the semantic and autobiographical memory of a postencephalitic amnesic patient who was intellectually virtually unimpaired. They found evidence for good retention of semantic material acquired before his illness but no evidence for any capacity to update semantic memory. They describe his autobiographical memory as being very impoverished but report no formal testing.

Zola-Morgan, Cohen, and Squire (1983) carried out a rather more systematic ivestigation of a wider range of patients. They conclude that autobiographical memory may be unimpaired in amnesia, and suggest that the neuropsychological evidence does not provide strong independent support for the semantic-episodic distinction.

*Procedure*

We, like Zola-Morgan, Cohen, and Squire (1983), adapted the technique devised by Galton (1883) to probe autobiographical memory. This involves presenting subjects with a cue word and asking them to try to recollect a personally experienced incident that could be related to the cue. If the subjects produce a general rather than specific recollection, they are urged to try to recall a specific incident. If they still fail to recollect a specific incident, they are cued by suggesting broad categories of events. For example, if the cue word were *break* the subject might be asked, "Have you ever broken a limb?" or "Have you ever broken a valuable object?" For each recollection, an attempt was made to establish the time and place of the incident and to assess how much associated detail was available. Hence, the patient might be asked if he or she could remember the time of day, the weather, the color of hair of participants, and so on. A detailed illustration of this method is provided by Crovitz (Chap. 15).

We were of course also concerned with the validity of our patients' recollections. Although it is rarely the case that one can check an autobiographical memory in detail, we were able in the case of our patients to retest them at a later time. In this respect there are advantages to working with amnesic patients because unlike normal subjects they typically do not remember the previous interview. If subjects did not spontaneously recall the same event in the retest, then they were given a broad orienting cue and asked for another recollection. A sequence of increasingly specific cues was then provided, if necessary, leading ultimately to a description of the event previously recollected and the request for a judgment of familiarity and provision of confirmatory further detail.

A series of 12 cue words were selected from Robinson (1976) so as to reflect a range of parts of speech and degrees of concreteness. The words were *letter, throw, happy, find, game, successful, river, lonely, dog, make, angry,* and *break*. Where possible, subjects were tested and retested on all 12 words. Because of the constraints of fitting this in with the demands of treatment, it did not invariably prove possible to test all 12 words. Maintaining a constant interval between the first and second test sessions proved even less practicable. We attempted to insure a delay of approximately a week, but on some occasions we had to test on successive days, and in one case, that of N.W., the retest occurred several months later when the patient returned to the rehabilitation center for a routine reassessment. The retest evidence for this latter case will therefore be interpreted with particular caution.

*The subjects*

Table 13.1 shows the characteristics of the subjects tested. All except the first two subjects showed evidence of memory problems. Some indication of the severity of these is given by the scores of patients on the WAIS Logical Memory passages from the Wechsler Memory Scale (Wechsler, 1945) and on the

Table 13.1. *The patients studied*

|  |  |  | Prose recall[a] | | RBMT score[b] | Intellectual status | |
|---|---|---|---|---|---|---|---|
|  | Age | Diagnosis | Imme-diate | De-layed |  | Verbal IQ | Performance IQ |
| R.P. | 49 | Nonamnesic "control" patient (right hemisphere stroke) | 17 | 16 | 12 | 133 | 130 |
| J.B. | 64 | Nonamnesic "control" patient (right hemisphere stroke) | 10 | 10 | 12 | 121 | 126 |
| M.O'C. | 52 | Alcoholic Korsakoff | 2 | 0 | 0 | 93 | 92 |
| A.B. | 46 | Alcoholic Korsakoff | 7.5 | 0 | 3 | 108 | 96 |
| K.J. | 59 | Postmeningitic/encephalitic | 12 | 0 | 0 | 133 | 131 |
| D.B. | 54 | Bilateral stroke | 9.5 | 0 | 0 | 133 | 121 |
| K.S. | 28 | Closed-head injury | 7 | 0 | 0 | 93 | 94 |
| S.J. | 20 | Closed-head injury | 8 | 0 | 1 | 120 | 96 |
| E.W. | 59 | Tumor/head injury/epilepsy | 3 | 2 | 2 | 78 | 76 |
| J.W. | 28 | Head injury | 1 | 0 | 0 | 80 | 69 |
| R.J. | 42 | Head injury | 3 | 0 | 0 | 100 | 76 |
| N.W. | 41 | Subarachnoid hemorrhage/anterior communicating artery aneurysm | 1 | 0 | 0 | 109 | 66 |

[a]Scaled score: normal performance = 10.
[b]Maximum score = 12.

Rivermead Behavioural Memory Test. The Logical Memory test involves the immediate and delayed recall of a prose paragraph, with performance scored in terms of the number of idea units correctly verbally recalled. It was included as a well-known and well-standardized test that has proved to be a good predictor of everyday memory problems (Sunderland, Harris, & Baddeley, 1983). The Rivermead Behavioural Memory Test (Wilson, Baddeley, & Hutchins, 1984) comprises a total of 12 subtests, each of which attempts to simulate an everyday memory problem such as remembering the name of a newly encountered person, learning a simple route, remembering to do something, or learning a new skill. Although detailed validation is still in progress, preliminary results were as follows: 20 non-brain-damaged normal subjects were tested, and all passed all 12 items; 5 brain-damaged patients who were rated by their occupational therapists as having no memory problems passed an average 10 out of 12 items; whereas 25 patients reported by their therapists as having memory problems sufficiently prominent to interfere with treatment passed an average of less than 4 items. On both the memory measures, it is clear from Table 13.1 that all except our two nonamnesic control patients showed clear memory impairment. The final column in Table 13.1 reports the degree of general intellectual impairment shown by the various patients. It will be clear that this ranges widely from patients with gross impairment to virtually intact cognitive performance.

## Measures of autobiographical memory

It rapidly became clear that intriguing qualitative differences were occurring among patients in their autobiographical memory performance, differences that were not predictable on the basis of the more traditional memory tests. We have therefore used a procedure of tape-recording and transcribing all sessions. This still leaves the problem of how the transcriptions should be analyzed so as to present the interesting qualitative differences in a reasonably compressed and manageable form. We have not solved this problem to our satisfaction, but as an interim measure we have used a set of rating scales based on those devised by Zola-Morgan, Cohen, and Squire (1983), supplemented by verbatim quotations. Although the ratings fail to capture many of the more interesting qualitative features of the patients' performance, they do show in a reasonably straightforward way some interesting differences in patterns of recollection. We shall therefore begin by using these measures before going on to give a more detailed and qualitative account of the performance of the two patients who showed clear signs of confabulation. The rating measures taken involved the fluency, episodicity, richness, and reliability of each recollection, together with an indication of the age of the incident recollected. These will be discussed in turn.

*Fluency.* In the case of the fluency measure, we simply rated whether or not the patient was able to produce spontaneously the recollection of a specific personally experienced event. The following recollection by the Korsakoff patient A.B., an ex-merchant seaman, to the cue word *river* would be a good example: "A near collision on the Hudson River . . . going back about twenty years, I suppose. Going up the Hudson River to New York and just missed a ship on the way out." He was able to recall the name of the ship, the time of year, and the weather with reasonable detail. A zero would be scored on this measure if no separable incident could be recollected, or if further prompting was required. If general encouragement with no specific suggestions was enough to evoke an autobiographical recollection, we scored it as a spontaneous recollection. If, however, this was not sufficient, then types of situations that might provide an effective cue were suggested.

We intentionally tried to maximize the chance of the patient recalling something, if necessary by very active prompting. Patients with memory problems are sometimes hesitant to display their difficulties and may be reluctant to

Table 13.2. *Episodicity rating scale*

| Rating | |
|---|---|
| 3 | *Episodic memory, specific time and place* (KJ postencephalitic in response to cue *throw*) |

KJ:      I can remember being taught how to use a hand grenade. I had to throw it, then duck very quickly.

ABD:    Can you remember any incident that happened during learning to throw the hand grenade?

KJ:      Yes I can. There was a Welshman in the squad who was a very nervous man; he pulled the pin out and dropped the hand grenade in the trench where we were, Sergeant Adams, the instructor, picked it up very quickly and threw it out.

2     *Personal but nonspecific event,* or *specific event but time and place not recalled* (KS, head injury, in response to cue *river*)

KS:      I can just remember going in boats along rivers, particularly in Wales when I just started work. I lived with my cousin and my auntie his mother in West Wales; I can't remember the name of the town which the newspaper I worked for was in.

ADB:    Can you think of a particular incident?

KS:      I can remember going fishing, I mean, just quite a simple thing it was, getting in a rather large boat with about 5 or 6 people in it to go fishing, you actually had rods. I didn't go fishing, I just watched the others do it because I wasn't sure how to fish or whether I could.

1     *Vague personal memory* (KJ in response to cue *game*)

KJ:      I quite like a game of chess.

ADB:    Tell me about a particular game.

KJ:      It's hard to remember a particular game, I've played so many times I can't say that one stands out.

0     *No response, or response based on semantic memory* (KJ in response to cue *throw*)

KJ:      My immediate thought was throwing a ball, then I thought of throwing up. . . . I can't think of a particular incident.

respond unless certain. We felt that it was better to prompt than to risk mistaking caution for impaired autobiographical memory.

*Episodicity.* The episodicity score is base on a judgment concerning the response produced, whether spontaneously or after cuing. Table 13.2 shows the rating scale used, together with examples. The results are shown in Table 13.3 (1), which also gives data on the previously described fluency rating. The number of ratings per subject in this and subsequent tables does not always total 12, because it was not always possible to test all subjects on all 12 words, nor did they always produce a classifiable response to each cue word given. It is clear that two patients, E.W. and J.W., stand out as being highly

Table 13.3. *Ratings of autobiographical memory*

| | R.P. (right hemisphere stroke) | J.B. (right hemisphere stroke) | M.O'C. (Alcoholic Korsakoff) | A.B. (Alcoholic Korsakoff) | K.J. (post-encephalitic) | D.B. (bilateral stroke) | K.S. (closed-head injury) | S.J. (closed-head injury) | E.W. (closed-head injury) | J.W. (closed-head injury) | R.J. (closed-head injury) | N.W. (subarachnoid hemorrhage) |
|---|---|---|---|---|---|---|---|---|---|---|---|---|
| *Spontaneous recollections (%)* | 45 | 50 | 40 | 50 | 58 | 33 | 20 | 73 | 9 | 17 | 60 | 67 |
| *1. Fluency rating*[a] | | | | | | | | | | | | |
| 3 | 7 | 7 | 7 | 11 | 8 | 8 | 5 | 8 | 1 | 2 | 7 | 11 |
| 2 | 3 | 4 | — | 1 | 1 | 1 | 4 | 2 | 1 | — | 3 | 1 |
| 1 | — | — | 2 | — | — | 2 | 1 | — | — | 3 | — | — |
| 0 | 1 | — | 1 | — | — | 1 | — | — | 9 | 1 | 2 | — |
| Mean rating | 2.45 | 2.64 | 2.09 | 2.92 | 2.42 | 2.33 | 2.40 | 2.80 | 0.45 | 1.50 | 2.25 | 2.91 |
| *2. Richness of detail* | | | | | | | | | | | | |
| 3 (very detailed) | 5 | 7 | 5 | 10 | 7 | 1 | 7 | 8 | — | — | 7 | 11 |
| 2 (main features recalled, details vague) | 5 | 4 | 2 | 2 | 2 | 6 | 3 | 2 | — | — | 3 | 1 |
| 1 ("real" memory but no detail) | — | — | 2 | — | 1 | 4 | — | — | 2 | 5 | — | — |
| 0 (no memory) | 1 | — | 1 | — | 2 | 1 | — | — | 9 | 1 | 2 | — |
| Mean rating | 2.27 | 2.64 | 2.10 | 2.83 | 2.17 | 1.58 | 2.70 | 2.80 | 0.18 | 0.83 | 2.25 | 2.92 |
| *3. Reliability rating* | | | | | | | | | | | | |
| 3 (spontaneous recall of same incident) | 8 | 8 | 5 | 7 | 12 | 4 | 1 | 5 | 1 | 4 | — | — |
| 2 (same incident recalled when prompted) | — | 3 | 2 | 5 | — | 3 | 2 | 2 | — | — | — | 1 |
| 1 (partial recall when prompted) | 1 | — | — | — | — | 2 | 3 | 3 | — | 1 | 2 | 4 |
| 0 (no confirmation or recognition) | — | — | — | — | — | 1 | 2 | — | — | — | 4 | 7 |
| Mean rating | 2.78 | 2.73 | 2.71 | 2.58 | 3.00 | 1.82 | 1.25 | 2.20 | — | 2.60 | 0.33 | 0.50 |
| Age of patient | 49 | 64 | 52 | 46 | 59 | 54 | 28 | 20 | 59 | 28 | 42 | 41 |

Table 13.3. (Cont.)

| | R.P. (right hemisphere stroke) | J.B. (right hemisphere stroke) | M.O'C. (Alcoholic Korsakoff) | A.B. (Alcoholic Korsakoff) | K.J. (post-encephalitic) | D.B. (bilateral stroke) | K.S. (closed-head injury) | S.J. (closed-head injury) | E.W. (closed-head injury) | J.W. (closed-head injury) | R.J. (closed-head injury) | N.W. (subarachnoid hemorrhage) |
|---|---|---|---|---|---|---|---|---|---|---|---|---|
| Time since onset of amnesia (mos.) | — | — | 7 | 6 | 20 | 48 | 5 | 21 | 6 | 18 | 6 | 6 |
| *4. Age of recollection (yrs.)* | | | | | | | | | | | | |
| 0–1 | — | 2 | — | — | — | 1 | 1 | 5 | — | — | — | — |
| 1–5 | 1 | 1 | 2 | — | — | 4 | 4 | 4 | — | 1 | 3 | 1 |
| 5–10 | — | — | — | — | — | — | 2 | 1 | — | — | 2 | 1 |
| 10–20 | — | 2 | 1 | 8 | 1 | — | 3 | 1 | — | 2 | 2 | 3 |
| 20–40 | 4 | 3 | 3 | 4 | 3 | 3 | — | — | — | — | 1 | 5 |
| >40 | 5 | 3 | — | — | 5 | 1 | — | — | 1 | — | — | — |
| Median age of recollection (yrs.) | 40 | 25 | 20 | 15 | 40 | 3 | 5 | 3 | — | — | 7 | 20 |
| *Autobiographical memory classification* | Normal | Normal | Normal | Normal | Normal | Clouded | Clouded | Normal | Non-fluent (?) | Non-fluent (clouded) | Confabulation | Confabulation |

<sup>a</sup>See Table 13.2. for details of rating scale.

defective in their ability to produce episodic autobiographical memories. These are both patients with evidence of frontal lobe damage; this is often associated with difficulty in initiating and controlling action (Shallice, 1982), and, in the case of E.W. at least, this was perhaps his most striking symptom. We shall return to this point later. In general, however, the remaining patients appear to be reasonably capable of generating autobiographical recollections.

*Richness.* Once again, we used a 0–3 rating scale to evaluate richness. Table 13.3 (2) shows the performance of our subjects when rated on this variable. Once again, patients E.W. and J.W. show impaired performance. However, there is also evidence for some impairment in the performance of the stroke patient D.B. This was qualitatively quite striking, and totally unexpected on the basis of his performance on other, more conventional cognitive tasks.

In response to the cue *break,* D.B. was asked if he had ever broken a limb and responded as follows:

> D.B.: No, well I have recently had an arm broken . . .
> B.W.: Can you tell me a bit about that?
> D.B.: Not so easily, no.
> B.W.: How did you break it?
> D.B.: I'm not sure now whether it was a break, I think it *was* a break, I thought it was just a strain, but I was lifting something heavy, laying lino, and I was lifting something heavy to get the lino underneath . . . but I have a suspicion that wasn't how it was caused. I fell, I think, out in the street, I fell and my right arm went back to break the fall.
> B.W.: So where were you when this happened?
> D.B.: In Bodmin.
> B.W.: Do you remember the name of the street?
> D.B.: I don't remember exactly where it was.

This happened about 2 years before, but his recall of much earlier events was equally uncertain. When asked about his time at university, for example, he could remember very little detail; he seemed to have difficulty remembering not only the date he went to university but also whether he went to university before or after being in the navy.

*Reliability.* Reliability is an assessment of the extent to which the incident recollected on the first interview was verified on the second. Table 13.3 (3) gives the rating scale together with data on the performance of our patients. The reliability is high for all but four patients; K.S., R.J., and N.W. show low reliability, and D.B. shows some signs of lack of consistency. The question of reliability forms the major theme of the second part of this chapter, but before proceeding to it we will consider one other measure and give a broad overview of the varieties of autobiographical memory deficit observed in our patients.

*Age of recollection.* Table 13.3 (4) shows the distribution of age of recollected incidents for the patients tested. Also recorded in Table 13.3 (4) is the time of onset of amnesia.

In general there appear to be no very clear patterns or obvious differences among patients other than those based on age. Most patients show some tendency to recall items from childhood, the most marked example being a control, R.P. There is also some suggestion of a tendency for recollections to cluster, often being associated with a common theme such as schooldays (R.P.), a period in the merchant navy (A.B.), or incidents from the war (K.J.). We suspect that there is a certain chance element here, with one memory triggering off another from the same period.

One further point of note concerns the dating of the recollections produced by the stroke patient, D.B., several of which came from *after* the onset of his amnesia. For example, one concerned a television program screened the previous week, and others concerned relatively recent incidents that his wife was able to confirm. This, together with his impoverished access to earlier memories, suggests the interesting possibility of a relatively specific *retrieval* deficit. A clear contrast to this is offered by the postencephalitic patient, K.J., who, although showing roughly equivalent performance on standard memory tasks, differs in having apparently normal recollection of early events together with no access to events subsequent to his illness, a pattern suggesting a learning rather than a retrieval deficit. Such a distinction at this stage remains speculative but seems worth exploring further.

### A taxonomy of autobiographical memory deficit?

It is clearly somewhat premature to postulate anything as ambitious as a taxonomy on the basis of a mere 12 patients. However, it is perhaps worth pointing out certain patterns of deficit that seem to be emerging.

There appear first of all to be several patients who though densely amnesic seem to have normal access to autobiographical memory, at least for events preceding their amnesia. The Korsakoff patients M.O'C. and A.B. fall into this group. In this respect our results are consistent with those of Zola-Morgan, Cohen, and Squire (1983), who found relatively normal autobiographical memory in their Korsakoff patients. This does not of course imply that Korsakoff patients always have relatively unimpaired autobiographical memory, a point that is made very clearly by the case P.Z. described by Butters and Cermak (Chap. 14). We also found apparently normal recollection in our postencephalitic patient, K.J. In other respects K.J. resembles the patient with a similar etiology studied by Cermak and O'Connor (1983). Both he and K.J. have relatively intact intellectual performance combined with dense amnesia. However, Cermak and O'Connor's patient appears to have very impoverished autobiographical memory, whereas K.J.'s autobiographical memory seems to be excellent. This, together with the data from autobiographical memory in Korsakoff patients, serves to emphasize a general point in neuropsychology, namely, that common etiology does not guarantee equivalent cognitive dysfunction.

A second category of patients shows what might qualitatively be described as clouding of autobiographical memory. A good example of this is the head-injured patient, K.S., who was able to recall events in some detail on one occasion but not subsequently. Consider, for example, the following recollection from the Falkland Islands campaign and his attempt to reaccess the same memory subsequently.

K.S.: I remember sitting with a typewriter in my cabin, which I shared with another reporter. . . . whenever I typed out things it was always late in the evening.

ADB: How long a letter?

K.S.: I can remember writing one on three sides of a sheet; I wrote it on the front and back of that letter and then another one. I can remember doing that. I don't think I wrote anything longer than that and probably a lot shorter. . . . I was just giving very brief details of what happened and that I was all right and that everything was going well.

Some 2 weeks later the word *letter* evoked other examples, and, when prompted to talk about writing letters in the Falklands, K.S. reported that he wrote to his parents quite a bit but was not sure whether he knew his current girlfriend at that time. When asked for a specific incident or a particular letter he replied:

I was being asked this yesterday; it wasn't yesterday, it was the day before yesterday, I was sitting down and my brother asked me if I could name incidents that happened in the Falklands, and I couldn't. I could remember sort of two of them and I couldn't remember more than that. I can't remember anything about writing letters in the Falklands; he asked me that as well, about writing letters. He said I used to write a lot of letters and did I know what I wrote in them and how I actually went on about it, and I said I didn't, whereas before I'd sat down in exactly the same place and told him a story about writing letters to somebody.

Although such clouding of autobiographical memory does involve inconsistency, the inconsistencies typically do not involve evidence of confabulation. They are more striking for the lack of ability to access information than for their production of implausible incidents. Such patients appear to be showing something equivalent to a partial retrograde amnesia, with information available on one occasion but not another. This point is well illustrated by the detailed transcript given by Crovitz (Chap. 15), who describes a successful attempt by a patient to penetrate the "cloud" and recall incidents from the period close to his head injury.

The third group of patients constitutes those with evidence of frontal lobe damage, who fall into two categories: patients (E.W. and J.W.) who show very poor fluency but little or no confabulation, and others (R.J. and N.W.) who are fluent but very unreliable. The remainder of the chapter will focus on these two groups, attempting to relate their dysfunction to the known effects of frontal lobe lesions on behavior.

## Autobiographical Memory in Frontal Lobe Amnesics

*E.W.*

E.W. was a 59-year-old man with a 20-year history of epilepsy. He worked as a handyman at a university and fell from a ladder while at work. A CT (computerized tomography) scan revealed extensive calcification in the frontal lobes characteristic of a meningioma. Some 6 weeks later, a bifrontal craniotomy was carried out to remove the tumor, and 2 months after this he was admitted to Rivermead for rehabilitation. At that time he was usually mute and expressionless, although he answered some questions appropriately and with no obvious signs of dysphasia. He also showed perseverative behavior, for example, pushing patients around and around in their wheelchairs and polishing the sink for hours at a time after washing his hands. On the National Adult Reading Test his estimated premorbid IQ was 116 although his current full-scale IQ as measured at that time was 76, that is, in the borderline retarded range.

E.W. was the least fluent of the patients we tested. This almost certainly stemmed in part from his great difficulty in initiating behavior, a characteristic of the frontal syndrome that E.W. showed in extreme form. It was extremely difficult to induce him to speak at all, and when he did his responses tended to be limited to one or two words. In the autobiographical memory test his most characteristic response was silence. He produced only two recollections, one to the cue word *happy.* When prompted with direct questions about his wedding he was able to say that it was a happy occasion and tell where and when he was married. When further questioned he was able to report the weather, the color of the bridesmaid's dress, and where the honeymoon had been spent. The only other recollection was in response to *dog,* when he spontaneously reported that he had been bitten three times by a dog. When questioned he was able to provide detail, that it occurred when he was a boy and that he was bitten by a white Sealyham Terrier on two occasions and by a brown dog on the third. Each piece of information emerged as a one- or two-word answer to a direct question. The other 10 cue words failed to evoke any response despite persistent prompting. On retesting, he again spontaneously recalled being bitten and again reported that it was by a Sealyham. On direct questioning he did clearly have access to some autobiographical memory, because he was able to report his current job and his two previous jobs, although again his responses tended to be limited to one or two words.

In conclusion, E.W.'s autobiographical memory does appear to be abnormal, but whether this is simply because of his all-pervading difficulty in initiating behavior, leading to a problem in recollecting, or because he has a further problem over and above this is not entirely clear.

## J.W.

J.W. was a hotel receptionist before suffering severe, primary global brain damage in a driving accident. She showed substantial intellectual impairment including signs of perseveration and the impaired performance on a test of verbal fluency that is characteristic of patients with frontal lobe damage.

In this case there was no problem in producing sentences, but great difficulty in accessing autobiographical information. Although specific incidents were sometimes recalled, the detail tended to be very impoverished; hence, she could not recall what subjects she did at school or any public exams she had passed, but she did remember, in response to the cue *make*, making something at school out of purple material with a 1950s pattern. On the other hand she did not remember what the garment was.

In the case of J.W., there is no doubt that her autobiographical memory is impoverished and patchy. There were some inconsistencies between recollections on the 2 days, but these were not sufficiently marked to identify clearly as confabulation rather than confusion. She was acutely aware of her difficulty in recalling details of her past life and in keeping to the point. For example, when asked about the name of a dog she had been very fond of, she began to recall an unhappy marriage and her divorce: "I can only remember things that we used to call him when I was married, but not now so it doesn't matter"; and when asked when the dog had been acquired she implausibly replied, "About a week ago."

In conclusion, then, J.W. appears to have similarities to D.B. and K.S. in having a grossly clouded autobiographical memory but in addition shows the characteristic frontal problem of having difficulty in keeping track and shows possible signs of confabulation.

*R.J.*

R.J. had been trained as a civil engineer and was working as a publicity manager when he was involved in a traffic accident at the age of 42 years. He sustained a severe head injury, which rendered him unconscious for several weeks. A CT scan showed intracerebral hemorrhages in both frontal lobes. When he was admitted to Rivermead five months after his accident, a psychological assessment was carried out. His behavior ranged from being passive and apathetic (e.g., on occasions he sat in the same chair without speaking or moving for 2 hours) to being amusing and charming. He could not remember his past reliably and frequently confabulated. His predicted premorbid IQ based on the National Adult Reading Test (Nelson & O'Connell, 1978), was 120, that is, in the bright average-superior range. His verbal IQ was assessed at this time as being in the average range and his performance IQ in the borderline retarded range. He showed classic signs of frontal lobe damage; that is, he perseverated in speech, writing, and other motor responses. For example, when asked to write the meaning of "Too many cooks spoil the broth" he wrote, "too many skills, skills . . . for such a mess of of of of of of a mess of of . . . ," and so on. He made 45 errors on the modified Wisconsin card-sorting test (Nelson, 1976), of which 43 were perseveration errors. He also had problems with verbal fluency, being unable to say any words beginning with *s* in 1.5 minutes, although he did say, "There must be hundreds of them." His reasoning skills were also impaired. He was totally unable to do the Tower of Hanoi task or answer questions such as "There were 18 books on two shelves. Twice as many books were on one shelf as on the other. How many books were on each shelf?"

One of R.J.'s most prominent features is his tendency to confabulate. This shows up very clearly in his description of the traffic accident that led to his brain damage. He was unconscious for many days following and almost certainly has no genuine memory of the incident but nonetheless readily gives an account of the accident, an account that varies with each telling. The following is characteristic. Note the implausibly detailed account of the various verbal interchanges that are said to have taken place and their tendency to become stuck in a loop of conventional social clichés.

> R.J.: I was driving along in South Wales, coming back from the steel company in Wales where I had been on business, and had an accident in my car; I pulled out to pass a lorry and a lorry came the other way and that lorry missed me; I then went to pull back in when I had passed the lorry I was overtaking and another lorry came along and he actually hit me, so there was I in the middle of the road with no car. He stopped and I stopped and he said, "I'm sorry, mate," and I said, "Don't worry about it, it was as much my fault

as yours," and he said, "Well, it was really." So I said, "Well there's nothing much I can do about it," so he said "Well, there isn't, is there really," and I said, "No, not really," so he said, "Well what's going to happen now?" I said, "Well, as far as I'm concerned nothing will happen at all because it was my fault, or most of it was my fault." He said "OK," so I then said, "Well, as far as you're concerned there's no need for you to do anything because it was my fault, or mostly my fault." He said, "Well, that's fine," he said it was, and I said, "Well yes, it was indeed," so he said, "Are you going to do anything about it?" and I said, "No," and he said . . .

He continued in this vein for another 10 verbal interchanges before concluding, "So we shook hands and said cheerio."

> B.W.: Were you hurt in the accident?
> R.J.: I was hurt, yes, not badly, but I was hurt.
> B.W.: How were you hurt?
> R.J.: I went back home and went to my wife, and she took me to Hereford Hospital and I went into Hereford Hospital for that night and the whole of the next day and the next day, and they looked at me and they said there's nothing wrong with you, you'd better bugger off home, and this is exactly what happened.
> B.W.: And how did you get to Rivermead then?
> R.J.: Well, when I came out of Hereford Hospital, which was the end of that following week, the sister in Hereford Hospital said the best place for you to go is Rivermead, which is near Oxford. She said, "You should go to Rivermead, it's the best place there is in the country for what you need." And I said, "Well, I'll go to Rivermead, where is it?" She said, "It's near Oxford," and I said, "Well, that's fine, there's no problem getting there. I'll get in my car on Sunday night and I'll drive down there." She said, "That will be great, and while you're down there take so-and-so with you," which is exactly what I did. So she said, "And when you come back let me know."
> B.W.: So who did you bring with you, then? Was it a friend or another patient?
> R.J.: Yeah, some girl, I can't remember her name, some big fat piece. And that's what happened, and then I went back and took her back with me. I rang up the sister of Hereford Hospital and said, "I'm back now and I've brought what's-her-name back with me." She said "That's terrific, what did you think of the place?" I said, "For what it is, it's fantastic."

Clear evidence of confabulation also occurred in R.J.'s autobiographical memory testing. For example, in response to the cue word *letter,* he produced the following spontaneous recollection.

> R.J.: I sent a letter to my great-aunt in South Wales when my younger brother was killed, saying just that.

He was able to provide detailed answers to a range of questions, including date (8 years ago), how he had heard (by telephone) how his brother had been killed, time of day, and time of year. When asked about the wording of the letter he replied:

R.J.: Dear Auntie Bertha, I am sorry to tell you that Martin has been killed in a car accident; it's all very sad and we're all terribly sorry, what can I say sort of thing, really.

B.W.: It must have been very painful.

R.J.: It was, yes.

B.W.: Have you just got one brother?

R.J.: I've got three now; I've got two now actually, one older and one younger.

B.W.: What are they called?

R.J.: Martin and John.

B.W.: Which one was killed, then?

R.J.: Martin.

B.W.: So did you have two Martins?

R.J.: We had actually in those days one Martin, then mother had another one and we called it Martin as well. I think she felt a bit sort of morbid about it so she called it Martin so we had two, I suppose, yes, or what would have been two.

B.W.: So how old was your younger brother, then, when he was killed?

R.J.: He's only five now so he wasn't born then.

B.W.: The one that was killed in the car accident that you've been telling me about, how old was he when the accident happened?

R.J.: He would have been about 12 or 13 I suppose.

In fact, R.J. does have a brother Martin who is adult and still alive and maintaining contact with him. The following week when retested he confirmed that he had an aunt in South Wales and a brother Martin but denied that his brother had ever been involved in a serious accident. He could not remember describing a letter of that type to his aunt.

Other similarly implausible recollections were produced. For example, in response to the cue word *game* he reported hurting his knee at a game some 3 or 4 weeks ago. The game was claimed to be rounders (English girls' baseball), organized on Christmas Eve for the patients of Rivermead.

Practically the whole of the complement of people here played, I think. The whole certainly of my year and the whole of the year below me and probably half of the year above me, and maybe some others as well, I don't know. But an awful lot of people were playing; we swam and played five-a-side football or rounders or whatever you call it that day as well.

The reference to the "year" suggests some analogy with school sports. In fact, the Rehabilitation Centre was closed for the period surrounding Christmas. Swimming in Oxford in December is very much a minority activity even among the fit and healthy; furthermore, because most of the Rivermead patients have difficulty in walking, the idea of them playing rounders is bizarre. Once again he was totally unable to recall the incident 1 week later.

Yet another incident in response to the cue word *river* described throwing a stone and hitting the eye of a niece he had taken there for an outing. He describes taking her to the hospital, where the doctor is reported as saying:

Well there is nothing I can do about that; it's damaged or the stone has done irreparable damage. The best thing you and I can do is fiddle around with it and if it gets worse you bring her back and I'll either close it or take it out, but I'll do something with it and if it doesn't get any worse take her somewhere else and they'll do exactly the same.

Again the incident was not recalled a week later. When given an account of his recollection, his response was that "it would have happened if I told you it happened; it would have happened, yes, no doubt about it."

Some of R.J.'s confabulations are so bizarre and delivered with such bland conviction that it is hard not to suspect that he is simply teasing the interviewer. We both considered this possibility very seriously. We ultimately regard it as unlikely, however, for the following reasons:

1. R.J.'s confabulation is not limited to test situations. He confabulates in interacting with therapists, fellow patients, and his family. For example, one weekend while at home with his family he sat up in bed and turned to his wife, asking her, "Why do you keep telling people we are married?" His wife explained that they were married and had children, to which he replied that children did not necessarily imply marriage. She then took out the wedding photographs and showed them to him. At this point he admitted that the person marrying her looked like him but denied that it was he.

2. The degree of conviction with which R.J. often asserts his confabulations suggests that he strongly believes them. As in some of the examples given earlier, when his statement is shown to be irrational he may still refuse to accept the fact.

3. Further evidence that he genuinely believes his confabulations comes from the way in which he will act on them. For example, on one occasion he was found wheeling a chairbound fellow patient down the highway and when questioned said that they were going to see a sewage works that R.J. had been involved in constructing. It seems that he had indeed been involved in the building of a sewage works,

but it was very many miles away and had been completed some 10
years previously.

4.    Actions stemming from his confabulation occur in the absence of an
audience and in situations that lead to inconvenience and no obvious
gain. For example, on one occasion he was found standing on the
lavatory seat attempting to reach the ceiling. On being questioned he
claimed to be attempting to find his baggage, which he reported was
stored in the loft above. He refused to give up the idea until eventually he was dissuaded by being shown that there was no loft. Indeed,
one of the major difficulties therapists and nurses had in dealing with
R.J. was his tendency to become fixated on some erroneous notion
and his extremely strong resistance to being persuaded otherwise. He
would insist, for example, that he should be in occupational therapy
next and not psychology, and in order to induce him to move the
occupational therapist would have to be called to confirm this.

In short, his behavior was not that of someone who merely produced tall
stories in order to cover up a memory problem. Nonetheless, we were concerned at how much weight could be given the results obtained from a single
highly atypical patient. We had, in fact, previously done some work on a
somewhat similar patient, N.W., who did not superficially appear to show
confabulation and whom we had not followed up in detail. However, when
N.W. returned for reassessment, we decided to retest his autobiographical
memory. Although initial recollections were slightly odd, they were not
nearly as bizarre as those of R.J., and we did not regard them as confabulation. When looked at in detail however, they proved to have a number of
implausibilities and, as we shall see, when subsequently followed up showed
no evidence of consistency.

*N.W.*

N.W. was a 41-year-old insurance salesman who had a subarachnoid hemorrhage due to a ruptured aneurysm on the right side of the anterior communicating artery. The aneurysm was clipped, but problems developed postoper-
atively. A CT scan showed a mild hydrocephalus and an area of low density
in both frontal lobes. It was believed that N.W. had a second hemorrhage prior
to his operation. His predicted premorbid IQ was 119 (top of the bright-
average range). His full scale IQ was in fact 90, that is, at the bottom of the
average range. He made 37 errors on the Wisconsin card-sorting test, of
which 32 were perseverative errors. He failed, when asked, to produce any
words beginning with *s* in 1.5 minutes. Both of these deficits are associated
with frontal lobe damage. His behavior was often bizarre, and he frequently

misinterpreted the situation he was in. For example, he sometimes thought the psychologist was his secretary and asked her to write for information on the game of bridge he mistakenly believed he had organized the day before.

The initial recollections produced by N.W. appeared to be rich and detailed, many of them associated with a farm in Scotland and many concerned with dissatisfaction with the grieve, or farm foreman. Some of the details seemed rather strange, and the excessive preoccupation with this one person seemed slightly odd and a little paranoid. An example of the former is an account given in response to the cue word *river* of a quarrel with a neighboring landowner. The quarrel apparently occurred when N.W. had gone to put lime on his land, "But we happened to have our solicitor with us together with this policeman and his dog," a rather odd group for liming the land, although it was just possible that they were taken along because trouble was anticipated.

It was however, only when we retested N.W. that we seriously began to suspect confabulation. The first reason for suspecting this was that, despite producing very detailed recollections on the initial interview, he was unable to repeat virtually any of the previous recollections. Because there was a delay of over 6 months between the two interviews, it is perhaps not too surprising that the same events were not spontaneously recalled, but it does seem surprising that the bulk were not even recognized. For example, on attempting to reevoke the memory of the argument over the land, which had involved in its first version the solicitor, the policeman, his dog, and the neighboring landowner, "an irate Etonian who became most abusive and took a swing [at me]," N.W.'s comment was, "I remember telling you that twenty minutes ago." (It was in fact 6 months.) When asked for details, he remarked that it is "not something that stays in my mind."

Another interesting example of inconsistency and ultimate implausibility is that suggested by the word *find*. On the first test, N.W. described finding pearl and diamond earrings. On being retested he recollected finding a stamp collection, a translation of a manuscript in ancient Persian, and then, when cued with the prompt *jewelry*, two separate occasions on which he had found diamond pins. He was then asked about earrings and reported that he did remember finding them but could not remember exactly what was involved. In the case of all these items, including the earrings, he also described how he was forbidden to keep them, either by his mother or on occasion by his grandmother. Indeed, in the second interview the slight paranoia was again present but this time directed against the various members of his family, in particular his mother.

In general, the plausibility of N.W.'s recollections was considerably greater than those of R.J. However, when pressed for further detail, his responses did become rather less convincing. For example, in response to the cue word *make*, in the first interview he described making a gramophone turntable while at school. On being retested, he initially produced no specific memory, but when he was asked to recall something he made at school the following ensued:

ADB: Can you think of anything you made at school that is striking?

N.W.: An Australian wombat.

ADB: An Australian wombat?

N.W.: Ashtray, something different.

ADB: That does sound different. How do you make an Australian wombat ashtray?

N.W.: Get a piece of wood, let your imagination go . . .

ADB: Did you make anything else that you can think of, a bit more conventional?

N.W.: No I don't think so; I made a daffodil, again in wood. That was all to do with the school play.

ADB: How was it to do with the school play?

N.W.: There was a bowl of fruit and flowers which had to be given to the queen, Queen Diadem. All the various people had to make a flower. We were told to make something out of wood; I happened to be asked to make the daffodil, one of the easier pieces.

As with R.J., confabulation was not limited to the distant past. For example, on arrival he was asked where he thought he was and replied, "Worcester" (close to where he now lives), whereas he was in fact being tested in Oxford. After he had been asked about the incident that happened on his farm in Scotland, a break occurred during which he was asked how they had driven to the Rehabilitation Centre, and he replied by describing a route in Scotland that was not only incorrect but would have been extremely lengthy. When asked where he thought he was, he replied "Just north of Crief" (Central Scotland). Again, although he did not confabulate nearly so freely as R.J., he did on one occasion complain to the ward sister that his gall bladder had been removed through his left testicle.

*Comparison with nonfrontal amnesics*

The fact that we have a range of patients with different characteristics allows us to ask a number of questions about the characteristics of confabulation and in most cases to come up with a clear answer. It is obvious first of all that confabulation is not an inevitable feature of amnesia. Indeed, in our experience confabulation is rare.

The term *confabulation* is defined as replacement of "the gaps left by a disorder of the memory with imaginary remembered experiences consistently believed to be true" (*Collins English Dictionary,* 1979). The term *confabulation* will be used in the present context to imply a substantial discrepancy between the patient's recollection and "the truth." Because we do not have an independent record of most of the events recalled, assessment of confabulation is not straightforward. We base our evidence for confabulation on two sources, inconsistencies within a given interview and inconsistencies between sessions. Within an interview, the patient may either contradict himself unequivocally or make statements that are to a greater or lesser degree implausible. Between sessions, the patient may make either contradictory statements or deny a previous statement. The decision as to whether confabulation has occurred thus depends on the accumulation of evidence. This raises the question of what represents an appropriate control group. What little evidence we have suggests that subjects with normal memory do not represent a fair comparison group, because they can recall their previous responses for most cue words, at least over the length of interval that it is practicable to use. For that reason we shall use the nonfrontal amnesic patients as controls.

Both of our Korsakoff patients did show minor discrepancies between their two recalls. For example, A.B. recalled the name of the ship involved in one 10-year-old recollection as "Esso Bernicia" on the first occasion and as "Esso Demetria" on the second. It is, however, hard to believe that similar inconsistencies do not crop up from time to time in the memory of normal subjects, although they would, however, be more difficult to pick up because, as mentioned earlier, normal subjects can usually remember what they said last time.

Given that amnesia does not inevitably produce confabulation, does defective autobiographical memory? The issue here is slightly less clear-cut because the head-injured journalist, K.S., and to a lesser extent the stroke patient, D.B., both show some evidence of inconsistency between successive sessions, although not within sessions. To what extent are such inconsistencies evidence of confabulation? It is of course very difficult to verify autobiographical memories, but insofar as this was possible, we did some cross-checking with the relatives and friends of K.S. and D.B. We found no evidence of confabulation. It appears therefore that autobiographical memory can be clouded without leading to confabulation.

## Discussion

We shall begin by giving a brief overview of what is known of the frontal lobe syndrome, together with a description of a particular interpretation of the viewpoint put forward by Shallice (1982). We shall then talk about the process of recollection before going on to offer a tentative explanation of the confabulatory behavior of our frontal lobe patients. This will be followed by some more general speculations as to the implications of our results for the normal functioning of autobiographical memory.

We would like to suggest a dissociation between the existence of a frontal lobe lesion, defined purely in terms of its *localization* within the brain and which may or may not have dramatic effects on behavior, and a particular syndrome whereby certain rather crucial features of *behavior* are disturbed, albeit typically in conjunction with damage to the frontal lobes. What are these functions? Shallice quotes Rylander (1939, p. 20) in describing the principal features of the frontal syndrome as follows: "disturbed attention, increased distractability, a difficulty in grasping the whole of a complicated state of affairs . . . well able to work along old routine lines . . . (but) . . . can not learn to master new types of tasks, in new situations . . . at a loss."

Shallice (1982) offers an interpretation of this syndrome in terms of a model of the attentional control of behavior produced by Norman and Shallice (1980). This assumes that behavior may be controlled at two separate levels. Well-learned skills will have built into them processes whereby they are run off and controlled. When two or more such skills, such as walking and talking, operate at the same time, possible conflicts between them are handled by a contention-scheduling procedure.

A major change in strategy or the initiation or cessation of a particular activity may however require the operation of the *supervisory activating system* (SAS), which is capable of overriding the contention-scheduling system. It is this system that is responsible for initiating behavior and for active intervention, a role that in the Baddeley and Hitch (1974) model of working memory is assigned to the central executive. Shallice (1982) suggests that it is this system that is malfunctioning in patients suffering from the frontal lobe syndrome.

Within a working memory framework, such patients could be described as suffering from a *dysexecutive syndrome*. This will be reflected in difficulty in initiating activity, for which the SAS or central executive is necessary, and also in the apparently opposite problem of difficulty in interrupting behavior, for which the same system is required. A tendency to mental inertia, reflected in difficulty in starting new activities, and a tendency to perseverate are very characteristic of the frontal syndrome. The distractibility that is also characteristic of the syndrome would be expected in cases where there is no well-structured ongoing activity. In a normal subject, the determinant of activity would be the SAS or central executive, whereas in the frontal patients, the absence of such control allows the system to be captured by any available stimulus. As we shall see, both these characteristics can plausibly be related to the task of autobiographical recall.

Although there are no well-developed theories of autobiographical retrieval, there have been a number of speculations. One of these is the process of active retrieval that has been termed *recollection* (Baddeley, 1982). Baddeley distinguishes between a relatively automatic component of retrieval, which is perhaps best captured by the processes assumed in Tulving's encoding specificity hypothesis (Tulving, 1983), and a more active and problem-solving activity termed *recollection*. This is assumed to involve the subject in searching for information by setting up a range of plausible retrieval cues and evaluating the information they evoke. Such evaluation involves deciding whether the information is veridical and, if so, whether it is that which is sought. If not, it may be used in order to generate further retrieval cues, which in turn will produce further information for evaluation. For example, Solso (1979) cites the case of an attempt to recall the name of a schoolteacher. This produced the first two letters, *A* and *L*, followed by the response "Alvira." Recall was also accompanied by the information that the name was also that of a province in Canada, allowing "Alvira" to be rejected in favor of the correct response, "Alberta."

A similar and much more extensive account of the process whereby a vaguely familiar face was recognized, leading through a slow and complex series of steps to the recognition of the person and his name, is described by Baddeley (1982), who suggests that amnesia may reflect a deficit in the capacity for recollection. In fact, data from the protocols obtained in the present study suggest that this may not be true of amnesia in general. In fact, most of our patients frequently rely on general knowledge to amplify and check their memory, particularly when it is unclear. For example, when the stroke patient, D.B., was asked how he had usually traveled to university, he relied on general knowledge of where he had lived and of the London transport system, because he seemed to have no direct memory of the many journeys he must have made at that time.

It seems likely then that the difficulty that amnesic patients have is not one of operating the recollective process of active memory search; it stems, rather, from a lack of the necessary mnemonic information on which such a search could take place. We would like to explore the possibility that frontal lobe amnesics, however, represent an example in which the process of recollection itself is disrupted. Let us consider our four frontal amnesics in turn.

There is little doubt that E.W. has substantial difficulty in initiating behavior, whether at an active motor level or at a more cognitive level of initiating speech or, we suspect, a search of memory. He can produce responses to questions about dominant features in his life but shows no evidence of an ability to sustain description of even these events and no capacity for retrieval of personal incidents in response to general cuing.

The case of J.W. is somewhat more complex because she seems to show a combination of the substantial clouding of episodic memory shown by K.S. and D.B., together with problems in initiating search and evaluating its outcome. However, because of the multiplicity of her problems, it is difficult to present a simple overall characterization of her autobiographical deficit.

The most striking evidence for our hypothesis comes from R.J. He shows the characteristic combination of perseveration and distractibility and hence is likely to find the task of autobiographical recall in response to a cue word to be very difficult, because it requires searching a defective memory for personally experienced events while rejecting other associations. The apparent fluency of his output suggests that he clearly can access information of some kind, but he appears to be unable to separate those experiences he has actually encountered from those he is simply generating. Because he shows signs of strongly believing the information he has generated, it seems unlikely that he merely omits to confirm the veracity of the item retrieved. It suggests, rather, a positive incapacity to perform the verification component of recollection, a component we will discuss further in connection with normal autobiographical memory. In conclusion, we would like to suggest that R.J. has a defective central executive that produces problems in initiating and controlling memory search. He solves the difficult problem of being pressed to recall an incident by following whatever the dominant association is at the time. This in turn leads to further associations and the generation of a story or incident, typically accompanied by the sort of detail and direct report of speech that is virtually never found in a genuine recollection.

The autobiographical memory of N.W. is similar, though much less extreme and bizarre. The events he describes tend in general to be reasonably plausible. Indeed, the only real cause of suspicion in the first interview was in the preoccupation with the misdeeds of the grieve, something that seemed odd but certainly not sufficient to assume confabulation. His second set of recollections were more obviously dubious in reliability. Australian wombat ashtrays and wooden daffodils do not play a very prominent role in most school woodworking courses. Clear evidence of perseveration showed up in his preoccupation with the grieve in the first interview; the second tended to be dominated by incidents demonstrating the unfairness with which his mother had treated him. Other evidence of perseveration occurred in his reporting a long succession of valuable objects found, each one being denied him by his mother or grandmother. As with R.J., there appears to be a lack of capacity to evaluate the plausibility of his recollections. In response to the word *game* he recalled "two recent games of golf, one of which I lost hopelessly and the other of which I won, surprisingly." Because he was confined to a wheelchair that seemed somewhat surprising, but when asked whether he played from the wheelchair he said, "Oh no, I walk," something that he was almost certainly incapable of doing.

*Implications for the understanding of normal memory*

We have clearly studied a highly varied group of patients. What do they tell us about normal memory? First of all, the fact that a number of our patients appear to have relatively unimpaired autobiographical memory together with dense anterograde amnesia casts doubt on the simple generalization that amnesic patients have a normal semantic but a defective episodic memory. Certain aspects of episodic memory in some of our patients at least appear to be quite unimpaired, whereas the ability to increment semantic memory appears to be generally defective in our group. This does not constitute evidence *against* the semantic/episodic distinction, but it does cast doubt on claims that such a distinction is supported by evidence from amnesia (Baddeley, 1984).

Our data are consistent with the emphasis on memory retrieval as an active process that is implied by the term *recollection* (Baddeley, 1982). The term implies the capacity both for directing memory retrieval and for evaluating its output. Our frontal patients appear to be defective in one or both of these. The difficulty in directing retrieval is also consistent with the tendency for frontal patients in general, and our four patients in particular, to have difficulty in generating items from specified semantic categories, although two of them are of course quite capable of producing an apparently effortless stream of unreliable memories and pseudomemories. The difficulty our frontal patients appeared to have in evaluating the output of their retrieval processes is also consistent with the tendency for frontal patients to perform very badly at tasks involving the use of "commonsense" knowledge in order to estimate answers. For example, a patient might be asked to estimate the height of Nelson's Column in Trafalgar Square. A tendency to produce bizarrely inappropriate responses is one characteristic of patients with a frontal lobe syndrome, suggesting that they have difficulty in applying their general knowledge in order to check any answers they produce.

This leads to the general question of how normal subjects verify their memories. The fact that we make mistakes indicates that this process is far from perfect, but the fact that most of our mistakes are plausible ones suggests that we do cross-check the results of our retrieval processes.

One final implication of our results is for the functional significance of autobiographical memory. This aspect of memory has until recently been largely ignored in neuropsychology. In the process of this investigation we found quite marked differences among patients who otherwise seemed very similar. For example, the postencephalitic patient, K.J., and D.B., the stroke patient, both have dense anterograde amnesia and are both highly intelligent with IQs in the 130s and apparently unimpaired intellect. And yet one, K.J., has apparently normal autobiographical memory whereas the other, D.B., has great difficulty in recollecting the past, a difficulty that appears to apply to both the remote and the recent past. The two patients also differ in their degree of adaptation to their memory problem, with K.J. having a much less enviable position (his wife had died, and he must live in an old people's home) but nevertheless appearing to cope much more stoically with the situation than D.B., who gives the impression of being much more frustrated by his plight. Although it is almost certainly the case that premorbid differences in temperament play a part in this, it is hard not to wonder to what extent having access to one's previous life is an important part of one's concept of one's self as a person. Of the frontal patients, J.W., who was acutely conscious of her problem in accessing information about her early life, appeared to be much more distressed by her memory problem than either R.J. or N.W. who typically appeared to be unaware of how unreliable their memories were.

In the case of the elderly, it has been suggested that disorientation is associated with a general deterioration in behavior and self-care. Programs of reality orientation training have been devised with the purpose of maintaining the patient's orientation (Holden & Woods, 1982). In their earlier versions at least, these concentrated heavily on reminding the patient where he was, what the date was, and what was going on in the world around him. Evidence for the effectiveness of such cuing was somewhat sparse, and more recently there has been a greater emphasis on linking the patient with his or her past life using the technique known as reminiscence therapy whereby old photographs and objects from bygone days are used to stimulate discussion among geriatric patients, with some reported therapeutic success (Merriam, 1980).

One interpretation of this might be as follows. For elderly and ailing patients to continue to cope it is important that they maintain self-respect. Self-respect by definition demands some coherent concept of the self, which essentially relies on autobiographical memory (c.f. Blythe, 1979). Hence, telling disoriented patients where they are at present and what the date is may not help very much because what they need to establish and maintain is not just *where* they are but *who* they are. Reminiscence therapy is a way of maintaining access to autobiographical memory despite the move from a familiar well-known environment to an institutional environment among strangers (Merriam, 1980).

Whether or not this interpretation of current therapies in geriatrics is in fact justified, there seems little doubt that autobiographical memory, by maintaining a record of the self, probably performs one of the most significant functions of human memory. As such, it now seems to us remarkable that it should feature so little in standard neuropsychological examination. The reason for this is of course clear. Although, as Linton (Chap. 4) points out, the range of techniques is increasing, we do not yet have an adequate range of tools for revealing and measuring deficits of autobiographical memory.

We ourselves have used only the cuing technique, finding it useful but far from ideal as a clinical technique. First of all, subjects are free to select their recollections from anywhere in their lives, so a patient having a few peaks of clear memory may well be able to perform apparently adequately on this measure, although subjects can be instructed to concentrate on a particular period of their lives, as in the case described by Crovitz (Chap. 15). In the absence of any such direction by the tester, however, no clear indication of degree of retrograde amnesia is obtained. It seems probable that some of our patients had a deficit that extended across the whole of their previous lives, whereas others had a relatively sharp dichotomy between memory for events before and after their illness. We have, however, at present no good means of ascertaining this in connection with autobiographical memory. A third problem concerns the detection of confabulation. We have used retesting as a means of checking the veracity of recall, but, as will be clear, such checks are both time-consuming and possibly quite difficult to evaluate. In particular, it is hard to know whether the failure to recognize a previous recollection means that that recollection was confabulated or simply indicates a clouding of autobiographical memory. From this viewpoint, evidence of internal inconsistency within the patient's protocol provides a more satisfactory source of evidence for confabulation.

We therefore plan to move to something approaching more closely a structured interview in which subjects are required to recollect incidents throughout their lives, with detailed probes of specific commonly experienced events at each point. We hope in this way to make our tests of autobiographical memory more genuinely autobiographical, with the long-term aim of producing tractable clinical techniques for studying this intriguing, difficult, but, we believe, very important domain of human memory.

# References

Baddeley, A. D. (1982). Domains of recollection. *Psychological Review, 89,* 708–729.
 (1984). Neuropsychological evidence and the semantic/episodic distinction. *Behavioral and Brain Sciences, 7,* 238–239.
Baddeley, A. D., & Hitch, G. J. (1974). Working memory. In G. Bower (Ed.), *Recent advances in learning and motivation, Vol. VIII* (pp. 47–90). New York: Academic Press.
Blythe, R. (1979). *The view in winter: Reflections on old age.* London: Lane.
Cermak, L. S., & O'Connor, M. (1983). The anterograde and retrograde retrieval ability of a patient with amnesia due to encephalitis. *Neuropsychologia, 21,* 213–234.
Galton, F. (1883). *Inquiries into human faculty and its development.* London: Macmillan.
Holden, U. P., & Woods, R. T. (1982). *Reality orientation: Psychological approaches to the confused elderly.* London: Churchill Livingstone.
Merriam, S. (1980). The concept and function of reminiscence: A review of the research. *Gerontologist, 20,* 604–608.

Morris, R. (1984, June). *Short-term forgetting in senile dementia of the Alzheimer's type*. Paper presented at the 2nd workshop of the European Society for the Study of Cognitive Systems, Cambridge.

Nelson, H. (1976). A modified card sorting test sensitive to frontal lobe defects. *Neuropsychologia, 12*, 313–324.

Nelson, H. E., & O'Connell, A. (1978). Dementia: The estimation of levels of premorbid intelligence using the new Adult Reading Test. *Cortex, 14*, 234–244.

Norman, D. A., & Shallice, T. (1980). *Attention to action: Willed and automatic control of behavior* (CHIP Rep. No. 99). San Diego: University of California.

Robinson, J. A. (1976). Sampling autobiographical memory. *Cognitive Psychology, 8*, 578–595.

Rylander, G. (1939). Personality changes after operation on the frontal lobes. *Acta Psychologica, Neurological Supplement*, No. 30.

Shallice, T. (1982). Specific impairments of planning. *Philosophical Transactions of the Royal Society London B298*, 199–209.

Solso, R. (1979). *Cognitive psychology*. New York: Harcourt, Brace Jovanovich.

Sunderland, A., Harris, J. E., & Baddeley, A. D. (1983). Do laboratory tests predict everyday memory? A neuropsychological study. *Journal of Verbal Learning and Verbal Behavior, 22*, 341–357.

Tulving, E. (1983). *Elements of episodic memory*. Oxford: Oxford University Press.

Wechsler, D. (1945). A standardised memory scale for clinical use. *Journal of Psychology, 19*, 87–95.

Wilson, B., Baddeley, A., & Hutchins, H. (1984). *The Rivermead behavioural memory test: A preliminary report* (Tech. Rep. No. 84/1). Oxford: Rivermead Rehabilitation Centre.

Zola-Morgan, S., Cohen, N. J., & Squire, L. R. (1983). Recall of remote episodic memory in amnesia. *Neuropsychologia, 21*, 487–500.

# 14 A case study of the forgetting of autobiographical knowledge: implications for the study of retrograde amnesia

*Nelson Butters and Laird S. Cermak*

## Introduction

There is little doubt that cognitive psychology has made a great contribution to the study of organic amnesia. Most of the published investigations of amnesia during the past 15 years have involved the application of cognitive concepts or theories to the severe memory disorders of patients with diencephalic or medial temporal lobe dysfunction. Theories stressing the distinction between *episodic* and *semantic* memory, the role of proactive interference in retrieval processes, and failures in encoding have all been thoroughly explored, with their limitations as well as their utility as heuristic models for guiding amnesia research duly recorded (for reviews, see Butters & Cermak, 1980; Hirst, 1982; Piercy, 1977; Squire, 1982).

This reliance upon a field that clearly emphasizes memory for recently acquired information (usually learned in the laboratory) has resulted in a disproportionate emphasis on anterograde rather than retrograde amnesia (RA). Most of the reported studies since 1970 have been concerned with information-processing deficits underlying amnesic patients' inability to learn new information presented subsequent to the onset of their amnesia (i.e., anterograde amnesia). Relatively few studies have been concerned with the amnesics' diminished ability to recall events and information learned prior to the onset of their neurological disorder (i.e., retrograde amnesia). Those that have been reported are generally more concerned with delineating the severity and duration of this impairment than with describing the cognitive processes that might contribute to the disorder.

Another reason for this benign neglect of retrograde amnesia is that anterograde amnesia is methodologically easier to assess than is RA. To investigate anterograde amnesia one must simply insure that learning materials

Support for the writing of this chapter and some of the research described was supplied by the Medical Research Service of the Veterans Administration and by NIAAA Grant AA-00187 to Boston University.

(e.g., word lists, lists of paired associates) are equated or systematically altered with regard to such variables as frequency of usage, meaningfulness, concreteness, and association value. Given the plethora of published norms for such factors, it is not difficult to find such experimentally sound materials to assess new learning. On the other hand, such is not the case for RA. As Sanders and Warrington (1971) have noted, it is an arduous task to develop either a public events questionnaire or a series of photographs of famous people in which the items are of equal difficulty and have had equivalent exposure over a prolonged period of time. For instance, 60-year-old veterans and nonveterans of World War II did not have equivalent exposure to the major events of that war. Similarly, when we ask a 48-year-old subject, "Who was president of the United States when the atomic bomb was dropped on Hiroshima?" are we assessing information that was acquired in 1945 or later in school in the 1950s or even now during public debates on the proliferation of nuclear weapons?

Despite these barriers, a limited number of investigators have tackled the issue, and the purpose of the present chapter will be to review this literature on retrograde amnesia, noting both the complexities of the problem and the advances that have been made. In addition, this chapter will demonstrate how extensive study of a single patient's autobiographical memory can provide the crucial evidence to explain the factors underlying at least one amnesic population's (patients with alcoholic Korsakoff's syndrome) retrograde amnesia.

Prior to beginning this review of the RA literature, it is important to clarify the definition of autobiographical memory that will be used in this paper. Unlike some contributors to this volume, we are not equating autobiographical memory with retrieval from episodic memory. It is certainly true that personal episodes tied to specific spatial and temporal contexts compose part of an individual's autobiographical memory. However, general knowledge, especially that shown by independent sources to have been acquired prior to the time of testing and to be pertinent to the individual's personal or professional life, ought also to be included. Documentation that a patient once knew a particular piece of information could easily be used as a critical factor for including it in a study of autobiographical memory. If little is known concerning a patient's past knowledge, one can only surmise that public events questionnaires and famous persons tests are truly assessing the retention and retrieval of previously learned information. However, if a patient has written an autobiography and/or provided written documentation (e.g., letters, diaries) of past knowledge, a retrograde amnesia battery constructed from this information could also be considered an assessment of his autobiographical memory.

### Recent investigations of retrograde amnesia

The patient with retrograde amnesia has difficulty recalling events that occurred before the onset of his illness. When asked who was president of the United States before Mr. Reagan, the patient may answer "Johnson" or perhaps "Kennedy." If asked whether any other presidents held office between Mr. Reagan and Mr. Kennedy, the patient may say no or at the very least be extremely uncertain as to the temporal ordering of the presidents he might ultimately recall. In general, this difficulty in retrieval of old memories is more pronounced for events immediately prior to the onset of the illness than for remote events from the patient's childhood. For the alcoholic Korsakoff patient, this loss of remote memories is severe, extends over several decades (e.g., 1930s–1970s), and is characterized by a temporal gradient in which memories for very remote events (e.g., from the 1930s and 1940s) are relatively well preserved (Albert, Butters, & Levin, 1979; Cohen & Squire, 1981; Marslen-Wilson & Teuber, 1975; Meudell, Northern, Snowden, & Neary, 1980; Seltzer & Benson, 1974; Squire and Cohen, 1982). These features of the Korsakoff patient's RA have been demonstrated consistently with a number of remote memory tests involving the identification of photographs of famous persons (e.g., Albert et al., 1979) and recordings of voices of famous people (Meudell et al., 1980) and the recall and recognition of public events (e.g., Albert et al., 1979; Cohen & Squire, 1981).

Zola-Morgan, Cohen, and Squire's (1983) recent investigation of remote episodic memory indicates that this temporal gradient is also apparent when alcoholic Korsakoff patients attempt to remember specific personal experiences. These investigators presented alcoholic Korsakoff patients and alcoholic control subjects with 10 stimulus words (e.g., *sad*) and asked them to recall specific episodes from their past that involved the stimuli (e.g., "I remember being very *sad* at my father's funeral twenty-two years ago. When I saw all my relatives at the funeral home, I began crying and continued to do so during the entire service"). If the patients did not initially recall an episode for a specific stimulus word, the examiner "probed" (i.e., cued) the patients by providing an example. The results showed that, although the Korsakoff patients and control subjects did not differ in their overall ability to retrieve episodic memories under cued conditions, they varied significantly in terms of the periods of their lives from which the memories emanated. Unlike the alcoholic control subjects, who remembered personal episodes from both the recent and the remote past, the Korsakoff patients recalled events almost exclusively from their childhood and early adulthood. Thus, with no temporal restrictions placed on their retrieval processes, the Korsakoff patients limited their recall to episodes that had occurred 30 to 40 years ago.

In contrast to the alcoholic Korsakoff patients' extensive deficits, systematic assessments of the RA of other patient populations have reported temporally limited (e.g., 1–4 years) forgetting of old memories. The well-studied amnesic patients H.M. (Marslen-Wilson & Teuber, 1975; Milner, 1966, 1970) and N.A. (Cohen & Squire, 1981; Squire & Cohen, 1982; Squire & Moore, 1979; Squire & Slater, 1978), depressed patients receiving ECT (Squire, Chace, & Slater, 1976; Squire, Slater, & Chace, 1975), and traumatic amnesics (Benson & Geschwind, 1967; Levin, Benton, & Grossman, 1982; Russell & Nathan, 1946) all have losses of remote memories limited to the 3- or 4-year period immediately preceding their illness or the beginning of shock treatment (ECT). Recall of public events that occurred prior to this circumscribed RA is normal, a finding consistent with the notion that old, very remote memories are more resistant to forgetting than are newly acquired engrams (Ribot, 1883).

Despite the consistency with which investigators have noted the relative or complete sparing of very remote memories, Sanders and Warrington (1971) have raised a serious issue concerning the validity of most test instruments used to measure the temporal gradient in retrograde amnesia. They also administered public events questionnaires and a test of facial recognition to a group of amnesic patients of mixed etiology. With their tests, they showed that amnesics were severely impaired with no relative sparing of very remote events. Their patients had as much difficulty recalling and recognizing public events from the 1930s as they did events from the 1960s. Sanders and Warrington proposed that other tests demonstrating a sparing of remote memories may have involved failures to control for the difficulty and overexposure of the faces and events associated with the decades under study. That is, events and faces from the 1930s and 1940s may be easier to recall than those from the 1960s and 1970s because the former have been overlearned and are of more lasting fame due to overexposure in subsequent decades. For example, pictures of Charlie Chaplin dressed as a tramp have been exposed to the public during every decade since the 1920s.

Warrington and Weiskrantz (1973) have interpreted this demonstration of an extensive and "flat" retrograde amnesia as consistent with their interference retrieval theory of amnesia. They proposed that all the memory difficulties of amnesic patients can be reduced solely to an inability to *retrieve* information from long-term memory and that there is no reason to expect memories from childhood, adolescence, and young adulthood to be spared.

Unfortunately, Sanders and Warrington's (1971) empirical data were flawed by "floor" effects (i.e., their amnesics performed at chance levels on the recognition tests), but their emphasis on the control of item difficulty and overlearning had face validity and forced a reevaluation of retrograde amnesia with more carefully developed test instruments. Albert, Butters, and Levin (1979) constructed an RA test battery that statistically controlled for item difficulty. Their battery included a famous faces (i.e., persons) test, a recall questionnaire, and a multiple-choice recognition questionnaire. Each test consisted of items from the 1930s to the 1970s that had been standardized on a population of normal controls before their inclusion in the final test battery. Half of the items were "easy" (e.g., picture of Franklin Roosevelt) as judged by the performance of the standardization group; the other half were difficult or "hard" (e.g., picture of Rosemary Clooney), judged by the same criterion. In addition, the famous persons test included photographs of some individuals both early and late in their careers. For example, photographs of Marlon Brando from both the 1950s and the 1970s were included in the test battery.

When this remote memory battery was administered to alcoholic Korsakoff patients and normal control subjects (Albert et al., 1979), little evidence supporting Sanders and Warrington's (1971) proposal was found. As shown in Figure 14.1, the alcoholic Korsakoff patients identified more faces from the 1930s and 1940s than from the 1960s, regardless of the fame of the individual pictured. Furthermore, although the normal controls were more accurate in identifying famous people later rather than earlier in their careers, the Korsakoff patients performed in the opposite manner. On the recall test of public events, the same pattern emerged. For both easy and hard items, the Korsakoff patients recalled more information from the 1930s and 1940s than from the 1960s. Similar gradients were reported for the recognition test of public events (Albert et al., 1979).

Recently, Squire and Cohen (1982) have suggested that Albert, Butters, and Levin's (1979) statistical approach to item difficulty may actually have confounded rather than solved the equivalence and overlearning issue. They questioned whether two public events (or pictures of famous people) from two separate decades (e.g., one from the 1930s and the other from the 1970s) can ever be considered intrinsically equal in difficulty, even if both are recalled by 80% of all controls. That one event occurred 40 years prior to the other and is still remembered as well suggests that the very remote event is more famous and overlearned than the recent one. The mere passage of 30 years since original acquisition should have weakened the memory engram more than a 5-year interval since original learning. From their viewpoint, statistical equality might simply be a mask for an intrinsic inequality manifested by the temporal gradients of amnesic patients.

Butters and Albert (1982) have offered some additional empirical evidence for their statistical approach, however. They reanalyzed their original data on the famous persons test so that "easy" items from the recent past could be compared with "hard" items from the remote past. They found that normal

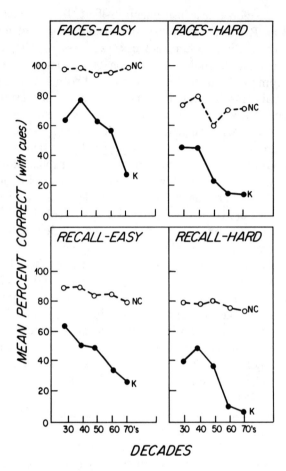

Figure 14.1. Mean percentage of easy and hard items correctly recalled by alcoholic Korsakoff (K) and normal control (NC) subjects on Albert, Butters, and Levin's (1979) famous faces test (*top*) and public events recall questionnaire (*bottom*). (From Albert et al., 1979)

controls, as expected, identified significantly fewer faces from the remote than from the recent past, but alcoholic Korsakoff patients evidenced the opposite trend. That is, the amnesic Korsakoff patients correctly identified more hard faces from the remote past (e.g., the 1930s and 1940s) than easy faces from the recent past (e.g., 1970s). Butters and Albert note that this relative preservation of very remote memories under conditions of planned statistical inequality offers strong support that temporal gradients characterize the RA of alcoholic Korsakoff patients.

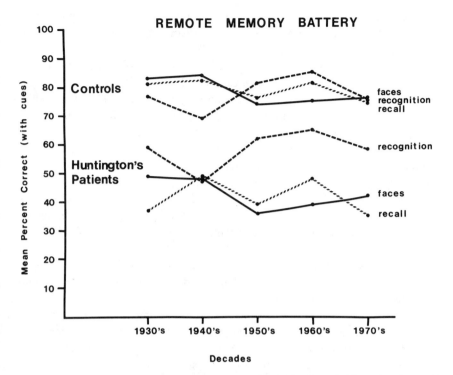

Figure 14.2. Performance of demented patients (Huntington's Disease) and normal control subjects on Albert, Butters, and Levin's (1979) retrograde amnesia test battery. Results for the famous faces test and the public events recall and recognition questionnaires are shown. (From Albert et al., 1981)

The investigations of the retrograde amnesia of demented patients with Huntington's Disease (HD) are also relevant to Squire and Cohen's critique (Albert, Butters, & Brandt, 1981). Huntington's Disease is a genetically transmitted disorder in which the patient undergoes progressive motor and intellectual deterioration due to atrophy of the caudate nuclei and other basal ganglia. During the early and middle stages of the disease the HD patient complains of memory problems, but his amnesic symptoms are only one aspect of a general intellectual dementia, as witnessed by his loss of visuoperceptive and conceptual capacities. When Albert, Butters, and Brandt (1981) administered their retrograde amnesia battery to such a group of HD patients, they found that these demented patients, unlike the amnesic Korsakoff patients, showed equal forgetting of public events and famous faces across all decades from the 1930s to the 1970s (Fig. 14.2).

Butters and Albert (1982) suggest that the HD patient's equal loss of very remote and recent memories weakens criticisms of the statistical approach to item difficulty. If the temporal gradients of Korsakoff patients were due to some intrinsic inequality in the difficulty of the faces and questions from the various decades, then the HD patients should have manifested a similar temporal gradient. Furthermore, like the amnesic Korsakoff patients, the HD patients should have identified more of the easy (from the 1930s and 1940s) than of the hard (from the 1960s and 1970s) faces and public events. To simultaneously accept the "flat" gradients of the demented patients and dismiss the temporal gradients of the amnesic patients, one must explain why Albert, Butters, and Levin's (1979) items from the 1930s and 1940s are not also intrinsically easy for demented individuals.

Squire and his colleagues have used a different approach to develop a remote memory test that also circumvents the overlearning and overexposure problems noted by Sanders and Warrington (1971). To insure limited but equivalent public exposure, Squire and Slater (1975) used the titles of television programs that had been aired for one season or less in the construction of their recall and recognition tests. The individual items on these tests could be matched for public exposure on the basis of known viewing histories, and because the items had a brief exposure period the time of learning could be specified. That normal subjects who resided out of the United States were unable to recognize the titles of the one-season programs aired during their absence provided strong support for the investigators' claim that the programs queried on the test were not overexposed or publicized in the years following their limited broadcast (Squire & Slater, 1975). A recognition form of this television program test requires the subjects to select from several alternatives the title of an aired program. On the recall test, the subjects were asked to supply details (e.g., names of characters and actors) about specified one-season television programs.

These tests of past television programs have been administered to depressed patients in the course of bilateral electroconvulsive therapy (ECT). The results of these studies also support Ribot's (1883) hypothesis. As shown in Figure 14.3, the RA following ECT is temporally limited. For both tests, the patients served as their own controls, with testing occurring prior to the first ECT and again 1 hour following the fifth administration of ECT. On the recognition form of the television test, the ECT patients were unable to recognize the titles of programs aired 1–3 years immediately prior to the ECT but had no difficulty recognizing titles of programs broadcast 4–17 years prior to ECT (Squire et al., 1975). For the detailed recall task, the patients were impaired in their recall of shows aired 1–2 years before ECT but did not differ from control subjects in recalling programs broadcast prior to that time (Squire & Cohen, 1979).

The vast majority of the published research with amnesic patients confirms

TELEVISION PROGRAMS TEST

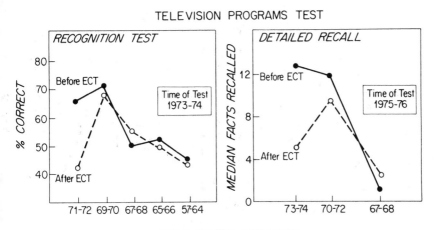

Figure 14.3. Retrograde amnesia following bilateral electroconvulsive therapy: (*a*) recognition of the titles of former one-season television programs; (*b*) recall of details about former one-season television programs. (From Squire & Cohen, 1982; Squire, Slater, & Chace, 1975)

the differential sparing of very remote memories, but it also underscores the heterogeneity of the RAs exhibited by different patient populations. Of the various amnesic patients who have been studied systematically, only the alcoholic Korsakoff patients (and possibly postencephalitic patients; see Butters & Cermak, 1980; Cermak, 1976; Cermak & O'Connor, 1983; Damasio, Eslinger, Damasio, Van Hoesen, & Cornell, in press) have remote memory losses that extend more than 10 years and involve all periods of the patients' lives. Although the alcoholic Korsakoff patients' memory for events that occurred during the 1940s is certainly superior to their recall of events in the 1960s, their retention of information from the more remote decades is still significantly impaired in comparison to the recall of normal controls (Albert et al., 1979; Squire & Cohen, 1982). As noted previously, this extensive *temporally graded* loss of old memories is much more evident and severe than the *temporally limited* retrograde amnesias (1 to 4 years) of depressed patients undergoing bilateral ECT, of patients with posttraumatic amnesia, and of the well-studied amnesic patients H.M. and N.A. More recently, Butters, Miliotis, Albert, and Sax (1984) have described the chronic amnesia of an electrical engineer (patient R.B.) following the clipping of an aneurysm of the anterior communicating artery. Despite an inordinate difficulty in retaining postsurgical life experiences and in learning verbal and digit-symbol paired associates, R.B.'s memory for events prior to his surgery seemed to be relatively intact.

This difference between the retrograde amnesias of alcoholic Korsakoff patients and of other amnesic populations has been addressed by Squire and Cohen (1982) and by Butters and Albert (1982). Both sets of investigators have suggested that the alcoholic Korsakoff patients' extensive loss of or access to remote memories may be secondary to a primary defect in establishing new memories (i.e., anterograde amnesia) during the 20 years of alcohol abuse that preceded the diagnosis of the amnesic syndrome. Although detoxified non-Korsakoff alcoholics have often been viewed as free of anterograde memory defects (for review, see Parsons & Prigatano, 1977), recent studies (e.g., Brandt, Butters, Ryan, & Bayog, 1983) have shown that detoxified alcoholics are impaired on some short-term-memory and paired-associate learning tasks. Consequently, if chronic alcoholics acquire less information each year due to a progressive anterograde memory deficit, then at the time an alcoholic patient is diagnosed as having Korsakoff's syndrome one would expect to find an RA with a temporal gradient. From this viewpoint, the Korsakoff patients' loss of remote memories would be considered an artifact related to a primary defect in establishing new memories. A corollary of this hypothesis is that true RAs, uncontaminated by deficiencies in original learning and cognitive retrieval strategies, are temporally limited and are far less severe and devastating than the amnesic patients' anterograde memory problems (Squire & Cohen, 1982).

To evaluate this "chronic" explanation of the Korsakoffs' retrograde amnesia, Albert, Butters, and Brandt (1980) administered their remote memory battery to detoxified long-term (non-Korsakoff) alcoholics and nonalcoholic control subjects. They felt that, if the learning deficit related to alcoholism was responsible for the alcoholic Korsakoff patients' difficulties recalling past events, two predictions could be made: (1) The alcoholics should be impaired in their identification of photographs of famous people and public events; and (2), because the detrimental effects of alcohol on the learning of new materials are likely related to years of alcohol abuse, the alcoholics' deficits in recalling past events should be most apparent for the years immediately preceding testing. The results partially confirmed these expectations. Although the alcoholics' mean recall scores for hard famous faces from the 1960s and 1970s were poorer than the scores of the nonalcoholic controls, these differences did not attain statistical significance. However, on the recall questionnaire the alcoholics had a significant, but mild, impairment in their recall of hard public events from the 1960s and 1970s. It is also pertinent that this deficit in the recall of remote events from the last two decades was consonant with the length of the patients' alcohol abuse (mean = 25.18 years). As further evidence, Cohen and Squire (1981) have also reported mild to moderate remote memory deficits in chronic (non-Korsakoff) alcoholics.

Although the results of Albert, Butters, and Brandt's (1980) and Cohen and Squire's (1981) studies are not of the magnitude to allow the alcoholic Korsakoff patients' RA to be reduced to an anterograde memory problem, they do suggest that two separate etiological factors may be involved. One factor is the impact of chronic alcohol abuse on anterograde memory processes. Because long-term alcoholics may have a progressive impairment in their ability to learn new information (Brandt et al., 1983), their store of remote memories for the recent past may be mildly or moderately deficient. Another factor may be a forgetting of, or a loss of access to, old memories that appears acutely during the Wernicke stage of the illness and results in a severe and equal loss for all time periods prior to the onset of the disease. When this acute loss of remote memories is superimposed on the patients' already deficient store, a severe retrograde amnesia with a temporal gradient would be expected. Patients should be impaired with respect to controls across all time periods, but memory for recent events should be most severely affected because less had been learned initially during this period.

## Autobiographical memory of patient P.Z.

The most convincing evidence for this two-factor model of the alcoholic Korsakoff patients' retrograde amnesia comes from a single-case study of autobiographical memory (Butters, 1984). This patient (with the fictitious initials P.Z.), an eminent scientist and university professor who developed alcoholic Korsakoff's syndrome at the age of 65, had written several hundred research papers and numerous books and book chapters, including an extensive autobiography 2 years prior to the acute onset of his amnesic condition in 1981. Like all alcoholics with Korsakoff's syndrome, patient P.Z. had severe anterograde and retrograde amnesia as assessed by both clinical and formal psychometric techniques. As seen in Figures 14.4 and 14.5, patient P.Z. was unable to learn both verbal–verbal (e.g., neck–salt) and symbol–digit paired associates. This latter task requires subjects to associate single-digit numbers with geometric forms such that when the form is presented alone the subject must recall the number that had been associated with it (for more detail, see Brandt et al., 1983). On Albert, Butters, and Levin's (1979) famous persons test, patient P.Z. was severely impaired in his identification of famous people but did evidence some sparing of memories of people from the 1930s and 1940s (Fig. 14.6).

In order to assess patient P.Z.'s amnesia for famous individuals within his scientific specialty, we constructed a famous scientists test. This test consisted of the names of 75 famous investigators and scholars, all of whom had been well known to P.Z. The vast majority of these names were mentioned promi-

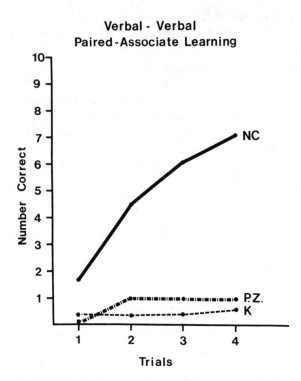

Figure 14.4. Performance of patient P.Z., patients with alcoholic Korsakoff's syndrome (K), and normal control subjects (NC) on a verbal–verbal paired-associate learning task. (From Butters, 1984)

nently in one or more of P.Z.'s books or major scholarly papers and, therefore, had been at one time part of his autobiographical memory. Still other names were chosen because of their documented professional interactions with P.Z. (e.g., editors of major journals in P.Z.'s area of expertise). Of these scholars, 28 had reached the pinnacle of their prominence prior to 1965, 24 had made major contributions both before and after 1965, and 23 had attained a high level of fame and visibility since 1965. Patient P.Z. was presented with each name and asked to describe the scholar's major area of interest and his or her specific contributions to this specialty. P.Z.'s answers were tape-recorded and later scored on a 3-point (0, 1, 2) ordinal scale in terms of their adequacy. For example, if P.Z. could identify the scientist's area of expertise but could not recall a specific major contribution, the response was rated as a 1. If, however, P.Z. identified accurately both the scientist's area of research and a specific scholarly contribution to this area, his response was assigned a score of 2. Only a total failure to recognize the scientist or to inaccurately identify the scientist's major area of interest resulted in a score of 0. To provide a standard

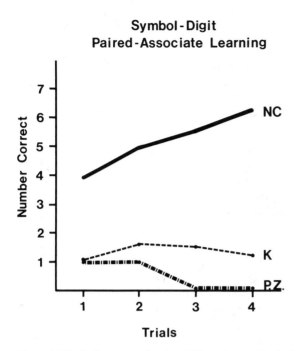

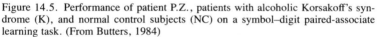

Figure 14.5. Performance of patient P.Z., patients with alcoholic Korsakoff's syndrome (K), and normal control subjects (NC) on a symbol–digit paired-associate learning task. (From Butters, 1984)

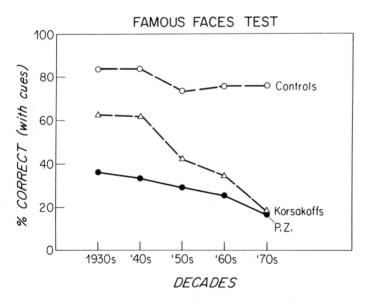

Figure 14.6. Performance of patient P.Z., alcoholic Korsakoff patients, and normal control subjects on Albert's famous faces test. (From Butters, 1984)

FAMOUS SCIENTISTS TEST

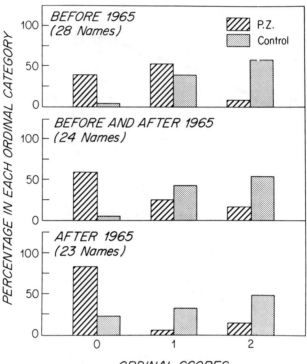

Figure 14.7. Performance of patient P.Z. and his matched control subject on the identification of famous scientists. Scores 0, 1, and 2 represent an ordinal scaling of the adequacy of the two subjects' responses. (From Butters, 1984)

for evaluating P.Z.'s memory for famous scientists, another 65-year-old, highly prominent scholar in P.Z.'s area of specialization was administered the same famous scientists test.

The results for this famous scientists test are shown in Figure 14.7. Even a casual inspection of this data makes it obvious that patient P.Z. has a severe RA for individuals who were once well known to him. This deficit is apparent for all three temporal categories, but it is most evident for those scientists who attained prominence after 1965. The percentage of 0 scores increases dramatically from the "before 1965" to the "after 1965" category, whereas the percentage of 1 rankings shows the opposite trend (i.e., highest percentage was for scientists prominent prior to 1965). Thus, P.Z. appears to have a temporally graded loss of knowledge for professional colleagues and ac-

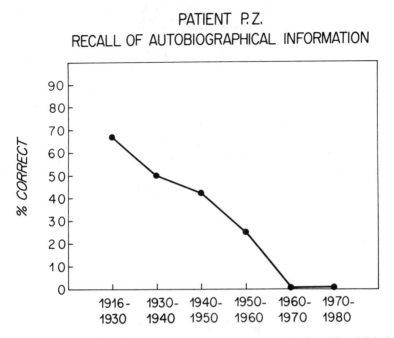

Figure 14.8. Patient P.Z.'s retrograde amnesia for information from his published autobiography. (From Butters, 1984)

quaintances who, by all accounts and documentation, were familiar to him prior to the acute onset of the Wernicke's stage of his disorder.

To determine whether patient P.Z. had also lost access to other autobiographical material familiar to him before his illness, a retrograde amnesia test based upon his written autobiography was developed. The test consisted of questions about relatives, colleagues, collaborators, conferences, research assistants, research reports, and books mentioned prominently in his autobiography.

P.Z.'s recall of these autobiographical facts is shown in Figure 14.8. As with the famous scientists test, two points are evident. First, P.Z. has a very severe retrograde amnesia for autobiographical events, with sparing of information only from the very remote past. Second, P.Z.'s retrograde amnesia for autobiographical material cannot be secondary to a deficiency in original learning. The fact that all the questions were drawn from his own autobiography eliminates the possibility that he had never acquired the information. Just 3 years prior to the onset of his Korsakoff's syndrome, P.Z. could retrieve this information, which he considered most important in his professional and personal life. Clearly, P.Z.'s illness marked the acute onset of his inability to access information once readily available to him.

The more severe impairment in retrieval of information acquired during the most recent two decades suggests that this autobiographical information might not have achieved as stable a level as information acquired earlier in patient P.Z.'s lifetime. There are a number of plausible interpretations. One possibility is that this instability represents a progressive loss of P.Z.'s ability to acquire new information during his 35-year history of alcoholism (Albert et al., 1980; Cohen & Squire, 1981). This is substantiated by the abundant evidence that alcohol is neurotoxic (for review, see Butters, 1984) and often results in mild to moderate deficiencies in the long-term alcoholic's capacity to learn new information (Becker, Butters, Hermann, & D'Angelo, 1983; Brandt et al., 1983). Thus, due to the increasingly deleterious effects of alcohol, P.Z.'s memory for episodes and facts from the past 20 years may have been based upon partial or "degraded" engrams. The more degraded or partial the memories, the more vulnerable they may have been to the acute brain damage that occurred in 1981.

A second plausible explanation for the temporal gradients that character-ized P.Z.'s retrograde amnesia involves the notion that information acquired decades previously might be retrieved from a more general knowledge system than is the case for recently acquired information. Cermak (1984) has sug-gested that newly acquired knowledge may be *episodic* in nature but that with time and continued rehearsal the memories become independent of specific temporal and spatial contexts (i.e., *semantic* memory). From this viewpoint, the gradients evidenced by P.Z. (and other alcoholic Korsakoff patients) are due to the greater vulnerability of episodic than of semantic memory to exten-sive damage to diencephalic or mesial temporal lobe structures. Knowledge of public events and personal experiences from the 1930s and 1940s may be part of semantic memory whereas public and personal happenings from the past decade may still be associated with specific spatial and temporal con-texts. This hypothesis stressing the loss of episodic memory is unique among theories of amnesia because it attempts to account for both the patients' an-terograde and their retrograde amnesias. Other investigators (e.g., Weingart-ner, Grafman, Boutelle, Kaye, & Martin, 1983) who have adopted Tulving's (1983) distinction between episodic and semantic memory have concentrated their analyses primarily upon amnesic patients' anterograde memory prob-lems.

Cermak's (1984) proposed shift of information from episodic to semantic memory has merit in our attempts to understand patient P.Z.'s temporally graded loss of autobiographical information, but it must be noted that seman-tic memory is not completely normal in amnesic conditions. It is relatively

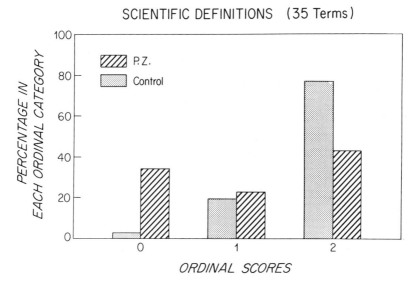

Figure 14.9. Performance of patient P.Z. and his matched control subject on the definition of scientific terms. Scores 0, 1, and 2 represent an ordinal scaling of the adequacy of the two subjects' responses.

more preserved than episodic memory, but, as our further explorations with P.Z. demonstrate, loss from general (i.e., semantic) knowledge also occurs following brain damage. Because we had access to P.Z.'s numerous books and journal publications, it was possible to construct a test consisting of definitions from P.Z.'s field of scientific expertise. All scientific terms on this test appeared in one or more of P.Z.'s written works, and thus they were, by our definition, part of his autobiographical, or personal, semantic memory. Patient P.Z. was read each term individually and asked to provide a complete definition with as many examples and details as possible. All of P.Z.'s responses were tape-recorded, later transcribed, and then rated on a 3-point ordinal scale (i.e., 0, 1, 2) similar to the one used on the famous scientists test (Fig. 14.7). A rating of 0 indicated that patient P.Z. was totally unaware of the meaning of a term, whereas a score of 2 meant that P.Z. supplied a full and accurate definition of the term. A score of 1 was used when P.Z. provided an incomplete, partial definition. The same control subject used for the famous scientists test was also asked to define the scientific terms.

The results for the scientific definitions test are shown in Figure 14.9. In comparison to his control subject, patient P.Z. is impaired in his ability to define scientific terms once well known to him. This lack of scientific knowledge not only is consistent with the previous evidence of an acute loss of autobiographical memories but also demonstrates that semantic memory is not completely intact in amnesic patients. If, as Tulving (1983) has suggested, the learning and retention of definitions can be used to evaluate the status of semantic memory, it is difficult to characterize P.Z.'s loss of autobiographical memory as a pure deficit in episodic memory. Taken together, the available data suggest that, although amnesic patients are relatively much more impaired in the acquisition and retention of episodic rather than semantic memories (Cermak, 1984), retrieval from both memory systems is adversely affected. The linkage of these two memory systems to specific brain structures still remains problematical. It is entirely possible, as Weingartner and his colleagues (1983) have suggested, that episodic memory depends upon the integrity of the limbic-diencephalic system whereas loss of semantic memory may be associated with damage to association cortex. Because most amnesic patients have suffered damage to both limbic and cortical structures, the validity of this proposed double dissociation remains difficult to assess.

## Conclusions

In summary, the intensive study of patient P.Z.'s autobiographical memory has yielded valuable insights into the retrograde amnesia of alcoholic Korsakoff patients. Because P.Z.'s autobiography, as well as his professional publications, provided us with extensive information concerning his episodic and semantic memories prior to the onset of Korsakoff's syndrome, it was possible to assess the acuteness, extent, and severity of his loss of remote memories. Based upon his current lack of knowledge of pertinent personal and professional information, there can be little doubt that his severe retrograde amnesia developed acutely with the onset of his amnesic disorder. Likewise, the temporal gradient so evident in his autobiographical memories suggests that this relative sparing of very remote memories cannot be dismissed as a methodological deficiency. Although there may have been a progressive degrading of new memories formed during his 35 years of alcohol abuse, the relative preservation of autobiographical memories from P.Z.'s childhood and early adulthood may also represent a shift of stored information from an episodic to a semantic store. Although P.Z. evidenced some significant loss of semantic knowledge concerning his profession, the possibility that amnesia represents predominantly a loss of episodic memories remains viable and worthy of future testing with amnesic populations of diverse etiologies.

## References

Albert, M. S., Butters, N., & Brandt, J. (1980). Memory for remote events in alcoholics. *Journal of Studies on Alcohol, 41,* 1071–1081.

(1981). Patterns of remote memory in amnesic and demented patients. *Archives of Neurology, 38,* 495–500.

Albert, M. S., Butters, N., & Levin, J. (1979). Temporal gradients in the retrograde amnesia of patients with alcoholic Korsakoff's disease. *Archives of Neurology, 36,* 211–216.

Becker, J. T., Butters, N., Hermann, A., & D'Angelo, N. (1983). Learning to associate names and faces: Impaired acquisition on an ecologically relevant memory task by male alcoholics. *Journal of Nervous and Mental Disease, 171,* 617–623.

Benson, D. F., & Geschwind, N. (1967). Shrinking retrograde amnesia. *Journal of Neurology, Neurosurgery, and Psychiatry, 30,* 539–544.

Brandt, J., Butters, N., Ryan, C., & Bayog, R. (1983). Cognitive loss and recovery in chronic alcohol abusers. *Archives of General Psychiatry, 40,* 435–442.

Butters, N. (1984). Alcoholic Korsakoff's syndrome: An update. *Seminars in Neurology, 4,* 229–247.

Butters, N., & Albert, M. S. (1982). Processes underlying failures to recall remote events. In L. S. Cermak (Ed.), *Human memory and amnesia* (pp. 257–303). Hillsdale, NJ: Erlbaum.

Butters, N., & Cermak, L. S. (1980). *Alcoholic Korsakoff's syndrome: An information-processing approach to amnesia.* New York: Academic Press.

Butters, N., Miliotis, P., Albert, M. S., & Sax, D. S. (1984). Memory assessment: Evidence of the heterogeneity of amnesic symptoms. In G. Goldstein (Ed.), *Advances in clinical neuropsychology* (vol. 1, pp. 127–159). New York: Plenum Press.

Cermak, L. S. (1976). The encoding capacity of a patient with amnesia due to encephalitis. *Neuropsychologia, 14,* 311–326.

(1977). The contribution of a "processing" deficit to alcoholic Korsakoff patients' memory disorder. In I. M. Birnbaum & E. S. Parker (Eds.), *Alcohol and human memory* (pp. 195–208). Hillsdale, NJ: Erlbaum.

(1984). The episodic/semantic distinction in amnesia. In N. Butters & L. R. Squire (Eds.), *The neuropsychology of memory* (pp. 55–62). New York: Guilford Press.

Cermak, L. S., & Butters, N. (1976). The role of language in the memory disorders of brain damaged patients. *Annals of the New York Academy of Science, 280,* 857–867.

Cermak, L. S. & O'Connor, M. (1983). The anterograde and retrograde retrieval ability of a patient with amnesia due to encephalitis. *Neuropsychologia, 21,* 213–234.

Cohen, N. J., & Squire, L. R. (1981). Retrograde amnesia and remote memory impairment. *Neuropsychologia, 19,* 337–356.

Craik, F. I. M., & Lockhart, R. S. (1972). Levels of processing: A framework for memory research. *Journal of Verbal Learning and Verbal Behavior, II,* 671–684.

Craik, F. I. M., & Tulving, E. (1975). Depth of processing and retention of words in episodic memory. *Journal of Experimental Psychology: General, 104,* 268–194.

Damasio, A., Eslinger, P., Damasio, H., Van Hoesen, G., & Cornell, S. (in press). Multimodal amnesic syndrome following bilateral temporal and basal forebrain damage: The case of patient DRB. *Archives of Neurology.*

Hirst, W. (1982). The amnesic syndrome: Descriptions and explanations. *Psychological Bulletin, 91,* 435–460.

Levin, H. S., Benton, A. L., & Grossman, R. G. (1982). *Neurobehavioral consequences of closed head injury.* New York: Oxford University Press.

Marslen-Wilson, W. D., & Teuber, H. L. (1975). Memory for remote events in anterograde amnesia: Recognition of public figures from news photographs. *Neuropsychologia, 13,* 347–352.

Meudell, P. R., Northern, B., Snowden, J. S., & Neary, D. (1980). Long-term memory for famous voices in amnesic and normal subjects. *Neuropsychologia, 18,* 133–139.

Milner, B. (1966). Amnesia following operation on the temporal lobes. In C. W. M. Whitty & O. L. Zangwill (Eds.), *Amnesia* (pp. 109–133). London: Butterworth.

(1970). Memory and the medial temporal regions of the brain. In K. H. Pribram & D. E. Broadbent (Eds.), *Biology of memory* (pp. 29–50). New York: Academic Press.

Parsons, O. A., & Prigatano, G. P. (1977). Memory functioning in alcoholics. In I. M. Birnbaum & E. S. Parker (Eds.), *Alcohol and human memory* (pp. 185–194). Hillsdale, NJ: Erlbaum.

Piercy, M. F. (1977). Experimental studies of the organic amnesic syndrome. In C. W. M. Whitty & O. L. Zangwill (Eds.), *Amnesia* (2nd ed., pp. 1–51). London: Butterworth.

Ribot, T. (1883). *Diseases of memory* (2nd ed.). London: Kegan Paul, Trench.

Russell, W. R., & Nathan, P. W. (1946). Traumatic amnesia. *Brain, 69,* 280–300.

Sanders, H. I., & Warrington, E. K. (1971). Memory for remote events in amnesic patients. *Brain, 94,* 661–668.

Seltzer, B., & Benson, D. F. (1974). The temporal pattern of retrograde amnesia in Korsakoff's disease. *Neurology, 24,* 527–530.

Squire, L. R. (1982). Comparisons between forms of amnesia: Some deficits are unique to Korsakoff's syndrome. *Journal of Experimental Psychology: Learning, Memory, and Cognition, 8,* 560–571.

Squire, L. R., Chace, P. M., & Slater, P. C. (1976). Retrograde amnesia following electroconvulsive therapy. *Nature, 260,* 775–777.

Squire, L. R., & Cohen, N. (1979). Memory and amnesia: Resistance to disruption develops for years after learning. *Behavioral and Neural Biology, 25,* 115–125.

(1982). Remote memory, retrograde amnesia, and the neuropsychology of memory. In L. S. Cermak (Ed.), *Human memory and amnesia* (pp. 275–303). Hillsdale, NJ: Erlbaum.

Squire, L. R., & Moore, R. Y. (1979). Dorsal thalamic lesions in a noted case of chronic memory dysfunction. *Annals of Neurology, 6,* 503–506.

Squire, L. R., & Slater, P. C. (1975). Forgetting in very long-term memory as assessed by an improved questionnaire technique. *Journal of Experimental Psychology: Human Learning and Memory, 104,* 50–54.

(1978). Anterograde and retrograde memory impairment in chronic amnesia. *Neuropsychologia, 16,* 313–322.

Squire, L. R., Slater, P. C., & Chace, P. M. (1975). Retrograde amnesia: Temporal gradient in very long-term memory following electroconvulsive therapy. *Science, 187,* 77–79.

Tulving, E. (1972). Episodic and semantic memory. In E. Tulving & W. Donaldson (Eds.), *Organization of memory* (pp. 381–403). New York: Academic Press.

(1983). *Elements of episodic memory.* Oxford: Oxford University Press.

Warrington, E. K., & Weiskrantz, L. (1973). An analysis of short-term and long-term memory defects in man. In J. A. Deutsch (Ed.), *The physiological basis of memory* (pp. 365–395). New York: Academic Press.

Weingartner, H., Grafman, J., Boutelle, W., Kaye, W., & Martin, P. (1983). Forms of memory failure. *Science, 221,* 380–382.

Zola-Morgan, S., Cohen, N. J., & Squire, L. R. (1983). Recall of remote episodic memory in amnesia. *Neuropsychologia, 21,* 487–500.

# 15  Loss and recovery of autobiographical memory after head injury

*Herbert F. Crovitz*

What follows is a transcript of two sessions with Mr. A., edited to protect his anonymity and to delete extraneous ramblings. These sessions are the data. Background literature and theoretical speculations may be found in the footnotes.

Mr. A. said he had had a head injury from a bad traffic accident, followed by a very long period of posttraumatic amnesia.[1] His continuous memory had not returned for almost a year, and that had been almost 3 years ago. What he really wanted was to remember events of personal importance to him that had happened *before* the accident, but whether weeks or months before he did not know. The method of seeking autobiographical memories in association with cue words led him on a fishing expedition in oblivion.[2]

This work was supported by the Medical Research Service of the Veterans Administration. I would like to thank Gregory Kimble, Raymond Horn, and David Rubin for making this chapter possible.

[1] Posttraumatic amnesia (PTA) is the period of variable length following head injury during which the person is confused and disoriented and during which new memories are not laid down normally or easily retrieved. During PTA people seem to act the way normals do while they are being distracted from a task. People sometimes have islands of preserved memory from during PTA. Such an island would be like a temporary removal of a distraction during a task. PTA ends when continuous memory begins again. When memories again can be stored and retrieved normally, it is as if the distraction has stopped. Retrograde amnesia (RA) is the period previous to the loss of consciousness that cannot be recalled. Usually, the length of the autobiographical memory gap termed RA shrinks quickly during recovery. It is difficult to understand retrograde amnesia in terms of commonsense concepts such as distraction, and the search for a convincing theory of RA is continuing. See Gronwall & Wrightson, 1980; Russell & Nathan, 1946; Russell & Smith, 1961; Schacter & Crovitz, 1977; and Levin, Benton, & Grossman, 1982, as well as Baddeley & Wilson (Chap. 13) and Butters & Cermak (Chap. 14).

Similar changes in memory functions occur in a great variety of neuropsychological disorders. For an extensive review of memory and other psychological functions from the point of view of clinical neuropsychology, see Lezak, 1983.

[2] The idea of using cue words to prompt associations appears to have originated with Francis Galton (1879; Crovitz, 1970). Recent studies that used such a method to elicit reports of autobiographical memories in patients with memory disorders include

Mr. A.: I want to know if everything I've been told is true. Some of the stuff interests me.

E. (Examiner): Now, you said there was a particular episode in the retrograde amnesia period you wanted to remember. Do you want to talk about that at all?

Mr. A.: It's just that my brother and I were trying to build something, and there was supposed to be a day when we had figured out how to get it to work. I'm curious about how we had solved the problem, what that day was like. It's blank in my memory.

E.: Okay, now we are going to use some cue words or prompts. They are like fishing hooks to use in going fishing in the pool of memory. *What I want to do is give you a cue word, and what I want you to hunt for is either the last one of these things you can remember from before the accident or the first one of these things you can remember from after the accident.* There will probably be a lot of slippage, but give me your best estimate of the time and place.[3] Okay, *animal.*

Mr. A. (*after a pause of 14 seconds*): I can see myself in Florida playing with a porpoise. I can see the porpoise and the beach ball in the pool. But that was just last year.

E.: The next word is *amount.*

Mr. A. (*after a pause of 34 seconds*): Sometime in the year after the accident. Sitting at my desk trying to do some calculations and thinking about

---

those of Schacter, Wang, Tulving, & Freedman, 1982; Wood, Ebert, & Kinsbourne, 1982; and Zola-Morgan, Cohen, & Squire (1983).

The cue words used in this attempt to stimulate Mr. A's autobiographical memory were a set of extremely common concrete, picturable nouns (Crovitz & Schiffman, 1974) and a set of words that appeared in undergraduates' retrieval of their early childhood autobiographical memories (Crovitz & Harvey, 1979; Crovitz, Harvey, & McKee, 1980). These words were chosen for use with Mr. A. not for any theoretically sound reason but because they were easily accessible in my files. Each of the two sets was presented in alphabetical order; however, a completely haphazard sequence of these cue words would have been better, for then the shrinkage of RA (and of PTA) toward the moment of head injury could be traced to time on the task; in this protocol the unlikely hypothesis that recovery is related to alphabetical order of the cue words remains possible.

[3] The accuracy of the times-ago assigned to autobiographical memories presents an interesting problem. On the one hand, the distribution of such memories with respect to claimed times in a person's life gives an opportunity for mathematical analysis (Crovitz & Quina-Holland, 1976; Rubin, 1982), and available evidence from diary keepers in Rubin's study indicates a high degree of accuracy in dating episodes. On the other hand, systematic errors have been found in the assignment of events to time-ago, rather than the assignment of times-ago to events. The errors that tend to occur in estimating the number of times one has been sick in the past year, for example, show *telescoping,* in which events outside the time period named tend to be drawn into it. See Loftus & Marburger, 1983; Schneider & Sumi, 1981; Sudman & Bradburn, 1973, 1974. Robinson (Chap. 10) and Brown, Shevell, & Rips (Chap. 9) show other forms of distortion in dates.

the amount of work I had to do. It seemed like a lot then. It would be simple to do now. I suppose early winter after the accident.

E.: This is in the period we say is your posttraumatic amnesia period?

Mr. A.: I can remember some little episodes.

E.: Just try to hunt for the closest association before or after the accident. Okay, *car.*

Mr. A. (*after a pause of 15 seconds*): From just last summer. I can't get rid of the memory, but I'll try to get one closer to the accident . . . yeah, the summer after the accident, driving as far as San Diego.

E.: The next word is *damage.*

Mr. A. (*after a pause of 16 seconds*): In the summer before the accident. I remember going into the firing range and blowing things up. I used to love to do that; that was fun. I still do sometimes.

E.: How about *brick?*

Mr. A. (*after a pause of 14 seconds*): Oh, heavens! A new one comes to mind. I remember . . . I'm not sure it's actually associated to brick, but it arises from brick. I remember the factory, which was a brick building. Which made me think of my ex-wife and me and my lab chief having a conference about my going back to work.

E.: That was when?

Mr. A.: That was the very end of August or the beginning of September after the accident. That's a new one, that's excellent! [*Grinning broadly*]

E.: You really look tickled with that memory. Enjoy it for a while. Does it bring back anything else?

Mr. A.: I remember a project during the autumn after the accident. I was in a different section because I couldn't use tools yet, so I got into a project in the sales department. That was not really great, actually; people weren't really helpful, and so I got switched to a different department after a couple of weeks. So this was in September for sure. I remember the supervisor, who was a royal pain in the neck.

E.: Is this the first time you've remembered that?

Mr. A.: So far as I know.

E.: Let's keep going. *Fear.*

Mr. A. (*after a pause of 35 seconds*): Afraid that that supervisor is scolding me. No, really it seems I was devoid of such emotion during the time after the accident. And I can't remember any particular incident before it.

E.: When did your emotions start picking up again, that you can remember?

Mr. A.: I still am rather stoic. I can't give you a definite time.

E.: How about *ink?*

Mr. A. (*after a pause of 14 seconds*): Yes. Trying to write in the sales department. Yes, I was trying to write, and the ink wasn't giving me any problems but I was having problems nevertheless.

E.: That was when?

Mr. A.: The first few weeks of September after the accident. September, or at the latest October.

E.: Okay, how about *knee?*

Mr. A. (*after a pause of 10 seconds*): Oh, this is far out! I can remember all sorts of things from that year all of a sudden. In that plant you were expected to be on all sorts of athletic teams but I wasn't in any condition to play football or anything, but I remember I went down to the gym trying to do exercises to get myself back in shape. I remember doing leg presses and all kinds of things. Aw . . . this is . . . yes! So I can remember the training room in the gym that autumn!

E.: Do you remember some particular event in the training room then? I'd like a memory like a flashbulb had gone off in your mind so you can see yourself at some specific time and place.

Mr. A.: Yes, I can remember the other men coming in to work out so I couldn't slough off any more. Why do I remember sloughing off?

E.: Probably because it happened a lot. I mean, frequency is a big thing in memory. Okay, *girl.*

Mr. A. (*after a pause of 23 seconds*): I have this really powerful memory that happened more than a year after the accident, of a girl I was seeing then. It was stormy and she was annoyed because she had forgot to bring along a hat. We were walking down First Avenue. I can picture the situation exactly in my mind, I have this incredible image in my mind. I can hear her voice, but I can't give you a worthwhile time. March or early April in the year after the accident.

E.: Okay, *moon.*

Mr. A. (*after a pause of 27 seconds*): I have been giving you all this afterwards junk; how would you like a before?

E.: Good.

Mr. A.: It was either one April before the accident, or the April before that, I'm not sure which. I was trying out a new telescope, and I remember very specifically noticing what looked like a reflection on the moon.

E.: Okay, *page.*

Mr. A. (*after a pause of 50 seconds*): Best thing I can think of is from May, a year after the accident. A page in a play about the Senate.

E.: *House.*

Mr. A. (*after a pause of 18 seconds*): Let's go back to the memory of me playing with the porpoise. I remember letting him out of a sort of underwater living quarters. I remember it flashing out to go after the beach ball. The same incident as before.

E.: The word is *suggestion*.

Mr. A. (*after a pause of 57 seconds*): Summer of 1980. In the next few months after the accident. I remember being in an uncle's house in Delaware and my mind wasn't too active yet, and my wife suggested I perhaps didn't want to go back to work just yet. Yeah, that was Paul's. I remember exactly where I was standing, right next to the coffee table in the living room under the skylight. A new one!

E.: Let me give you just a little theoretical vacation here. This is fascinating to me because one possibility has been that when you recover memories from a period of amnesia they don't have the same sensory autobiographical quality. Recall sometimes seems to depend on a similarity of brain states at the time of encoding and the time of retrieval. But these memory reports seem like any other ones. *Mother.*

Mr. A. (*after a pause of* [*missing data*] *seconds*): I can remember a hospital in Nevada, where I had gone to have plastic surgery and to visit my mother who lives there. I specifically remember it was my birthday, September second. I wanted to go out for my birthday to one of the gambling houses but I couldn't because I was in the hospital.

E.: How about the word *play?*

Mr. A. (*after a pause of 22 seconds*): April or March before the accident. I was standing at a ball park, a sort of pickup softball game. A few of my friends were trying to act like real pros, but they weren't succeeding.

E.: So that's in the retrograde period?

Mr. A.: I guess so. Yeah. Yeah. [*Laughter*]

E.: Can you find any other memories, looking around at the same time? Or the same place?

Mr. A.: And my brother, the one I'm trying to remember working with me on that invention, I remember he was also playing. He and I were tossing a ball.

E.: And that was two or three months after the incident you are trying to remember?

Mr. A.: Yeah, I guess, June – yeah, so it was two months *before* the accident. About two months before.

E.: How about *tongue?*

Mr. A. (*after a pause of 14 seconds*): [*Grinning*] I can't tell you when that was. Sometime during the year before the accident. My brother and I were down in the basement and he took his shoe off and we were looking at the way tongues are put in shoes.

E.: So that was approximately when? Between when and when?

Mr. A.: It could have been anytime between September 1979 and June 1980 – he moved into that house in September, I think. Yeah, when he went back to school.

E.: And June 1980 is the time of the accident? How about *school?*

Mr. A. *(after a pause of 8 seconds)*: I have a very vivid memory of the cafeteria at the technical school I was teaching a class at. I was joking around with some of the students who were wearing light clothes, no coats, so it must have been March or April.

E.: And this is somewhere in the time period you are looking for?

Mr. A.: Yeah, it's close.

E.: Can you find the day after?

Mr. A.: Oh, wow. I wonder how I know that! I was in class. The best student I ever had. Maybe that's why I remember it. Right after lunch in the cafeteria. I can see that student and hear her voice, giggling. *[Laughter]*

E.: Okay, let's move on. How about *water?*

Mr. A. *(after a pause of 57 seconds)*: No . . . I want to tell you about another memory, not one I've already talked about, but I'm not having much success so far . . . gee, I can remember all these things about my brother, but I can't remember that day . . . I can remember holding the water hose for my brother. It must have been mid to late June of 1980. I was holding the water hose for my brother. I don't have any idea why I'd remember that, because there's nothing very spectacular about what happened. I can't remember any conversation, I just remember doing it.

E.: Can you see the position you were standing in? Or where he was?

Mr. A.: Um, he was getting a drink out of the water hose and I was standing; let's see, the water hose was attached to a spigot behind a bush, and he was facing the bush and I was to his right, facing away from it.

E.: That was only a couple of weeks before the accident?

Mr. A.: That was only a couple of weeks before, I guess. Right. Wow. But why did I find that one? It's so illogical.

E.: I don't know why you pull out certain things when you put the hook down into the pool. Very often it isn't clear what the reason is one pulls up the memory one does.

Mr. A.: I think that's one of the pieces of seaweed.

E.: Okay, how about *worm?*

Mr. A. *(after a pause of 15 seconds)*: I can't blot out a memory of fishing with worms as bait last summer. The summer of 1982. Nothing close to the time of the accident.

E.: How about *bucket?*

Mr. A. *(after a pause of 17 seconds)*: On that trip in the summer of 1980. I can remember playing basketball in their yard. They had a dumb bucket up at the backboard instead of a net. But I don't care anything about that time period anyway.

E.: How about *apple?*

Mr. A. (*after a pause of 37 seconds*): I – I have this very momentary, almost instantaneous vision, I can't call it back now, of my brother's kitchen, cutting an apple. It won't come back. Damn it! No, I can't remember cutting it any more. It won't come back. But that was when he was living on Mount Street and there were apple trees in the yard. When was that? Maybe the fall of 1979.

E.: How about *arm?*

Mr. A. (*after a pause of 45 seconds*): The best I can give you is from early 1982.

E.: Let's try to get closer to the accident. *Baby.*

Mr. A. (*after a pause of 31 seconds*): I wonder if this is because I'm trying to focus on my brother, but I can remember a girl coming up to my brother and saying "Baby" and kissing him.

E.: When was that?

Mr. A.: That was [*long whistle*], oh, I hope it isn't my own mind creating it, but for some unknown reason, it seems like the time just before the accident. Late May or early June 1980. I don't know why it seems that way to me though.

E.: Okay, how about *bird?*

Mr. A. (*after a pause of 53 seconds*): Nothing of any import comes to mind.

E.: Okay, how about *board?*

Mr. A. (*after a pause of 31 seconds*): Holy crap! That must have been, yeah, it has to be June of 1980. Helen's house is next to a park where there is a merry-go-round made out of ordinary boards. I was pushing Helen around and around, faster and faster. The weather had become quite warm. And it started to rain. Reason for knowing these things I can't tell you, but I can remember these things. I can remember telling Helen about what my brother and I were doing.

E.: But the episode you want to remember is before June 1980.

Mr. A.: Or during. It must have been during. That becomes clear now because I remember telling her about the thing we were building, but it hadn't reached the stage that my brother told me about, that I'm trying to remember. Of course this incident at the park with Helen could have been very late in May. The weather could have been late May or early June.

E.: Okay, what about *book?*

Mr. A. (*after a pause of 20 seconds*): I can't give you an exact time for this one, but it must have been in the couple of weeks I was working in the sales department. I remember looking at the cover of a catalog and thinking what a rotten, ugly cover it was. Sometime in September of 1980.

E.: How about *bottle?*

Mr. A. (*after a pause of 87 seconds*): Absolutely nothing.

E.: How about *boy?*

Mr. A. (*after a pause of 20 seconds*): Helen. Apparently I did tell her something about my brother that really tickled her. I can't remember what I told her now, but it seems funny now. Because I was laughing about it then.

E.: That was also in June 1980?

Mr. A.: Yeah.

E.: You thought you had lost this stuff forever?

Mr. A.: Well, I hoped I hadn't.

E.: I guess this is an interrupting, but . . .

Mr. A.: That's okay, that's fine. I think I need a break for a second anyhow.

E.: When we met last week and when we were talking earlier this morning, you thought you had a retrograde amnesia from November or December 1979 to the accident at the end of June 1980. Why did you think that?

Mr. A.: Why did I think that? Because I can remember some of the things I did in the autumn of 1979, but during the period after November or December they are very hazy. Though they are clearer now than they were. Some of them are clearer now than they were.

E.: When people say their retrograde covers a certain period of time, the problem is, what do they really mean? How do they decide that? What you suggested was that there was a period that was clear but there was a period that was hazy, and I guess you made some estimate of when the hazy period started. Is that right?[4]

Mr. A.: Yeah. I've talked about this with family and friends et cetera, since then, and it has become apparent that the things I can remember with much greater ease were prior to Christmas 1979, I guess you could call it.

E.: Okay, shall we get back to this for a while and see if we can find the missing episode? *Cat.*

Mr. A. (*after a pause of 7 seconds*): No, that would have been a year before, say June 1979. I have a really clear memory of a cat being run over by a car. Hmm. I'm trying to find something during the period we care about. I can't really find one to *cat.*

E.: How about *church?*

Mr. A. (*after a pause of* [*missing data*] *seconds*): About a year ago, Saint Patrick's cathedral in New York. But that is also in the wrong time period.

---

[4] A former head injury with loss of consciousness is claimed by 25% of male and 15% of female randomly selected college students. Usually, these were very mild head injuries; at the time of testing most students with a former head injury had no retrograde amnesia, and the median length of reported PTA was only 3 minutes. For a retrospective study of 1,000 college students, see Crovitz, Horn, & Daniel, 1983.

**Two days later**

Mr. A.: During the past few days I have thought about and thought about all the things I remembered, and nothing new came.

E.: A question occurred to me during the past couple of days that is interesting to me. If you find any more memories from the PTA period in which you had impaired consciousness, let's pay attention to whether they differ in vividness from ones from other times. Memories from before the accident got encoded in full consciousness, but those soon after the accident were about things happening when consciousness is impaired, so there might be a difference between them.[5]

Mr. A.: It interests me that my most vivid memory is from the post-traumatic amnesia period; it is a remarkable clear island in the middle of nothing. That doesn't seem to make sense.

E.: I don't know. Maybe the brain, or the memory machinery, fluctuates into periods of working great. I don't know – that's too hard. I can't think about hard things.

Mr. A.: [*Laughter*]

E.: Now, today, I will continue giving cues from the list, and we are seeking memories, particularly, that you are *absolutely certain you had been amnesic for* prior to our session a couple of days ago. Would that be fun?

Mr. A.: Yeah, yeah.

E.: Okay, just like last time, I will say a word and you will try to find a memory associated to it and, I hope, from sometime in the period you are sure you had been amnesic for. Okay the first word is *clock*.

Mr. A. (*after a pause of 43 seconds*): Nothing that seems to register except for a time I'm pretty sure I wasn't amnesic for, the beginning of last summer, seeing a clock at a gas station. Nothing spectacular at all.

E.: Okay, let's hope for better. *Door.*

Mr. A. (*after a pause of 71 seconds*): Blast. That's two in a row. I can't think of anything for that one either.

E.: How about if I make a suggestion? There's the door to your house, there's the door to your brother's place, there's doors to cars . . .

Mr. A.: I can remember walking in the door, yeah! I remember walking in the door to that conference after the accident, right before I started working again. We already got that episode though.

---

[5] When a person is in an abnormal rather than a normal biological state (e.g., distracted or delirious or intoxicated or drugged or recovering from head injury), ongoing experience may be perceived and encoded differently from normal, and less of it may be stored. "Memories" are more likely to be made accessible later, when retrieval cues are provided externally. See Eich, 1980; Petersen, 1977; Weingartner, Adefris, Eich, & Murphy, 1976.

E.: Okay, how about *engine?* Car engines, cars breaking down, cars at gas stations . . .

Mr. A. (*after a pause of 138 seconds*): A new one! I can see my wife out in the driveway washing her car. She does that all the time. And I can see, lying in the corner of my driveway, the motorcycle that we were going to throw out because it was so incredibly mangled, by a truck that had hit it. My wife kept it because she knew I would want to see it afterwards. And she was right.

E.: That was from the accident?

Mr. A.: That was from the accident. *The* motorcycle. So that had to be the same summer as the accident, about when I was going back to work, later August or early September. You got me interested again.

E.: Shall we try another word? *Flag.* How about the last flag you can remember from before the accident.

Mr. A. (*after a pause of 237 seconds*): I can picture myself riding the motorcycle. Right out the parking lot from work, *that* motorcycle out of the parking lot. I can't think how long I had had that motorcycle. I don't think it was very long. Sometime between April 1980 and June 1980. I can see the motorcycle under me. It has the manufacturer's name right here.

E.: Okay, lets go for another one. Ready? *Horse.*

Mr. A. (*after a pause of 17 seconds*): Sure, I can give you one of those. I said I didn't remember most of the year before the accident, right? Sometime between November 1979 and February 1980 I was riding a horse that shied and threw me. I know it was winter; I can't time it better.

E.: Okay, *hospital.*

Mr. A. (*after a pause of 24 seconds*): I wonder if this is something they told me. I have this vivid picture in my mind of what it might have looked like. I wonder if that's memory.

E.: What's that about?

Mr. A.: I can see the nurse taking me out of the hospital in a wheel-chair. Starting to take me out in it. I was perfectly able to walk myself. But hospital policy. That might be a vision; it's unclear enough it might be some-thing somebody told me – that I have this vivid image in my mind of what it would have looked like. Or it might have been posttraumatic amnesia period stuff. It was on the day I know I left the hospital, a month after the accident.

E.: Did your brother come to visit you in the hospital?

Mr. A.: Christ, *everybody* came to visit me in the hospital. But wait, I *think* I remember this. I've been told it several times, that it is true, but I think I remember it! Sally came to visit me, and that was the first conscious emotional sign I had given since the accident. It was just about three weeks after the accident. And I – and I reacted to her although I didn't say anything yet. I think it is a memory. I really – it is much more vivid than when I was told about it in the past, anyhow.

E.: You were lying in bed?

Mr. A.: I was lying in bed.

E.: Were you lying on your back or your side?

Mr. A.: I was lying on my back and I had a bunch of tubes in my throat, and did I have tubes up my nose then? That was to feed me. Oh, oh yeah! I've been told about really hating those tubes that were always in me, and pulling them out. And it *seems* like I might be *remembering* it.

E.: What do you mean, you might be remembering it?

Mr. A.: Well, in the past I've always had a picture of what that would look like. And I've seen the hospital room I was in, so I know what it looks like, and I can picture it. But now I can picture it more precisely. The image in my mind seems much more vivid.

E.: Give me some details.

Mr. A.: Give details. I see the sun through the window. It wasn't quite white. It was rather off-white green. A green-tinged wall. I had straps on my chest so I couldn't thrash around. I looked down at the tube and it annoyed me, so I reached up and pulled it.

E.: Do you remember that?

Mr. A.: I think so . . . yeah . . . yeah . . . *yeah!* Blast! Maybe I would be more sure if I hadn't gone through three years of not remembering it, but I'm pretty sure, yes I'm sure, that was the real thing.

E.: All right, are you ready for another one?

Mr. A.: All right.

E.: Okay, *library.*

Mr. A. (*after a pause of 36 seconds*): I was always in the library. Whenever I could be. Reading the journals and the patents and anything else.

E.: How about a library in *June?*

Mr. A.: I was interested in chemistry. I was reading a lot of chemistry. I can remember talking to Herman about a molecule. About the results of a test he had done on a sample.

E.: Can you give me time and space features of that?

Mr. A.: Unfortunately, space, the labs all look the same. Time, it was pretty early in the morning. Quarter of eight or eight o'clock. Bright and early anyway.

E.: On what day would it be?

Mr. A.: I can't remember what day of the week. If anything, if anything, I'd call it Tuesday. I don't know why, but it – I'd call it Tuesday.

E.: This was early in June?

Mr. A.: It was, let's see, one week after [*inaudible*].

E.: What was that? Say that again.

Mr. A.: I was hit one week after Herman went on vacation. One week from when we got that sample. So I was hit – that would be two weeks before I was hit.

E.: So around June thirteenth?

Mr. A.: Yeah, somewhere around then. That was [*inaudible*] June.

E.: Okay, let's do another. *Nail*.

Mr. A. (*after a pause of 92 seconds*): That's a memory I've already had. Pushing the merry-go-round. There were nails sticking out of it that we had to avoid.

E.: No nail memories from the June of the accident?

Mr. A.: I'm trying, but I can't find any.

E.: Okay, *picture*.

Mr. A. (*after a pause of 94 seconds*): How'd you like a memory one week before the accident?

E.: I certainly would. Let me just make a note.[6]

Mr. A.: Poker game on my brother's porch. Hanging plants coming down from the ceiling. Bushes outside the screened-in porch. Through the door to the living room a Picasso picture, some bright-colored print with flowers and people, dancing people. I can remember, now I'm certain, that the memory I want to remember is *before* that poker game, because I remember looking into the living room and, uh, remembering. Wow! I can remember remembering!

E.: So the episode you want to remember *did* happen?

Mr. A.: I don't remember it, but I remember grinning at my brother across the table and him grinning at me and I was remembering it.

E.: Try hunting around there for the memory of the episode itself, the one you've wanted to remember.

Mr. A.: There's this [*inaudible*] walking past that picture. Oh, that picture was identical to a poster in one of the labs at the engineering school I went to. We walked past the picture and went down into the basement and . . .

E.: That's a *very* broad grin!

Mr. A.: Ha, ha. You bet. I got it! *I got it! I got what I was looking for!* My brother and I were down in the basement and we started up the machine, and I was adjusting some of the components, and the machine didn't stop the way it always had before. I remember thinking, why isn't it stopping,

---

[6]It was 94 seconds from the time the cue word *picture* was said until the time that Mr. A. first spoke. When a smile first appeared on his face, 70 seconds had passed, and 15 seconds after that, about 5 seconds before he first spoke, the smile had broadened and one could easily imagine the cartoonist's lightbulb going on over his head at that time.

why isn't it stopping? Who *cares* why it isn't stopping? What's the difference? It's not stopping! [*Clearing his throat*] And from there it carried on.

E.: When was that?

Mr. A.: Oh, blast. That was – that was, I guess, the weekend before finals week at the technical school, so that would have been two weeks before the accident. Yes. It was, yes! It was after the exam I gave, and that was Thursday, probably Thursday. I don't have any idea why I know that, but it was Thursday, it seems like it was Thursday, but it could have been Friday, but what difference does it make?

E.: So you found it.

Mr. A.: Yes. [*Giggle*] Yes. [*Laugh*]

E.: So you got what you came for.

Mr. A.: Yep, I got it! Astonishing!

E.: But do me a favor . . .

Mr. A.: I'll keep . . .

E.: Just a few more of these.

Mr. A.: I'm having a very good time learning the rest of these, too.

E.: Okay, so we got stuff now a week and two weeks before the accident.

Mr. A.: Exactly.

E.: Which were in the retrograde amnesia period.

Mr. A.: Yes. For sure. I've been trying to remember it for almost three years. It is suddenly *very* vivid.

E.: The question is, how did you remember it?

Mr. A.: It was *very* slow. Very slowly came the memory of me standing at the picture. Looking toward the door to the stairs to the basement. And my brother following me down the stairs. And that all came back very slowly. Very hard to pick up on. And then, when I tried to remember me and my brother downstairs – I want – I can remember easily, the two of us when we got everything going; that came like a snap of the fingers, all at once, it was *there*. Walking past the picture, walking down the stairs, walking up to the machinery, that was all like thinking I can sort of remember that, that must have been the time, so let's see, can I remember it, can I remember it, can I remember it? It was sort of very, very hazy, but when I got the first thread of it, adjusting the component, it was just, bang, there. Right there! There it was! Ha!

E.: All right, now what I'd like you to do on the remaining cue words, what I really want to do, mostly to see if it can be done, *is to get right before the accident.*

Mr. A.: Yes, yes. That is another thing I have wanted to remember, swerving to avoid the truck.

E.: Let me just say that usually people don't remember the moment of impact, that's a permanently forgotten event after a severe head injury that gives amnesias. But what does usually eventually come back is memory up to a few seconds before the sudden loss of consciousness. But you might remember everything.

Mr. A.: I'm game.

E.: Okay, ready for the next cue word? *Potato*.

Mr. A.: [*Silence*]

E.: Or foods in general. You must have eaten sometime soon before the accident. A meal before the accident?

Mr. A. (*after a pause of 14 seconds*): No, in fact I didn't have a meal yet; I was working at home that day and just came in to check my mail.

E.: How do you know that?

Mr. A.: I've been told that several times. I had gone in after the lab had let out, but Smitty was still there, and he said we chatted and I got my mail and left.

E.: Give me the *potato* closest to the accident.

Mr. A.: I'm not sure a potato has ever made an impression on me. I haven't anything specific in mind. I used to go to the farmer's market pretty often, but that could be from any time, before or after or during or anything. Sorry about that.

E.: That's all right. You got what you came for; this is just some added science.

Mr. A.: Added science. That's what *you* came for.

E.: That's what I came for. The cue word is *prison*.

Mr. A.: (*after a pause of 2 seconds*): Prison. There's jail. Judge. Cops. Robbers, bang, bang. I think it was, when? Before the accident I think, yes. I was over at Dudley's, I was at his condominium; was it his TV set? I think it was his TV set. There was a very funny shoot-'em-up crime movie on TV. We were watching the movie and drinking beer.

E.: That would have been when?

Mr. A.: I can't tell you why, but it seems like it was June of 1980. The week before the accident. I think. But I have no idea why; it is very unclear.

E.: Okay, let's go for another one. *Ship*.

Mr. A. (*after a pause of 60 seconds*): The best thing I can think of now is that – Christ!, the memory I've had for years, the terribly vivid island of memory. From August 1980. Sitting on the deck of a ferry off Long Island. Watching the sea gulls. My ex-wife's arm around my shoulders.

E.: Was she sitting to your left or your right?

Mr. A.: It's very vivid. She's sitting to my left, wearing a red scarf. Why do I remember that?

E.: There may be some emotional meaning to that moment. That may be why it sticks in your mind.

Mr. A.: We're on the deck. For some reason it seems her sister was there too. Standing at the railing. We were sitting at the very stern of the boat. These details aren't as clear as the second or two watching the sea gulls. That's what I've always remembered. Those seconds with the sea gulls.

E.: Did you always also have the memory of your wife sitting with you, of her sister?

Mr. A.: I think I always had those details too. When it was first discovered I couldn't remember things, like when I remembered that one incident, my ex-wife said, "Yeah, you are right, I remember it that same way, but why do you remember that that way?" The doctors at the hospital warned my wife I might have some slight memory problems, but I don't remember if they warned me.

E.: Okay, let's go for another cue word. And, again, let's try to find the accident. *Star.*

Mr. A.(*after a pause of 30 seconds*): I really would like to have a memory from June. But all I can find is that drive to San Diego, the summer afterwards. Driving through Nevada and remembering then that way back in my childhood I had looked up in the sky and seen how incredibly many stars there were.

E.: You remembered having seen stars when you were a child?

Mr. A.: Yes, and thinking that there seemed to be less stars now.

E.: Right. Okay, another one. *Street.*

Mr. A. (*after a pause of 39 seconds*): This is very unclear. Maybe a fabrication of my own mind. *But,* I think I can remember. Uh-oh! I think I can remember riding my motorcycle. Down from the lab. *The day of.* I knew the truck was coming around the corner. For some reason I thought he would come to a stop, or slow down. I remember thinking to myself . . . that truck can't hit me, how can that truck hit me?

E.: Can you picture it?

Mr. A.: Yes. I was coming to the corner and the truck was there, and I was very unconcerned, starting to turn before I got worried at all, and then I thought, I can make it, and I took that corner. And I would have made it except for that fender. The last memory I can get is – I hope, not a fabricated one – starting to go around the corner and being very confident I could make it. I can sort of remember my feeling of confidence, of overconfidence. Wow.

E.: Why do you say "Wow"?

Mr. A.: I can – I can sort of remember my feelings of immortality. I thought, I really used to think, even more than I do now, that nothing can destroy me.

E.: You still do?

Mr. A.: I still have feelings like that at times, but I try to settle them down so I don't get killed again. Or killed once, or something like that.

E.: My goodness. We seem to have got close to the accident.

Mr. A.: Within a few seconds. So far as I know – I've been thinking about it just now – I can probably remember as much now from that year as the year before it or the year before that. Or any time previous. So I guess that means my retrograde amnesia has shrunk to a few seconds.[7]

E.: The thing that is worth calling to your attention is that these memories, on the average, take *over a minute* from the cue word, so that if you try to remember something and give up without waiting . . .

Mr. A.: After fifteen seconds.

E.: As people usually do.

Mr. A.: Always! Right. Without fail![8]

---

[7] Here's the question: Are these recovered autobiographical memories valid? Might they be confabulations? Baddeley & Wilson (Chap. 13) give examples of confabulation in autobiographical memory reports, and illustrate it in the cases of R.J. and N.W. Baddeley & Wilson's criteria for suspecting confabulation include the bizarreness of the incidents and the unreliability of the reports on retests. Butters & Cermak (Chap. 14) are in a very strong position to determine errors in autobiographical memory in their study of P.Z., because material that P.Z. had written before his illness was available. Similarly, one would be in a strong position to determine confabulations in one's own recollections of life episodes if one kept a diary and later used it as a criterion of accuracy of recollection.

How can you tell if any of *your* autobiographical memories is valid? The credibility of a memory is enhanced if an objective record was made of the episode at the time or if other people remember the event in the same way. Juries judge the credibility of courtroom evidence in a similar manner. When neither objective validation nor consensual validation is available, the specification of details "from memory" may seem convincing, but details may be intentionally or unintentionally fabricated. Ulrich Neisser has argued that even when details are wrong, the meaning behind a claimed episode may be quite correct; see Neisser, 1981.

People are relieved when they are satisfied that they have recovered autobiographical memories from periods they had been unable to remember. However, some evidence from analogous experimental studies using hypnosis suggests such claims may sometimes be invalid; see Dywan & Bowers, 1983; Laurence & Campbell, 1983. These studies indicate that pseudomemories may occur when pressure is applied to enhance recall and that well-intentioned subjects may claim strongly that the pseudomemories refer to episodes that, in fact, did not exist. See also Loftus & Loftus, 1980, and Baddeley & Wilson (Chap. 13).

[8] One theory of the time required to retrieve material from verbal long-term memory is Anderson's spreading activation theory; see Anderson, 1983. One usually finds that a cue word leads normal college students to a claimed autobiographical memory before 10 seconds have elapsed. However, the reaction times in this protocol are extremely long.

Head injury leads to a slowing of cognitive processing, but recovery of speed has usually occurred within a month or two (see Gronwall & Wrightson, 1974). It is not known whether the extremely long latencies found here indicate a residual slowing of cognitive processing or whether future research will find that long-lost memories laid down in an abnormal brain state require extensive time-consuming search to find and claim as one's own.

# References

Anderson J. R. (1983). Retrieval of information from long-term memory. *Science, 220,* 25–30.

Crovitz, H. F. (1970). *Galton's walk: Methods for the analysis of thinking, intelligence, and creativity.* New York: Harper & Row.

Crovitz, H. F., & Harvey, M. T. (1979). Early childood amnesia: A quantitative study with implications for the study of retrograde amnesia after brain injury. *Cortex, 15,* 331–335.

Crovitz, H. F., Harvey, M. T., & McKee, D. C. (1980). Selecting retrieval cues for early-childhood amnesia: Implications for the study of shrinking retrograde amnesia. *Cortex, 16,* 305–310.

Crovitz, H. F., Horn, R. W., & Daniel, W. F. (1983). Inter-relationships among retrograde amnesia, posttraumatic amnesia, and time since injury: A retrospective study. *Cortex, 19,* 407–412.

Crovitz, H. F., & Quina-Holland, K. (1976). Proportion of episodic memories from early childhood by years of age. *Bulletin of the Psychonomic Society, 7,* 61–62.

Crovitz, H. F., & Schiffman, H. (1974). Frequency of episodic memories as a function of their age. *Bulletin of the Psychonomic Society, 4,* 517–518.

Dywan, J., & Bowers, K. (1983). The use of hypnosis to enhance recall. *Science, 222,* 184–185.

Eich J. E. (1980). The cue-dependent nature of state-dependent retrieval. *Memory and Cognition, 8,* 157–173.

Galton, F. (1879). Psychometric experiments. *Brain, 2,* 149–162.

Gronwall, D., & Wrightson, P. (1974). Delayed recovery of intellectual function after minor head injury. *Lancet, 2,* 605–609.

(1980). Duration of posttraumatic amnesia after mild head injury. *Journal of Clinical Neuropsychology, 2,* 51–60.

Laurence J.-R., & Campbell, P. (1983). Hypnotically created memory among highly hypnotizable subjects. *Science, 222,* 523–524.

Levin H. S., Benton, A. L., & Grossman, R. G. (1982). *Neurobehavioral consequences of closed head injury,* New York: Oxford University Press.

Lezak, M. D. (1983). *Neuropsychological assessment* (2nd ed.). New York: Oxford University Press.

Loftus, E. F., & Loftus, G. R. (1980). On the permanence of stored information in the human brain. *American Psychologist, 35,* 409–420.

Loftus, E. F., & Marburger, W. (1983). Since the eruption of Mt. St. Helens, has anyone beaten you up? Improving the accuracy of retrospective reports with landmark events. *Memory and Cognition, 11,* 114–120.

Neisser, U. (1981). John Dean's memory: A case study. *Cognition, 9,* 1–22.

Petersen, R. C. (1977). Retrieval failures in alcohol state-dependent learning. *Psychopharmacology, 55,* 141–146.

Rubin, D. C. (1982). The retention function for autobiographical memory. *Journal of Verbal Learning and Verbal Behavior, 21,* 21–38.

---

The long reaction times found here, however, may be most likely to be explained by demand characteristics of the task. Mr. A. had extremely long reaction times, but so did another otherwise fully recovered subject who was run the same way. He had had an extensive old RA associated with quite a different etiology (delirium induced by excessive cimetidine medication for a stomach disorder), had very long reaction times, and also claimed to find episodes that had been in his extended memory gap. The most likely explanation may be that both subjects found it necessary to take time for rejecting memorial associations from the *wrong* time periods, until episodes were reported that could be assigned to times close to the amnesic period.

Russell, W. R., & Nathan, P. W. (1946). Traumatic amnesia. *Brain, 69*, 280–300.

Russell, W. R., & Smith, A. (1961). Post-traumatic amnesia in closed head injury. *Archives of Neurology, 5*, 16–29.

Schacter, D. L., & Crovitz, H. F. (1977). Memory function after closed head injury: A review of the quantitative research. *Cortex, 13*, 150–176.

Schacter, D. L., Wang, P. L., Tulving, E., and Freedman, M. (1982). Functional retrograde amnesia: A quantitative case study. *Neuropsychologia, 20*, 523–532.

Schneider, A. L., & Sumi, D. (1981). Patterns of forgetting and telescoping: An analysis of LEAA survey victimization data. *Criminology, 19*, 400–410.

Sudman, S., & Bradburn, N. M. (1973). Effects of time and memory factors on response in surveys. *Journal of the American Statistical Association, 68*, 805–815.

(1974). *Response effects in surveys: A review and synthesis*. Chicago: Aldine.

Weingartner, H., Adefris, W., Eich, J. E., & Murphy, D. L. (1976). Encoding-imagery specificity in alcohol state-dependent learning. *Journal of Experimental Psychology: Human Learning and Memory, 2*, 83–87.

Wood, F., Ebert, V., & Kinsbourne, M. (1982). The episodic-semantic distinction in memory and amnesia: Clinical and experimental observations. In L. S. Cermak (Ed.), *Human memory and amnesia* (pp. 167–193). Hillsdale, NJ: Erlbaum.

Zola-Morgan, S., Cohen, N. J., & Squire, L. R. (1983). Recall of remote episodic memory in amnesia. *Neuropsychologia, 21*, 487–500.

# Author index

291

# Subject index

adolescence, 124–5

affect, 44, 57, 59–60, 66, 90–3, 104, 108–9, 123, 127, 168–72, 191, 193

aging: deficits in autobiographical memory from, 250; effects on autobiographical memory of, observed, 64–5, 66, 209–17; effects on autobiographical memory of, possible, 206–8; effect on retention of, 206

amalgam, 58–9, 63, 64

amnesia, 14–16, 223: *see also* closed head injury; frontal lobe damage; Korsakoff's syndrome

biography, 20, 22; literary, 11, 84–6

causal chains, 107, 114–16, 117–18

childhood amnesia, 119–20, 131, 217–19; definition of, 191–4; evidence for, 194–9

closed head injury, 280n, 288n; case study of, 273–88

clustering, 173–4

confabulation, 237–45, 248, 251

context-plus-index model, 102–4

copy theory of memory, 41, 43–4

cryptomnesia, 96

cued recall: of autobiographical memory, 36–8, 54–5, 181–2, 195, 196–8, 202–5, 209–17, 226–7, 251, 273n–4n; of words, 163–8

dating events, 63, 140–3, 147, 274n; effects of a temporal reference system on, 180–7; reaction times and, 151–6; role of autobiographical events in, 143, 146, 148–9, 150–6; strategies for, 143–50

definitions of autobiographical memory, 8, 32–5, 71, 122, 254

déjà vu, 96

development, 6–7, 21, 123–5, 202; of symbolic process, 125–6

directed search, 100–1; *see also* retrieval strategies

dysexecutive syndrome, 246, 248

ecological approach, 76, 79–80

electroconvulsive therapy, 260–1

emotion, *see* affect

episodic memory, 33; *see also* semantic/episodic distinction

extendure, 10, 13, 57, 66, 74

flashbulb memory, 8, 35–6, 41, 79, 83, 127, 140, 157

free recall: of autobiographical memory, 204; temporally cued, 54, 59–65, 172–3, 195, 198

frontal lobe damage, 236–45

historical methods, 21, 138–9

history of the study of autobiographical memory, 19–23, 39–40

Huntington's disease, 259–60

identity crisis, 87

imagery, 26, 29, 31–2, 34–6, 38, 40, 61–2, 124–5, 127

incidental recall of context, 139–40

individual difference, 40, 51

involuntary memories, 53–4, 63, 65, 66, 85, 122, 127

Korsakoff's syndrome, 234–5, 245, 255–63; case study of, 263–70

measures of autobiographical memory: episodicity, 230–3; fluency, 229–30; richness, 233; reliability, 233–4

methods of study of autobiographical memory, 19–22, 36–40, 52–7; *see also* cued recall; free recall; reaction time; recognition

DATE DUE

ILL
4-28-94

MAY 17 1996

JUN 16 1997

Sent
12-15-98

JUN 2 9 2004

ILL
4-1-11

GAYLORD                                        PRINTED IN U.S.A.